PENGUIN BOOKS

THE PENGUIN BOOK OF THE RENAISSANCE

Professor Sir John Plumb was born in 1911 in Leicester where he was educated at the University College and afterwards at Christ's College, Cambridge. He began research under Professor G. M. Trevelyan on the social structure of the House of Commons in the reign of William III. In 1939 he was elected to the Ehrman Fellowship, King's College, Cambridge. During the Second World War he worked in a department of the Foreign Office. On his return to Cambridge he became Fellow and Tutor of Christ's College and University Lecturer in History. In 1957 he was awarded a Litt.D. for his work on eighteenth-century history. He was Professor of Modern English History at Cambridge from 1966 to 1974, now Emeritus, and elected a Fellow of the British Academy in 1968. From 1978–82 he was Master of Christ's College, Cambridge, and in 1982 he received a knighthood. He has written books on *Chatham*, *The First Four Georges*, *West African Explorers* and *The Renaissance* and is the author of *Crisis in the Humanities* (1964) and *The Growth of Political Stability in England, 1675–1725* (1967). His life of Sir Robert Walpole was acclaimed both in England and America as one of the outstanding biographies of our time. He is editor of the multi-volume *History of Human Society*. He was visiting Professor at Columbia University for 1960, and Ford's Lecturer at Oxford University, 1965–6. He is the European Advisory Editor for *Horizon*, the advisory editor for history for Penguin Books, and editor of the Fontana *History of Modern Europe*. His other books include *England in the Eighteenth Century*, *Royal Heritage* (1977), *Royal Builders and Collectors* (with Huw Wheldon, 1977), *George III* (1978), *Georgian Delights* (1980), *Royal Heritage: The Reign of Elizabeth II* (1980), *The Making of an Historian* (1987) and *The American Experience* (1988).

The Penguin Book of the Renaissance

By J. H. Plumb

with essays by
Garrett Mattingly
Kenneth Clark
Ralph Roeder
J. Bronowski
Iris Origo
H. R. Trevor-Roper
Denis Mack Smith

PENGUIN BOOKS

PENGUIN BOOKS

Published by the Penguin Group
Penguin Books Ltd, 80 Strand, London WC2R 0RL, England
Penguin Putnam Inc., 375 Hudson Street, New York, New York 10014, USA
Penguin Books Australia Ltd, Ringwood, Victoria, Australia
Penguin Books Canada Ltd, 10 Alcorn Avenue, Toronto, Ontario, Canada M4V 3B2
Penguin Books India (P) Ltd, 11 Community Centre, Panchsheel Park, New Delhi – 110 017, India
Penguin Books (NZ) Ltd, Cnr Rosedale and Airborne Roads, Albany, Auckland, New Zealand
Penguin Books (South Africa) (Pty) Ltd, 24 Sturdee Avenue, Rosebank 2196, South Africa

Penguin Books Ltd, Registered Offices: 80 Strand, London WC2R 0RL, England

www.penguin.com

The English language edition of this book was first published in the USA by
American Heritage Publishing Co. Inc.,
and in Great Britain by Collins, 1961, under the title
The Horizon Book of Renaissance

Published in Penguin Books 1964
Reprinted as *The Pelican Book of the Renaissance* 1982
Reprinted as *The Penguin Book of the Renaissance* 1991
Reprinted as a Classic Penguin 2001
1

Set in Monotype Bembo
Printed in Great Britain by The Bath Press, Bath

CONTENTS

The Penguin Book of the Renaissance

An angel, by Filippino Lippi
Janos Scholz Collection, New York

INTRODUCTION

J. H. Plumb

Art reflects society – its aspirations, confusions, and inheritance. But the future is there as well as the past and the great ages of man only have meaning so long as they create modes of expression and behaviour which will hold unborn generations in unconscious subjection. And this was peculiarly true of the Renaissance in Italy which started themes capable of infinite variation, so that Shakespeare and Poussin, and even Isaac Newton and Edward Gibbon, were carried along by its impetus into new worlds of creative achievement. Iconoclastic scholars have belittled the originality of the Renaissance; attempts have been made to isolate it; to demonstrate its overwhelming debt to former ages; to confine it to the realm of art. Not even the most prejudiced medievalist, however, can deny the astonishing vigour and originality of fifteenth-century Italy in painting, in sculpture, and in architecture. True, it adds depth to our understanding to realize the power of Gothic influence in the tragic nudes of Michelangelo and to appreciate the ironic handling of his inheritance by Uccello. Yet, as these splendid pages show, artists from the days of Masaccio to the death of Tintoretto not only equalled the triumphs of Greece and Rome, to which they were so deeply indebted, but excelled them. By their exploration of perspective, of landscape, of the nude, and of the human face, they opened up fresh dimensions in art. Although there were aspects of Renaissance painting that are as private and as esoteric as anything that modern art can produce, yet mostly it possessed a universality of appeal that shows little sign of diminishing, even as the last relics of the social

9

structure which gave rise to it vanish from the Western world. Both capitalist and communist can gaze at Leonardo's self-portrait and be moved by the dignity of man and feel pity for his lonely fate. Perhaps the most profound themes of Renaissance painting and sculpture are concerned with the destiny of men, caught in the inexorable process of Time. And the originality of its greatest artists lies not in the virtuosity of their technical experiments, or the boldness with which they explored landscape and the naked body, but in their concentration on the uniqueness of the human temperament and the significance of individual experience. This became the preoccupation of Renaissance society; of its poets, philosophers and educators as well as its artists.

Renaissance art possessed, however, mundane roots: and the dung that fertilized them was golden. Without patrons, without the careless extravagance of popes and princes, cardinals and merchants, it could never have flourished. Italy in the fifteenth century was once more really rich; not as affluent as in the days of Imperial Rome but wealthy enough to support an extravagant and self-indulgent merchant aristocracy. The devastations of the barbarian invasions, the onslaught of Vikings, Magyars, Slavs, and Moslems had destroyed the fabric of European society and impoverished its peoples. For centuries rich men had been few, money hard to come by, and what profits there were from agrarian toil and feeble commerce were needed for castles and cathedrals and the courts of kings. There were always pockets of luxury and sophistication, which provoked occasional originality in art and in thought; at times an eagerness for knowledge, and even a love for the classics, so that much of the Renaissance seems foreshadowed in earlier centuries. Foreshadowed, yes, but never achieved. Before Dante and Petrarch, and even after them, the iron dogmas of theology limited speculation, inhibited change, and gave preference to argument over observation.

In spite of setbacks, however, Italian cities, particularly Venice, Genoa, Florence, Milan, Naples, and Palermo grew in population and in wealth: their merchant communities, vigorous, competitive, questing, increased steadily until their numbers, strength and riches began to bring into being a new form of society, that involved a fusion of aristocratic and bourgeois principles which found its expression in Italy of the Renaissance.

This fusion took place slowly, for the inertia of medieval society was very strong. Religion was neither overturned nor undermined. The Madonnas, Pietàs, Crucifixions, and the innumerable saints of Renaissance art speak eloquently of the traditional faith of Machiavelli's princes or of the Borgias' cardinals; plenty of painters of pagan nudes remained ardent Christians, Michelangelo did, so also Botticelli. Nor was the aristocratic structure of society submerged by the growth of the merchant class: indeed the Renaissance witnessed as much, if not more, penetration of the ideas and manners of the nobility into the ethos of the bourgeoisie as the other way about. In the fifteenth-century Italian world of violence, in which soldiers of fortune secured a dukedom for their prowess, noble birth was never necessary but always desirable, and feudal genealogies were manufactured with alacrity. Yet the prosperous and sophisticated merchants of Florence and Venice helped to promote civility and to widen the horizons of aristocratic life. A knowledge of the ancient classics, an appreciation of art, of literature, of music, and of conversation became the hallmark of a gentleman, whether he was a soldier, statesman, priest, or merchant. As wealth spread and the rich multiplied, their sophisticated demands created new tastes and encouraged new techniques. Permanent theatres for the performance of operas and plays became a necessity for any city with pretensions to civilized living. The rapid exploitation of the invention of movable type in 1451 made libraries possible for men of modest means and so revolutionized education. Culture was constantly extended, thereby creating opportunities for advancement for those without the privilege of birth or the security of wealth. The gradations in society increased as well as thickened: individual enterprise, creative imagination, and weight of temperament became of great potential value in a world in which the lines of class structure grew blurred. Pietro Aretino, the scourge of princes and the first man to live in splendour by his pen alone, is as much a part of Renaissance Italy as Michelangelo, Machiavelli, or Pius II, whose lives are discussed in this book.

As the old certainties slowly dissolved or grew more limited in application, curiosity took their place; of course, previous ages had contained men of ample curiosity, but society had not encouraged its practice nor inflamed its appetite. It had had to find its satisfaction in argument based on the dogmatic certainties of revealed religion. During the Renaissance it became easier for a few men to look at the world about them with the desire to understand it on its own terms, not God's. In the drawings of Leonardo that explore the formation of rocks or the turbulence of water, one can see this habit of truth being formed; so, too, in the political writings of Machiavelli or Guicciardini there is a quest for truth, no matter where it may lead. Nor did Renaissance society discourage these tentative steps towards an open mind to man and his nature: other forces – particularly the great discoveries of continents beyond Europe – nourished and strengthened an attitude which was often during the Renaissance intermittent and unrealized. Such stirrings might have withered had not the circumstances of society been appropriate for their growth. And they would have lost all significance had not Italian society of the Renaissance been the prototype of those great empires that were to grow in Western Europe as the trade of the Atlantic flourished. Humanism took root elsewhere and its greatest triumphs were not to be Italian: but open minds, the use of trial to discover error, and the acquisition of knowledge for its own sake were vital for the growth of the commercial, and increasingly secular, societies of Western Europe. Italy of the Renaissance began hesitantly to experiment with what they so greatly developed. Attitudes of mind are difficult to pin-point in an historical context, but it is obvious that neither Machiavelli nor Leonardo could have pursued their own genius in the Middle Ages as they did in the Renaissance. And this Renaissance in Italy is as important for understanding the intellectual attitudes of Western Europe as for its art.

As will be seen from the pages that follow, Italian society, which gave rise to this stupendous achievement, was complex, exciting, dramatic, a world of violence that threw up geniuses with the ease of a juggler. An age of genius and one of extraordinary *panache*, it has never in all its variety ceased to entrance generations of men and women.

THE DAWN OF THE RENAISSANCE

THE face of medieval Europe was scarred with the ruins of its past. In Rome itself, the Colosseum housed the barbarous Frangipani and their armed retainers, greedy, lawless, destructive; the Forum provided a quarry for churches and rough pasture for the cattle market, and beneath the broken columns of the temple of Castor and Pollux the bullocks awaited their slaughter. The Campagna was littered with the crumbling ruins of its aqueducts; the pavements of those splendid Roman roads were narrowed by the returning wilderness. Elsewhere scraps of walls, the ruins of arena, temple, and triumphal arch, sometimes embedded in the hovels and houses of a town struggling to regain its life or lost forever in the countryside, constantly reminded the man of the Middle Ages of the fleeting life of man, of the unknowable nature of Providence. For him the past was dead, and its relics but morals in stone, a terrible warning of the wickedness which God had punished.

The wealth that was wrung from the soil and the tenuous trade of those dark centuries was poured into the splendid barbaric churches, noble if grotesque, that soared to heaven in violation of all the harmonies of ancient art. Or it served a grimmer purpose, and from it grew the towering fortresses, the embattled towers, the walled cities that were a necessity in a society in which the clang of armour was as common as the church bell.

Yet relics there were, and the miracle is that so much survived the ravages of violence. The barbarian hordes had swept away the thin veneer of Roman culture in north-western Europe and broken

The Kiss of Judas. Detail, by Giotto
Scrovegni Chapel, Padua

the powerful web of trade, law, and government that had bound the Mediterranean world in unity. This breach, on which time had worked, was widened by the surge of Islam which swept across and absorbed not only northern Africa, the islands of Sicily and Sardinia, but also the huge peninsula of Spain, and poured over the Pyrenees only to be checked on the plains of France. Under the hammer blows of Vikings, warrior colonists and traders by the sword, Europe and its culture had nearly bled to death. Violence, insecurity, and poverty reduced trade and city life to pitiful dimensions. Yet even in the worst of times, groups of peasants spread like a virus through the wastes and forests, colonizing those vast tracts of Europe which the Romans had dominated but never peopled.

Their lives were controlled by a warrior caste which attempted to give them protection, but battened on their labour; or by priests and monks who controlled the ritual of their existence and taught them that life was as fleeting as the crops they harvested. Men of this western world lived simple, isolated, primitive lives in which pestilence, famine, and war marked the passage of the years.

Yet the past was never quite destroyed, the structure of society never utterly broken. Trade with the great civilizations of Islam and Byzantium transfused a little wealth into the shattered society of the West. More than wealth – ideas, too, could leap across the frontiers of hate and heresy to stimulate the cunning of men. So Byzantium lured men, warriors as well as traders, and so did the challenge of the Moslem world, which called the knights to battle and sanctified the blood-crazed warriors of Europe, offering them riches in life or glory in death.

This curious society of peasant and priest and warrior, which drew its strength from individual men rather than from nations or countries, was held together by the Catholic Church and by feudal law. The secular ideal, often expressed but rarely achieved, was of an ordered, graded society, unchanging and unchangeable, compounded of obligations and rights fixed by law, both written and customary. At all times the majority of men, including the most bloodstained baron, accepted unquestioningly the superior merits of the religious life; the liturgical worship of God and the contemplation of the spirit, by which man subordinated his nature and exorcized his desires, became a social ideal. And like all ideals dreamed of by many, it was attained by few. The institutions for its fulfilment were everywhere created, but frequently they served mere mundane ends. For the sake of power and wealth, men forgot their obligations and found it sufficient to expiate their sins in age or defeat. Even for those who genuinely sought the ideal in the most ascetic monastery, the instincts of men broke through and compelled them to draw, to paint, and to sing for the glory of God.

In the darkest decades, there was a force at work – trade – which was inimical to this world of warriors, priests, and peasants. Trade drew Moslem, Jew, and Christian together; trade fattened towns, sometimes bred them. In so primitive a world, the personalities of kings and popes could lead either to strong government or to social anarchy; peace and good harvests could lift prosperity with outstanding rapidity; war and disease and famine could hold in check all progress, all growth, for a generation. At times it seemed as if the forces of expansion would lift Europe to a higher level of civility than it had known since the decay of Rome; at others that it would vanish and leave nothing but barbarism. In the eleventh century, towns and trade and craftsmanship grew rapidly. An intense interest in ancient learning, particularly in Aristotle, followed; the surging success of the Crusades promised new power and new prosperity. But the prospect faded and disaster followed. The Western Christians savaged the Byzantine Empire; the Moslem world revived under the powerful leadership of the Ottoman Turks; the scourge of the bubonic plague emptied the towns and reduced Europe's population by at least a third. A new death rather than a rebirth seemed Europe's prospect. Indeed, the dance of death became a threnody of life, haunting the imagination of men. Yet in the middle of the fourteenth century there were forces working like yeast in the economy and in the spirit of Italy. During the Renaissance these were to ferment and turn life into a new form, not only in Italy itself but throughout the western world.

Throughout the Middle Ages, Italy never belonged wholly to Europe. The Romans had thoroughly colonized the land, creating an urban life which neither Goth nor Lombard nor Saracen ever totally destroyed. Feudalism was planted in Italy but never rooted deeply there. Gothic art achieved one or two outstanding successes, but never dominated the Italian imagination. Italy remained a prey of, not a breeding-ground for, warriors. During the waves of invasion there were times when it seemed that Italian society might be destroyed or transmogrified. The haemorrhage of war weakened Italy's strength, emptied her towns, diminished her trade, and enfeebled all institutions save the Church of Rome, whose universality endowed it with some of the authority, if little of the strength, of the Caesars. But always there was trade, there was an urban life. When Belisarius landed in the sixth century at Naples with his Byzantine troops, intent on recapturing Italy for the Eastern Empire, his leading ally was a Syrian businessman, Antiochus. Aistolf's laws for the Lombards, in about AD 750, legislated for merchants. A pair of Venetian traders, in 828, stole the relics of St Mark from Alexandria. By 836 there was at least one merchant, Semplicianus, rich enough to endow a monastery at Milan. Indeed, during these barbarous centuries, Venice was laying the foundations of its future greatness by exploiting the natural advantages that Italy possessed as the link between the primitive world of the North and the sophisticated East. The most valuable traffic was probably in men, women, and children, who were shipped to Alexandria where there was a ready slave market. Paid in coin, the Venetians then bought luxuries – the silks which the concubines of Charlemagne's court found so ravishing, the great silver dishes which might find their way into the ship-graves of chieftains by the northern seas, the papyrus that the papal Curia needed for its administration. As well as slaves, the Venetians traded the salt from their lagoon for the products of the Lombard plain. Nor was Venice the only mercantile community among Italian cities. Ships from Pisa, Genoa, and Amalfi ventured to the eastern Mediterranean, carrying pilgrims to the Holy Land, trading with the Greeks or the Moslems or the Jews, creating a spider's web of commerce. Yet progress was neither steady nor constant. Pirates infested the inland seas, war was endemic, and risks, like profits, were huge. Nor must the amount of trade be exaggerated; often it consisted of nothing more than a pedlar plodding dusty roads by the side of the Rhône, carrying his pack laden with eastern marvels to the rural fairs of Champagne.

Trade, however, was not the only catalyst at work in Italy and medieval Europe. The world of armed knights was not cheap; the courts of kings have never tolerated poverty; and though princes of the Church might preach self-denial, they rarely practised it. As war became more highly technical, it became more costly; as kingdoms grew in strength, their administration needed larger funds; as the network of churches and monasteries honeycombed Europe, so the wealth and expenses of the Church became more vast. The result was that the merchants quickly found themselves in fresh and lush pastures. They became financiers. As with trade, so with finance, the seeding-ground for the rest of Europe was Italy. The great banking street of London was, and still is, called Lombard Street after the Italian moneylenders who settled there in the thirteenth century. Of course, this high finance of popes, emperors, and kings could be as dangerous as trade. The Venetians rarely made any loans to a prince: the risk was too great and default too common. Yet in the handling of taxes, in the loans for war, in the purchased rights of justice, there were men who amassed fortunes. And by the High Middle Ages the structure of international finance, based on Italy, was as advanced as that of the ancient world. This helped to make Italian life more complex and more secular.

The burgeoning both of trade and of finance rested primarily on the growth of Europe's population. The great empty lands of Gaul, Britain, and Germany absorbed generation upon generation of men; in the struggle to conquer the forests, the marshes, and the wastes, few could be spared from the toil of the land save for prayer or for war. Although Italy was ravaged often, its thickly-spread peasant population possessed remarkable powers of recuperation from famine, pestilence, and war, and this numerous people nourished crafts and industries. Wealth and commerce aided their growth, and the old walled Roman cities gave them protection. Cities, not states or kings or princes, dominated the land. The sole exception was the Pope, whose superiority in the hierarchy of universal power even emperors had, after bitter conflicts, reluctantly admitted. The popes intended both to protect the Patrimony of St Peter and to prevent any secular ruler from achieving the hegemony of Italy. To achieve this aim they were rarely reluctant to call to their aid the warriors of France – an ominous precedent for the future. To check the Pope's territorial ambitions, some cities were not averse to asking on occasion for military help from the Emperor, to whom they owed a certain allegiance. It is true that the powers and rights of the Holy Roman Empire were more often ignored. Theoretically, the emperors claimed universal secular authority as the popes claimed universal spiritual power, but in practice the emperors' strength was based on the lands that they possessed in Germany, their estates in Italy, and a vast, ill-defined collection of rents, dues, and legal powers over the cities and states of Italy, the Netherlands, and parts of Burgundy. And any threat to the riches of Italy brought the imperial armies across the Alps. Invasion and war, sometimes desperate and tragic and bloody, threaded the history of Italy for a millennium, making her poets and philosophers dream of freedom, of unity, of peace. No great power ever succeeded for long, and the absence of a powerful state-system, the lack of any corpus of national law or secular jurisdiction, bred an openness to political experiment that was in itself a powerful stimulus to the new age which dawned in Italy toward the end of the fourteenth century, an age which was dominated by the city-state that was born in the violence and anarchy of medieval Italy.

Trade, high finance, a large and partially urbanized population, quickening industry, the absence of a deeply rooted all-powerful political structure – all of these were seminal. There were, however, other forces – equally important, if less measurable – that were needed to change the whole life of Italy at the Renaissance as cer-ainly and as dramatically as the Industrial Revolution changed the face of Britain in the late eighteenth century. Ideas, like heresy, travelled in the Middle Ages along the lines of trade. From Byzantium, from Islam, from the prosperous and flourishing lands of France, Burgundy, and the Flemish towns came ideas in art, in technology, in science, and in philosophy. And even in the most barbarous times, cultivated Italians never forgot the great traditions of their imperial past nor their splendid achievements in literature. Throughout the Middle Ages the classics had been copied, studied frequently for their moral virtues, occasionally enjoyed for themselves. Monks appreciated Horace as well as Seneca, and even Ovid was not unknown to the cloister. There were high points of excitement and discovery. The recovery of many of Aristotle's works in the twelfth and early thirteenth centuries, from Arabic sources, created an intellectual ferment in scholastic circles. As secular life grew in complexity and stability and urbanity, the laws of Justinian became the object of devoted research, and long before the Renaissance, Roman ideas of law, of order, and of government had permeated Italian city life. This complex society, never far from barbarism yet close to civility, threw up men of great intellectual stature and brilliant literary gifts. Long before the Renaissance dawned, St Thomas Aquinas had provided a philosophic argument for dogma that was to serve men for century after century. Dante, the Florentine, produced the first great poem in Italian – a poem that is medieval in spirit but modern in technique – and Petrarch, who followed, showed that Dante's achievement was not likely to remain unique. These were but the brightest stars in a luminous firmament.

Europe of the Middle Ages was not a closed world. The Crusades had ripped open the Near East and given the hordes of warriors a taste of sophisticated, cultured society which previously had only been the experience of merchants and pilgrims. And Italy was the door through which the Crusaders passed. There had been more distant seekings, too. Marco Polo had reached Peking; links, unfortunately to prove as fragile as gossamer, had been made with the long-lost Nestorian Christians of India and China. At one time it seemed as if the Great Khan himself might turn Christian and link Europe with the eastern seas. The glimpse of the wider world proved brief – the Khan remained a Buddhist, the Chinese threw off Mongol control, and Ottomans swept the Christian powers out of Asia Minor, seized the Balkans, and threatened Italy itself. Yet this ebb and flow of European power interlocked the Christian and Moslem worlds. Methods and materials passed from one to the other. At the splendid court in Sicily of Frederick II, it was an Arab who taught geography and presented the Emperor with a silver sphere on which the map of the world was drawn. Indeed, at that court the Renaissance itself seemed at hand. Frederick, ruthless, amoral, violent, a realist in politics as in philosophy, might have been an uncle of Cesare Borgia. Although he was the Holy Roman Emperor, possessing vast lands and vaster rights beyond the Alps, the core of Frederick's strength and power lay in his kingdom of Sicily, which contained most of southern Italy as well as the island itself. Here he introduced laws based on Justinian's code, fostered city life, and favoured the bourgeoisie. He patronized the arts; encouraged literature, poetry, science; kept an astrologer; dabbled in alchemy; brought together a menagerie of rare animals and an exotic collection of mistresses. He lived flamboyantly and realistically and delighted in the creative activities of man. But he was a portent, not a man of his time. Legends festooned his name, and they called him *stupor mundi* as much from awe as from flattery. The delight of his court in literature and in philosophic inquiry, the efficiency of his administration, the energy of his diplomacy, and above all the openness of his mind to all ideas, whether Moslem or Christian or pagan, struck a rare chord in thirteenth-century Europe. Yet about him and his courtiers there is still an air of barbarism, a lack of sophistication, even of experience, that makes his world, in truth if not in appearance, closer to that of Charlemagne or Otto I than that of Lorenzo de' Medici or Lodovico Sforza.

By the time of Lorenzo and Lodovico, Italy had changed fundamentally and dramatically, and this change is rightly called the Renaissance. In Rome broad streets had been driven through the chaotic slums that crouched amid the rubbish of antiquity. A new city had arisen about the Vatican, and the plans for the huge Basilica of St Peter were slowly taking shape. The palaces of the cardinals proclaimed the tastes, the interests, the sophistications of this new age. As in Rome, so in Florence. The great towers in which families

23

had sought refuge during the furious vendettas of the Middle Ages had been razed. In their place stood the opulent homes of patrician families – Strozzi, Medici, Rucellai, and the rest. These great houses were designed according to the austere classical harmonies that the great architect of the Renaissance – Brunelleschi – had made fashionable. Out in the Tuscan countryside the first villas of modern times rivalled those of Augustan Rome. The style as well as the decoration of these buildings was in sharp and vivid contrast to the Gothic which so many men and women of the Renaissance thoughtlessly despised, not realizing the extent of their debt to their recent past. But such unawareness was scarcely surprising, for their age was astonishingly fresh, and the achievements of the fifteenth century as remarkable as they were original. Historians, concerned with origins and remote influences, stress how deeply interlocked this age of the Renaissance was with the medieval world: how much it owed to Flanders, to Paris, to Byzantium. True as this may be, it also distorts reality by the nature of its emphasis. It would be folly to underestimate the creative strength and originality of fifteenth-century Italy. This stretched far beyond architecture, dramatic though the structural changes of the Italian cities were. In sculpture and in painting the change was, perhaps, more profound. In both these arts there had been precursors – Giotto, the great Florentine painter, Duccio, the Sienese, and Andrea Pisano, the sculptor – and the break with the past was neither so sharp nor so vivid as in building. The achievement, however, was far greater. For the next four centuries the themes, the traditions, the techniques, and the preoccupations of the artists of fifteenth-century Italy were to dominate Western Europe. The roll call of their names – Fra Angelico, Bellini, Botticelli, Donatello, Ghiberti, Leonardo, Lippi, Mantegna, Michelangelo, Pollaiuolo, Signorelli, and Verrocchio, a list that could be doubled with scarcely any loss of quality – speaks for itself: such a constellation of artistic genius, spread over a mere century and a half, would alone make the Renaissance one of the great epochs of human achievement.

Yet art was only one aspect of the brilliance of Renaissance Italy, which created an image of man, a vision of human excellence, that *still* lies at the heart of the Western tradition. Rarely achieved, it has nevertheless haunted men like a mirage. The Italians, particularly the Florentines, revered antiquity – its wisdom, its grace, its philosophy, and its literature. Sensitive and deep-thinking men had done so, of course, ever since the Roman world had crumbled into decay; in monastic schools and universities Plato, as well as Aristotle, had been studied intensively. Yet such knowledge had been largely part of the private world of scholars. At the time of the Renaissance these humanistic studies spread through the upper and middle ranks of society and became a formidable part of the education of those who were to wield power and authority. The timely invention of the printing press not only multiplied the works of antiquity so that they were readily available to hundreds of thousands of men and women, but also helped to create a public for their study. What had been private became public, and a study of the classical heritage became a necessity for a gentleman; indeed, his familiarity with the classics was the hallmark of civility. A man might still be a warrior, a priest, a merchant, with a professional outlook and professional mores, yet if he wished to be regarded as the complete man, *l'uomo universale*, more was expected of him. He needed to be well-bred, and the breeding of a gentleman was defined by Italians of the Renaissance. They insisted on a refinement of taste, an ease of manner, combined with a capacity for manly pursuits, a knowledge of the classics, an acquaintance with history and philosophy, an appreciation of music, painting, architecture, and sculpture, a connoisseurship of the rare and the beautiful whether books, jewels, coins, or scraps of antiquity. All of these interests were to be lightly borne, without pedantry or excessive professionalism. This was the image that Castiglione created in his famous book, *The Courtier* – an image which was drawn from the knowledge he acquired of men such as Lorenzo de' Medici and Federigo da Montefeltro.

Saints Ambrose, Michael, and Augustine, by Simone Martini
Fitzwilliam Museum, Cambridge

To acquire, let alone indulge, such sophisticated tastes required money, for education in so many disciplines and interests, even if superficial, took time, and no one could patronize the arts without wealth. As patronage grew competitive, the arts themselves became more costly. Renaissance society was designed for rich men, rich cities, rich popes. To maintain so vast an expenditure required an active and most profitable commerce; to indulge it a prodigious concentration of costly talent was necessary. And the Italian cities possessed both. Venice, Florence, Milan, and Rome were full of exceedingly rich men, and money, which was the base of all Renaissance achievement, nurtured genius. The transmutation of gold into works of art was the result of a complex social process, the marriage between aristocratic extravagance and bourgeois ambition. The aristocrats of medieval Europe did not vanish overnight; they still lived on, maintaining their sense of caste, providing a snobbish goal towards which the rich merchant could direct his social ambition. The patricians of Florence, Milan, or Venice might be merchants, but they wished to live like nobles in Italy of the Renaissance; therefore, aristocratic and bourgeois attitudes fused to create a pattern of life, a tradition of social expression that was to be adopted by societies of the West as the wealth of the New World and of the Indies poured into their cities. Commercial capitalism, struggling in the framework of feudalism, learned, through Italy, not only how to express itself in art and learning, but also how to make an art of life itself.

It is a sobering thought that the great Italian achievements in almost every sphere of intellectual and artistic activity took place in a world of violence and war. Cities were torn by feud and vendetta: Milan warred against Venice, Florence against Pisa, Rome against Florence, Naples against Milan. Alliances were forged only to be broken, the countryside was constantly scarred by pillage, rapine, and battle, and in this maelstrom the old bonds of society were broken and new ones forged. After a brief period of peace, in the

second half of the fifteenth century, the confusion and carnage grew
worse through the great French invasions of Charles VIII, Louis XII,
and Francis I, a time of agony that did not end till the dreadful sack
of Rome in 1527 by the Holy Roman Emperor, Charles V. Yet this
violence worked like yeast in the thought of men, and profoundly
influenced the way they were to regard problems of power and
government for hundreds of years. They ceased to look for answers
to the fate of man in the dogmas of the Church. They searched the
histories of antiquity for precedents that might guide them to the
truth, but they also sought to explain, as Machiavelli did, the world
in which they lived by what they knew to be the nature of man.
Indeed, it was during the Renaissance in Italy that many men came
to feel that truth was elusive, a mood afterwards strengthened by the
discovery of the world beyond Europe. The old dogmatic certainties
did not vanish at once, and the habit of trying to nail truth down
by argument from fundamental principles was not lightly cast aside.
Some of the most original minds, however, particularly Machiavelli
and Leonardo da Vinci, sought truth not in argument but in
observation. Machiavelli brooded on men and events, on the effects
of political action, and on the consequence of chance; Leonardo
grew preoccupied with the flow of water, the flight of birds, the
formation of rocks. The growth of ideas and the development of
mental attitudes are difficult to pinpoint in the course of history, but
this, at least, can be said: the men of the Renaissance, by the range
of their inquiries, by the freshness of their scepticism, and by the
sharpness of their observation, gave impetus to, and helped to
acquire intellectual acceptance for, the search for truth on earth
instead of in heaven.

Artistic expression, intellectual inquiry, social attainments – the
Renaissance enriched all these things in an original and creative way.
Its influence spread throughout Europe and continued for centuries.
It was the work of hundreds of gifted men and a score of remarkable
cities – Vicenza, Rimini, Ferrara, Urbino, Mantua, Parma, and the

rest all made their contributions. They had their artists, philosophers, poets, and craftsmen of genius and distinction, yet the full force of the Renaissance flowed most strongly in four cities – Florence, Milan, Rome, and Venice. Florence, a very small city by modern standards, cradled the Renaissance and produced an astonishing array of genius which Rome and Milan, both far richer than Florence, patronized. The full tide of the Renaissance reached Venice late, but it lingered there longer, creating an island of delight in a world made brutal by the new clash of religious ideologies as the Reformation broke Europe asunder. Neither Reformation nor Counter-reformation, nor the economic decline of Italy, brought on by the discovery of the New World, could check the spread of the Renaissance. Its ideas and its achievements ran like an ineradicable dye through the fabric of Europe, and its monuments have become a part of the world's heritage.

Chess game
Jacopo de Cessolis, Libro di Giuocho di Scacchi
Florence, 1493

'HORROR waits on princes,' wrote Webster, the Elizabethan dramatist for whom the bloodstained annals of Italy had a compulsive fascination. Certainly, the way to power was strewn with corpses; men murdered their wives, wives poisoned their husbands, brother slaughtered brother, family raged against family, city sacked city. In 1402 the chief members of the ruling house of Lodi were burned alive on the public square; at Bologna in 1445 the people, enraged by the slaughter of their favourite family, the Bentivoglio, hunted down their enemies and nailed their steaming hearts to the doors of the Bentivoglio's palace, as a token of their love.

Yet Bologna was a tranquil city compared to many, and even bloodless when matched with Foligno; there a noble – Pietro Rasiglia – cuckolded by his prince, took his vengeance. He flung his faithless wife from the turrets of his castle and killed two brothers of the prince. Retribution rapidly followed. The whole Rasiglia clan, men, women, and children, were butchered and chopped up; their joints, hung like meat, were paraded through the streets. Of course, the ghoulish chroniclers liked to heighten the horror, and their macabre imaginations rioted in sadistic fantasy. Yet all allowance made, politics became a murderous game in which death in bed came only to the skilful or the lucky. The savagery used by men in pursuit of power was due to the nature of society and the prizes which it offered.

The city-states of Italy had won their independence by playing off the two greatest powers of medieval Europe – the Papacy and the Empire. In theory, the Pope ruled men's souls, the Emperor their bodies; the facts accorded ill with theory. The Church had acquired property which no emperor or king could match; its real estate, its pecuniary rights – first fruits, Peter's pence, and the like – made it formidably rich, rich enough to challenge the Empire and to claim the supremacy of the spiritual over the temporal power. Yet bishops were princes as well as bishops; abbots and their monasteries owed feudal obligations on their lands. The great baronage of the Empire bred too many sons to view the Church's dependence on Rome with equanimity. Who should or should not select or confirm the bishops in their rights became a vital matter for emperors. And although the great struggle between the Empire and the Papacy expressed itself in the language of theology, its roots were mundane enough – land, money, power. Behind the Papacy stood the great estate of the clergy, formidable in numbers, in learning, and in authority; the Emperor had his own resources. His major strength was drawn from his lands and rights in Germany, Austria, and the Netherlands, but he was also King of Lombardy and, as such, possessed important and valuable lands in Northern Italy; yet his presence was rare in these territories, and his enemies flourished at his expense. The chief of these was the Papacy, rendered strong and inflexible by the great reforming popes of the twelfth and thirteenth centuries.

The Papacy, conscious of its God-given role in the *respublica Christiana*, had not been reluctant to encourage the revolt of the Italian communes, any more than it had hesitated to call to its aid the ferocious Norman barons, to help it in its conflict with the emperors. This great struggle unleashed on town and village and countryside the fratricidal war between the Pope's party, the *parte Guelfa*, and the Emperor's, the *parte Ghibellina*, which continued long after the defeat of the Hohenstaufen emperors had destroyed the hopes of the Ghibellines. It left behind two poles of feeling about which passion and anger and rivalry could crystallize – often to the point of absurdity, as when the Ghibellines of Milan tore down the Christ from the high altar in the Cathedral of Cremona because His face was turned to His shoulder in the manner of a Guelph. Yet the great conflict between Pope and Emperor left behind more than a tradition of internecine war. It unleashed chaos; an anarchy of power in which the strong devoured the weak, in which trivial wars, scarcely more significant than riots, alternated with struggles that involved the lives of thousands. From 1350 to 1450 Italy scarcely knew a month, let alone a year, of peace. Yet during this time the great states – Florence, Milan, Naples, Venice – emerged as the arbiters of Italy's destiny. None powerful enough to overthrow the others, they lived in an uneasy equilibrium of power that lasted for nearly fifty years until, in 1494, welcomed by Milan, the French king invaded Italy to assert his dynastic claims. Wars more terrible and more violent than Italy had ever known ravaged the land and turned Lombardy into a cockpit in the struggle between the Habsburg emperors and the French kings, a struggle that lasted until the sack of Rome in 1527, when Charles v brutally reasserted the Imperial power and tied the destiny of Italy to the house of Habsburg.

In war or in peace, in freedom or in subjection, the towns grew, and in growing changed the nature of their government, sliding from hopeful democracy into greedy oligarchy. They varied greatly in size and power – a few like Florence, nearly a hundred thousand strong, a hive of trade and manufacture, and many like Orvieto of about twenty thousand, busy market towns of farmers, shopkeepers, and artisans. Yet, great or small, they had each undergone a novel political experience – the flowering of a qualified democracy in the midst of feudalism. Within these cities the *popolo* – not the people but the members of craft guilds – had acquired power and taken over or devised their own institutions of government. Usually they possessed no written authority or fundamental constitution; they exercised power, solved their problems, *ad hoc*. They represented not only the wealth and the enterprise of the city, but also that oligarchy of families which could hold and maintain authority. Force, and the consent of their immediate supporters, was the basis of their government. There was rarely unity in any commune – the nobility both of the surrounding countryside, known as the *contado*, which acknowledged the authority of the city, or of the city itself, had long been divided by feuds and rivalries before the division between Guelph and Ghibelline gave their hatreds a sharper edge. And although the artisans and merchants dominated the life of the city, they frequently needed the skill and the training of the nobility both in diplomacy and in war. Furthermore, the unformalized nature of these city constitutions enabled men seeking power to manipulate the quasi-democratic methods of government, as the

The grand entry of Charles VIII into Naples
Page from a contemporary MS.
Pierpont Morgan Library, New York

Medici were to do with supreme skill in Florence. And the relics of the nobility, or in the large towns the great merchant oligarchs, had little difficulty in acquiring the leadership and the control of seemingly 'popular' movements. Hence there was a pronounced tendency for all communes to drift, either secretly or openly, to the despotism of a family or a clique. This was the ground swell that was to lift the Renaissance prince to power.

Chance, however, in the shape of the great bubonic plague that ravished Italy in the middle of the fourteenth century, also took a hand. Men and women died like flies, and death ate up the cities more rapidly than the countryside. Chronicler after chronicler tells of the empty streets, the pillaged houses, the yawning pits in the graveyards, and the resulting poverty from the decay of trade. In this blighted world it was naturally easier for tyranny to flourish.

Yet plague or no plague, tyranny probably would have thrived. From the earliest days of these communes, force and expediency had governed all. Their urbanism had been as militant and as aggressive as any nationalism. They had seized villages and lesser towns by force; and war had been the lifeblood of their growth. A small town such as Orvieto, perched on its impregnable fortress of rock, quickly absorbed great tracts of countryside, stretching south to the Lake of Bolsena, westward to the coast, eastward to the Tiber, and north almost to Lake Trasimeno – almost, because greater cities than Orvieto were expanding too. Siena and Perugia wanted the territory that Orvieto coveted. Neither was without enemies on its own northern borders. Florence hated Siena and attacked or courted Perugia according to her need. So war was endemic, and the citizens were constantly marching out to do battle with their neighbours.

The further dimension of diplomacy, with the vast paraphernalia of chicanery and pressure and secrecy, found its breeding ground in the rivalries and conflicts of these city-states, for what was true of Orvieto, Siena, Perugia, and Florence was equally true of the cities of the Lombard plain or the Patrimony of St Peter. Only in the

35

south, in the kingdoms of Naples and of Sicily, was the conflict of cities held in check by the rule of hereditary monarchy. The Papacy, which might have given coherence to the Patrimony of St Peter, had been transferred to Avignon in 1309, where it remained until 1378. From then until 1417 the Great Schism provided yet additional causes for division and strife not only in the Papal States, but also throughout Italy. And it was not until 1421 that Martin v re-established the Papacy firmly and securely at Rome. The Emperor, after the defeat of the last of the Hohenstaufen, lacked the power to influence, let alone control, Lombardy's political development. Hence the appetites of the city-states for their neighbours' lands went unchecked, and war was constant. And not only war – so was treason, murder, and plot, for this reason. Some states lacked constitutions, they were without the constitutional formalization of social, economic, and political power that was sanctioned by tradition or by law. Power was captured by groups, by inter-related families, sometimes depending on oligarchic, sometimes on popular, support, and occasionally on the help of other city-states and, in time, on foreign invasion. Exiles from all states abounded, to become the instruments of aggression: murder, trickery, and civil war were accepted elements of political activity. Gradually, as war diminished the localization of power, the great city-states emerged. Florence battered down Pisa and Pistoia; Venice absorbed Padua and Verona; Milan ate up Pavia and Lodi; by skilful alliances a few smaller states – Ferrara, Mantua, and others – survived to act as pawns in the chequer-board of power. Such states were too large and too rich to rely on the citizen army, which had been sufficient in the earlier days when the enemy was but a day's march away. Also, war was becoming too technical for simple peasants and workers. The cities had the need for, and the money to hire, the professional soldiers – the condottieri – who roamed Italy in order to ravage a living from its people. As the wily Venetians realized, the condottieri prevented armed power from being placed in the hands of a citizen or his

Condottiere, by Leonardo da Vinci
British Museum

faction; and so it became a fixed principle of Venetian administration that no Venetian born could command its army. At first the condottieri were foreign – Sir John Hawkwood, an Englishman, had a famous band of ravishers, the White Company. Soon the tyrants of petty states put themselves and their citizens out for hire. Some, like the Montefeltro of Urbino, kept their states, their heads, and their reputations; others, like Francesco Sforza, won a duchy;

The condottiere Roberto Malatesta, detail
From Piero di Cosimo's Passage of the Red Sea
Sistine Chapel

most died violently, executed, murdered, killed in battle. They lived for hire, but they could not be trusted, since bought troops meant treacherous troops. Always the danger loomed of a condottiere turning against the state that employed him. This the Venetians and the Florentines realized clearly enough, and they saw to it that the camps of their condottieri were riddled with spies. The use of hired professional armies reduced violence even though it increased treachery, for no captain wished to waste his greatest asset – his fighting men. As a result, battles were rare, sieges infinitely prolonged. And increasingly, to the alarms and rumours of war and conspiracy were added the deliberate exaggeration and the hidden subterfuges of diplomacy.

Diplomacy as we know it arose in Italy of the Renaissance. It grew strong in the fifteenth century through the equilibrium of power created by the three great northern states of Italy – Milan, Venice, and Florence. It appealed to the leaders of these mercantile societies. They enjoyed and believed in the efficacy of hard bargaining, nor were they unaware of the merits of partnership for the destruction of rivals (and partners need supervision as well as persuasion). The collection of intelligence, the assessment of personalities and contingencies, was early the stock in trade of bankers. The application of these commercial techniques to the service of the state was effortlessly made. Every Venetian abroad was expected to spy for his country. Nor was intelligence required solely for the purpose of foreign affairs; internally it was of equal if not greater importance. The fear of tyrants intensified their suspicion as well as their cruelty; thus their citizens and followers were encouraged to spy and to betray. Such behaviour was not peculiar to despotisms: in Venice men were encouraged to report anonymously their suspicions of their neighbours. These calumnies were meticulously sifted, at times with the help of the rack and the boot, by the republic's inquisitors. Elsewhere fear took on more fantastic shapes, and friends, relations, and children of tyrants lived on a volcano of violence that could erupt on the slightest suspicion. Naturally, such insecurity bred a desire to survive that overrode all claims to loyalty or affection, and frequently poison or the dagger momentarily cleared a state of its bloodstained ruler. Yet such actions and attitudes were an accepted part of the political and military life.

The frequency of assassination, the perennial plots, the constant vicissitudes encouraged superstition and a romantic view of Fate. Men felt themselves to be the prey of strange destinies and turned to astrologers and magicians to strengthen their hope, to check despair, and to help them meet the uncertain future with confidence. The stars were studied as intensely as diplomatic dispatches, as a guide to action; and superstitious dread threaded the daily course of men's lives. Even the popes felt more secure in their faith when the heavens were propitious. Julius II fixed the date of his coronation on the advice of his astrologers, and Paul III arranged his consistories at the dictates of the stars.

The ever-present sense of death and danger heightened instinct as well as superstition. The possession of power, naked and absolute, removed the barriers for its gratification, no matter how quaint the desire might be. At the courts of the despots sexual licence was as common as treachery. And in the rampages of the flesh, as in the pursuit of power, the popes were second to none. The princes and the republics of the Renaissance lived in a dangerous, excitable, and exciting world of power. Morality was not involved, only success. But, of course, only a few princes, nobles, and merchants were concerned in any state. The mass of the people eschewed office, and the disasters of government troubled them only in military defeat.

Yet it would be wrong to consider the tyrants of Italy as concerned only with the pursuit of power by the most cruel methods. Many were intelligent, some sensitive; all desired fame. Since fame involved outward expression – buildings, statuary, art, pageants, tourneys, and even public benefactions – patronage, in its widest aspects, was an illustration of power, or rather of social and political

Assassination attempt
Detail from Scene from the Life of San Bernardino
Pinacoteca Vanucci, Perugia

grandeur. Splendour added stature to the Doge as well as the Pope, and the Visconti with their Cathedral of Milan and their Certosa at Pavia glorified their state as well as their dynasty. Display became a part of the art of government, and the wealth of Italy permitted an extravagance that would not have been unbecoming to an ancient Roman emperor. Pageantry was also a part of the aristocratic tradition, but the riches of the Medici, the Sforza, the Gonzaga, or the Este, and the skill of their painters and sculptors, raised this art to an intenser level. The tourneys which celebrated the wedding of Beatrice d'Este and Lodovico Sforza were prolonged, extravagant, drenched in mythology, a vast spectacle that took months to prepare and days to enact. And for this Leonardo da Vinci directed his genius to the design of the costumes. The power of princes and the glory of

Tempio Malatestiano, Rimini, by Alberti

cities could be expressed less ephemerally. All raised monuments to their greatness in buildings, in painting, and in sculpture. Leonardo da Vinci sought the patronage of Cesare Borgia as well as Lodovico Sforza; Raphael began his career in the most bloodstained and power-ravaged city of Italy – Perugia. The patronage of tyrants took delight in all that gratified the mind as well as the senses of men. Exquisite and extravagant food, fabulous and sumptuous clothing,delicate and intricate jewellery, masterpieces of craftsmanship in silver and gold, lightened the strain and soothed the anxieties of princes. So did the memorials of antiquity, the broken torsos, the green, encrusted bronzes, the coins and medallions which the earth yielded. Books were novel not only in their contents but also in their new printed form, and it was not long before they became as worthy of collection as the illustrated manuscripts of the recent past. The animate world also distracted the mind and ennobled the possessor. Strange animals or misshapen men were collected like curios. Popes and kings, cardinals and princes outbid each other to persuade the great in art, letters, and science to join their entourage; rarely has so great a premium been placed on men of creative ability. These strange courts of princes – so close to violence, yet so alive to beauty, so transient in power, yet so permanent in expression – need a closer focus, both the best and the worst.

At Mantua, high above the Piazza Sordello, swings an iron cage; throughout the fourteenth and fifteenth centuries it was usually occupied by a dead or dying man. The grim, embattled palaces of the Bonacolsi and the Gonzaga provided a fitting background to the sagas of their princes. The lords of Mantua had their quota of fratricide, of treasonable sons and murderous uncles, of wives caught in adultery and killed for their crime. Its citizens, as well as its princes, had their times of horror, their years of tribulation. Like all city-states it was born in feudal anarchy and nurtured by inter-urban strife. Gifted with a superb natural strength (on three sides the Mincio swells out into large, wide lakes that proved difficult to probe), Mantua quickly dominated the surrounding countryside and held it against the most formidable assaults of its combined enemies Still, it is doubtful whether it could have survived but for the aid of Venice. It was too strong and too remote for Venice to absorb, yet its powerful princes were an excellent buffer against their common enemy, Milan. So the Venetians hired the Gonzaga as condottieri and, to pay them, ceded Lombard towns that were too weak to maintain their independence and too poor for Venice to covet. The Gonzaga were too clever to allow a tradition of dependence on Venice to develop, and from time to time they sold their skill to the rulers of Milan. The balance of power kept Mantua independent, and the needs of Venice or Milan made it rich. Violent though its history was, it enjoyed more peace and greater security than was the common lot of Italian cities. The unruly, battle-scarred Gonzaga were never mere condottieri; they governed as strongly as they fought. Under Lodovico Gonzaga, in spite of plague and pestilence and flood, trade in wool and silks flourished, and the population grew to forty thousand or more. Money from war and trade was spent not only to delight the eye, but also to train the mind. Opportunities for pageantry proved frequent enough. Pius II called a council there in 1459 to declare a Crusade against the Turks. In 1474 the King of Denmark paid a state visit and found a royal welcome. Powerful neighbours – the Sforza from Milan, the Este from Ferrara – expected and received extravagant hospitality. The births and marriages and deaths of Gonzaga princes were celebrated with appropriate solemnity and expense. So were their triumphs: few public occasions matched the reception of Francesco Gonzaga, the first cardinal of his house, a prince of the Church at seventeen and a symbol of his family's greatness.

As became Renaissance princes, the Gonzaga sought a permanent expression for their wealth and power and destiny. Lodovico (1414–78) was, perhaps, the most gifted of his family and possessed abundantly those wide-ranging tastes and abilities that were so much

Francesco Gonzaga, by Gian Cristoforo Romano
Museo Bardini, Florence

admired in his day. He embodied the skill and decision of a man of action with the sensitivity of a scholar. He proved himself ruthless in war, adept in diplomacy, yet more generous towards his treacherous brother Carlo than was usual in a despot, a sign of that human warmth which infused his private life and his artistic sensibilities. By 1460 he had persuaded Andrea Mantegna to make Mantua his permanent home and to become his court painter. The result was a splendid series of frescoes that still adorn the Camera degli Sposi in the Castello of Mantua; other frescoes have been destroyed, and pictures that were painted for Lodovico dispersed, but what remains is one of the great achievements of the Renaissance. As with painting, so with architecture: for Lodovico's taste was sure. He employed Alberti – a man of universal genius and a leading Florentine figure in the Classical revival – to design his churches, and urged Mantuans to give generously so that plans for Sant' Andrea could become a reality, which, as Lodovico said, 'from its vast size and noble simplicity should be superior to any building of the kind in the leading cities of Italy, and worthy to stand beside the magnificence of Rome herself'. Huge buildings, sumptuous palaces, brilliant paintings – these were the common extension of a prince's greatness. Lodovico, however, was a man of wider and deeper sympathies. He encouraged philosophers and poets to stay at his court. Pico della Mirandola, Platina, Poliziano, Ognibene, Guarino da Verona, and Filelfo: all, at one time or another, brought distinction to the Mantuan court. Lodovico himself took a delight in books; he collected not only manuscripts of the classics, but also of Dante, Petrarch, and Boccaccio, and employed the most gifted craftsmen to illustrate their books.

The width of Lodovico's interest was due partly to his native genius and partly also to his education, for it was in the education of princes that Mantua made one of its most remarkable contributions to the Renaissance. Lodovico's father had established the great humanist Vittorino da Feltre at Mantua. Vittorino's ideas were to influence European education profoundly for centuries. He believed that education should concern itself with the body as well as the mind, with the senses as well as the spirit. Wrestling, fencing, swimming, and riding alternated with hours devoted to Virgil, Homer, Cicero, and Demosthenes. Luxury was eschewed, and Vittorino educated the poor with the rich. Nor was he prejudiced about the sexes; the Gonzaga princesses enjoyed the same extensive education as the princes. Above all, he encouraged the belief that individual greatness was part of the nature of man, and a desirable part, one that was in no way in opposition to the obligations which men had to their fellow men. To Vittorino the virtues were innate; they were human. Although a devout Christian and insistent on regular religious practices, he nevertheless cherished an optimistic view of man's capacities. Certainly in Lodovico, as in the great Federigo da Montefeltro, Vittorino found an apt pupil, and the traditions which he helped to create kept the Gonzaga from gross excesses and saved Mantua from the terrible sufferings which were so frequently the lot of other Italian cities. And Lodovico was as lucky in his children and his grandchildren as Mantua was in its dynasty. His son Federigo proved himself as skilful a condottiere, as wily a diplomat, and as sensitive a patron as his father, but it was his grandson Francesco and his wife, Isabella d'Este, who lifted the court of Mantua to its highest fame.

There were few among the lesser cities which enjoyed such serenity as Mantua or were led by so able a man. Ferrara under the Este, Bologna under the Bentivoglio, and Urbino under the Montefeltro were perhaps its nearest rivals, but the common lot of cities was more grievous, their tyrants more terrible. Orvieto, in little more than fifty years, was sacked and ravaged eight times, and sacked and ravaged with a brutality that was exceptional even for those murderous times. Yet even in an age which had grown immune to violence, the thought of Perugia and its tyrants made men quail.

The cities of the papal states experienced the most unfortunate

47

The Rout of San Romano. Detail, by Uccello
Uffizi, Florence

fate of all the Italian communes. The absence of the popes at Avignon had given an opportunity for princely anarchy to flourish; the Great Schism had encouraged lawlessness and rapine; and the return of the popes to Rome merely led to punitive wars. Both by geographical position and by reason of its size, Perugia was regarded as one of the most important cities of the Patrimony. By the middle of the fifteenth century its history was steeped in bloodshed that none other could equal. Chroniclers delighted in exaggeration and enjoyed recounting blood-curdling deeds, yet after making every allowance, the Perugian story is horrifying in its utter cruelty and in its wanton disregard of human suffering. The great families, who with their armed ruffians raged and stormed and slaughtered in its streets and churches, failed to exterminate each other; some always seemed to escape; to live to plot revenge. Naturally, the cities that feared Perugia were ready to succour them and to provide them with arms and money for their campaigns of revenge. And the oppression which Perugians suffered too often lured them into thinking that any change of master might be for the better.

Here are but a few examples of Perugia's tribulations, of the curse of blood that seemed to its great chronicler Matarazzo to be the city's fate.

In 1488 the Baglioni and their enemies the Oddi fought a pitched battle in the Piazza, and the governors of the city were helpless to stop it. In 1491 the Baglioni strung up before the Palazzo dei Priori 130 men, supporters of the Oddi, who had found their way into the city. Shortly after this the Baglioni were only saved by the bravery and skill of Simonetto, a boy of eighteen, who held a narrow street with a few followers until they were nearly hacked to pieces. Then came the great betrayal in which four of the leading Baglioni were slaughtered in their beds – including Simonetto. Between 1520 and 1535 practically all who were left of the Baglioni were either publicly executed or murdered by each other. Nor were these fratricidal vendettas the only horror that the Perugians had to suffer. War was waged in their *contado* with a ferocity unusual for the fifteenth century, for the Baglioni, as condottieri, did not believe in half-measures. And to give an additional taste of horror, the plague found in Perugia a happy playground – between 1424 and 1486 there were eight severe epidemics.

Violence and sickness, suffering and death, made the Perugians susceptible to the more evangelistic expressions of religious fervour. The slaughters by, or of, the Baglioni were usually followed by days of solemn ritual and purification. On one occasion the cathedral was washed with wine and reconsecrated; on another over thirty altars were erected in the Piazza, and Mass was continuously solemnized. It is not, therefore, surprising that the vivid preaching of Fra Bernardino of Siena found a fruitful soil in Perugia. The people of the city responded eagerly to his denunciations of the vanity of all earthly life. He condemned the crimes of its citizens,

Design for a fortress, by Francesco di Giorgio Martini
Trattato di Architettura Civile e Militare
Biblioteca Nazionale, Florence

called them to repentance, reconciled enemies, and made a large bonfire of worldly delights in a great act of public repentance. The results of Bernadino proved as fleeting as were the reconciliations of the Baglioni and the Oddi later in the century, yet this thread of religious revivalism, of sensational open-air preaching, of the sudden need for public repentance, was not an unusual theme in city life of fifteenth-century Italy – it was a common response to the insecurities created by war and pestilence and crime.

Although the constant strife proved inimical to trade, although the population declined, these things failed to kill the vigorous artistic life of Perugia. In the midst of the turmoils, paintings of exceptional beauty were produced: Perugino and Raphael shared the city with the Baglioni and the Oddi. Perugino's frescoes of quiet, ecstatic saints, and Bonfigli's charming, tender, personal vision of the merciful Madonna, provided the background for fratricidal slaughter in a piazza reeking with blood and festooned with the grotesque shapes of slaughtered youths and men. At no other place were the dark and the light of Renaissance life brought to a stranger contrast.

Sensitive, thoughtful men realized that this was a world like to none other. They searched the histories of antiquity – Livy, Suetonius, Plutarch – looking for the keys that would unlock for them the problems of princes and of cities. What made men succeed? Or fail? Why did some cities grow great and rich only to dissipate it all in war and rebellion? Why did free citizens become the prey of professional thugs? What were the causes of tyranny? Was tyranny bad? Did cities have a natural life like men – youth, maturity, age? And were learning, art, and the practice of humanism bound up with the nature of institutions? Did philosophers make the best citizens? They ransacked antiquity, read again and again Plato and Aristotle and, above all, Cicero, who seemed to demonstrate more clearly than any other the virtues of a philosopher at large in civic life. What they did not turn to was theology, to St Thomas Aquinas, to St Ambrose, or to St Jerome. The theological way of thinking about men and events was as alien to them as a salon painting to Picasso. The key to their problems they knew to be rooted in the lives and actions of men, not in universal mysteries or the attributes of God. Consequently, there is an astonishing freshness about the historians and the political philosophers of the Renaissance, and, as with the painters and sculptors, the greatest by far were the Florentines, and the greatest of the Florentines was Niccolò Machiavelli, whose speculations about the nature of men's political actions are as remote from the thinkers of the Middle Ages as Leonardo da Vinci's drawings are from the illuminations of missals. Yet Machiavelli is no isolated phenomenon – from Salutati to Guicciardini, men were following the same quest. What general rules can be derived from political experience? As history enshrines political experience, thinkers grew profoundly interested in the past. In the Middle Ages political philosophers were theologians, in the Renaissance they were historians. This change had been brought about by the conflict of cities, the problems of despotism, and the crisis of liberty.

Niccolò Machiavelli, by Santi di Tito
Palazzo Vecchio, Florence

MACHIAVELLI

by Garrett Mattingly

For most of us, Renaissance statecraft is typified by a single man, Niccolò Machiavelli – or rather, by a single name, a reputation, an epithet. After all, not many people have any clear recollection of the life and character of the man Machiavelli (not many, even, of the relatively few who have ever bothered to read anything about him). But everyone knows what the name stands for: all the complicated devilry, hypocrisy, intrigue, secret murders, and public treacheries which for four hundred years the Western world has held typical of the Italian Renaissance. Seventy-five years ago a learned Frenchman identified the whole high Renaissance – the last decades of the fifteenth century and the first ones of the sixteenth – as the Age of Machiavelli. Certainly he realized the incongruity of labelling that bustling time after the drab little servant of a third-rate state, a man whose name even those princes and prelates to whom he had bowed probably never knew or, unless they were Florentines themselves, promptly forgot. But Maulde la Clavière was writing about Renaissance politics, and the name imposed itself. It came as naturally as saying the Age of Augustus, or of Louis le Grand, or of Napoleon, and it carried, like those labels, its own connotations, it own peculiar and, in this case, definitely sinister aura.

In a way it was appropriate that Niccolò Machiavelli should have become the interpreter of Renaissance politics to subsequent ages. He was a Florentine of the Florentines, and the citizens of his city were the quintessence of the new spirit that was then stirring in Italy. Not at first, of course: in the years after the great Guelph victory, after the popes had broken the power of the Empire in Italy forever, Florence was only one of the vigorous, turbulent city republics with which northern and central Italy swarmed. Some of these paid a token allegiance to the Papacy, although the popes knew how little that really meant, and some professed a loyalty to the Holy Roman Emperor, since no Emperor could endanger their liberties any more, but in fact they had all torn clean away from the hierarchical system in which the rest of Christendom was enmeshed, and were engaged in an external struggle against all their neighbours and an internal one of faction against faction, in which the only reality was the naked fact of power.

At first most of these new states were republics. Then, as the bigger fish devoured the smaller, not only were there fewer independent cities, but fewer of the survivors were republics. Presently came the anxious moment when on the Italian mainland only one republic was left, or only one that mattered. By force or guile the great Duke of Milan, Giangaleazzo Visconti, was building himself a kingdom. All Lombardy yielded to him from Piedmont to the Adriatic, and then Genoa and Pisa, Perugia and Siena, and finally proud Bologna. Guarded by its lagoons, the Republic of St Mark turned its aristocratic back on Italy. Only Florence still held out.

Florence had had as chequered a political history as any of her neighbours. In the century since she had exiled her greatest poet, the bitter factional strife which Dante lamented so pathetically and joined in so energetically had never ceased and only occasionally diminished. In the moment of crisis there was, of course, a clique to say that it would be madness for Florence to pit her unaided strength against the wave of the future, that it would be better for Florentines to live as the subjects of a tyrant than to die as his victims. But the Florentines chose to resist. Apparently they preferred the uneasy vigilance which is the price of freedom to the smug lethargy of the Milanese, and were willing to risk death as free men rather than embrace life as slaves. They did not have to make so hard a choice.

As he advanced against Florence, the plague struck down the tyrant, and his jerry-built kingdom fell into ruins. By resisting, the Florentines saved not just their own liberty but the liberties of Italy.

In a series of masterly studies Hans Baron has recently shown how the outcome of this crisis altered the whole tone of Florentine and so of Italian thought. Florence became the centre from which spread a new humanism, a new appreciation of political liberty and civic virtue, a new attitude towards the place of man in society. It was this attitude which insured the independence of the major Italian states, and consequently that vigour and diversity of Italian artistic and cultural development which characterized the Renaissance. Now that the point has been made, it seems strange that we did not see it before, but even without Baron's fresh insight, Florentine civic humanism has long been recognized as characteristic of one aspect of the Italian Renaissance. Although he was himself no humanist, if we make that term include a polished mastery of Greek and Latin letters, Niccolò Machiavelli was soaked in the spirit of Florentine humanism.

He was soaked, too, in the Florentine obsession with politics. He came of a family which had played a great role in the political life of his city for more than two centuries. Ancestors of his had been honoured, time and again, with the republic's highest offices, and if his father was too stiff-necked a republican to hold a place in a government which was becoming a more and more transparent mask for the boss rule of the Medici, we may be sure that papa Bernardo saw to it that son Niccolò was thoroughly imbued not only with the history of ancient republican Rome, but also with the great traditions of his own city. When he was forty-four, Niccolò wrote that politics was the passion of his life, that he could think and talk of nothing else, and we may guess that this began to be true when he was still young.

For fourteen years he had a chance to indulge his bent in action. When the French invaded Italy in 1494, the Florentines, who had begun to be restive under the scarcely disguised rule of Lorenzo the Magnificent and had become more so under Lorenzo's incompetent son, rose up to reclaim their ancient liberties and drove the Medici out of Florence. Niccolò was then twenty-five. We do not know whether he held any kind of post in the first years of the re-established republic, but when the revolutionary fanatics who were swayed by Savonarola's eloquence gave place to a solider, less hysterical government in 1498, Niccolò Machiavelli, just turned twenty-nine, was appointed second chancellor of the republic. Shortly afterwards he was given the additional charge of secretary to the influential committee known as the *Dieci di Balia*, the Ten of Liberty and Peace, as they were sometimes grandiloquently called, or, more realistically, the Ten of War.

War was the chief preoccupation of the restored republic. Foreign armies were tramping back and forth across Italy. Spaniards slowly tightened their grip on Naples; Frenchmen periodically invaded the kingdom and were periodically chased out of Milan; Switzers and Germans were in the field, fighting sometimes for foreign paymasters, sometimes for their own hands; around Rome, first the bastard son of the Borgia Pope and then that warlike old man who succeeded to the Papacy as Julius II were trying to unify the anarchic Papal States; and once all the warring powers put aside their quarrels in order to combine against the one powerful, independent Italian state, the Venetian republic. In the midst of these big wars Florence was busy with an interminable little war, trying to reconquer Pisa, which, in the confusion of the first French invasion, had slipped from under the Florentine yoke. Since his nominal chief, the first chancellor, was more interested in Greek poetry than Italian politics, Machiavelli took a large part in these affairs. He was deep in the business of war and the diplomatic bickerings and hagglings which were the normal Renaissance accompaniments of war. Most of the correspondence of the republic passed through his hands. He wrote memoranda to inform and advise his masters on a variety of subjects, and the Signory sent him on numerous diplomatic missions in Italy, Germany, and France.

Early in his diplomatic career his path crossed that of the man

Fleet of Ferrante I in the Bay of Naples after the Battle of Ischia, 1464
Museo di San Martino, Naples

who for most of us typifies the prince of the Age of Machiavelli, the typical prince of the Italian Renaissance – largely because he is the leading figure, the ostensible hero, of Machiavelli's famous little book. Actually, Cesare Borgia was not much more typical of the princes of Italy in his time than Caligula was a typical Roman emperor, or than Al Capone was a typical tax dodger of the Age of Herbert Hoover, but there is no denying that for a few years Cesare cut a wide swath and attracted a lot of attention, even eclipsing his notorious father.

The Battle of Fornovo, woodcut in A. Verard's Mer des Histoires *Paris, ca 1503*

Throughout his papacy, the whole family of Rodrigo Borgia, who ascended the papal throne as Alexander VI, was surrounded by a buzz of scandal. Gossiping about popes has always been a favourite Italian pastime, but probably no pope has ever afforded so much occasion for juicy gossip. Other popes had kept mistresses in the Vatican, and simony and immorality were no more rife in Rome under the Borgia pope than they had been under his predecessors and would be under his successors. But there was a sort of childlike shamelessness about Alexander VI which invited comment. Other popes had auctioned off high ecclesiastical offices, double-crossed their associates and allies, and used their exalted position for the advancement of their families and for base personal ends, but usually they had pretended that they were doing something else. Rodrigo Borgia had either an honest scorn for hypocrisy or a naïve ignorance of the force of public opinion. Other popes had thrown wild parties at the Vatican, but no other pope had made the parties so flamboyant or so public. And no other pope had had a portrait of his official mistress, robed as the Virgin Mary, painted over the door of his bedchamber or, at the same time, given his official mistress so many transient but reasonably well publicized rivals. Temperate, even ascetic in most respects (in spite, or perhaps because of his gross body, he drank little wine and ate sparingly of coarse food), Rodrigo Borgia was a great lover of women, and this alone was the source of innumerable stories which grew more outrageous with each retelling.

But neither his private conduct nor his carelessness of concealment can account for all the stories about the Borgia pope. The trouble was that, although far from a saint, he was a first-rate administrator, with enormous energy and a driving will. He tried to police not only the streets of Rome, but even the Roman *campagna*, he tried to control the disorderly Roman nobility, he tried to make sure that the papal treasury received its proper cut of all the sums which the swollen papal bureaucracy and their hangers-on extorted from suitors at his court. He tried, and in part he succeeded, and this made him very unpopular with the Romans. Besides, he tried to assert the rights of the Papacy and his jurisdiction over the Papal States wherever it was challenged, whether by the Duke of Milan or the republics of Venice or Florence, by the King of Naples or the anarchic Neapolitan barons, or by the petty tyrants of Umbria and the Romagna. This made him unpopular with the ruling classes throughout Italy. Worst of all, he was a foreigner, a Spaniard, and Italians have always resented a non-Italian pope. Hence another whole cluster of stories, different and more sinister.

Two of Rodrigo Borgia's children, his eldest son, the Duke of Gandia, and his daughter Lucrezia, were less than ideal targets for malicious gossip. Gandia, although he inherited to some extent his father's disposition to run after women, was otherwise a conventional and colourless type. Lucrezia, although she had a chequered and somewhat smirched history of successive marriages before she was out of her teens – a foundation on which Roman scandal-mongers readily erected a towering superstructure – was really a bland, vapid creature with nothing remarkable about her except a cow-like disposition and long blonde hair. But the Pope's younger son Cesare was something else again. Even as a mere stripling, just turned seventeen and newly made a cardinal, he was already a spectacular figure, taller by a head than most tall men, with massive shoulders, a wasp waist, classically regular features, a leonine mane, and blazing blue eyes. It was said that he could leap into the saddle without touching pommel or stirrups, bend a silver *scudo* double between his fingers, or straighten the iron of a horseshoe with a twist of his wrist. And he was a show-off. He dressed himself and his household with insolent magnificence, and he used to organize *corridas* in the Piazza Navona so that the Romans could watch him behead a bull with a single stroke of a broadsword. Before long he was trailing a legend gaudier and more lurid than that attached to his father.

It was said that he was his father's rival for his sister's incestuous bed. (Almost certainly false.) It was said that after the horrible sack of Capua he seized forty beautiful highborn maidens and added them to his personal harem. (Highly unlikely. Cesare does not seem to have shared his father's excessive appetite. The maidens were probably commandeered by Cesare's captains, though perhaps in his name.) It was said that he seduced that gallant youth Astorre Manfredi, and when he tired of him had him murdered. (Possible, but the motive for the murder was more probably purely political.) It was said that he had murdered his brother, the Duke of Gandia.

(Probable. At least his father seems to have believed it.) And that he had his brother-in-law, Lucrezia's second husband, murdered. (Pretty certainly true.) But it was a dull week when one, at least, of the embassies in Rome did not chalk up another murder to Cesare's credit, sometimes by poison, sometimes by the hands of hired assassins, sometimes by his own dagger. Probably he really was responsible for a fair share of those bodies hauled out of the Tiber. Freed by his brother's death from his cardinalate, Cesare became Duke de Valentinois (Valentino, the Italians called him) and Gonfaloniere of the Church, cousin and ally of the King of France, and commander in chief of the papal army. As he marched through the anarchic Papal States, seizing one town after another, by bribery or trickery or the sheer terror of his name, his legend hung over him like a thundercloud.

When Machiavelli first encountered the Duke, the spell of the legend must have been already at work on him, and it must have been heightened by the manner in which Valentino received him and his chief, at night, by the light of a single flickering candle which showed only dimly the tall figure clad in black from head to foot without jewel or ornament, the still, white features as regular as a Greek statue and as immobile. Perhaps the cold beauty of those marble features was already beginning to be marred by the pustules which led Valentino later on usually to wear a mask. Perhaps the eyes, lost in shadow, already held that glare which another ambassador noted in them shortly afterwards, the look of a savage beast at bay. And perhaps a shrewder observer might have reflected that there was the smell of comedy about these negotiations, the Duke endlessly repeating the same banalities about his eternal friendship for Florence and how wise the republic would be to employ the services of so good a friend, while his captains warned the Florentine envoys that the Duke's patience was growing short, that France would support him against Florence and the Venetians would not stir, that the army was poised to spring and could be at the city's

AES·BORGIA·VALENTIN

Cesare Borgia
Palazzo Venezia, Rome

gates before the news of its coming. It was really one of the cruder forms of blackmail, but something about the Duke's personality put the act over, and the Florentine envoys carried away the image of a great prince, subtle, inscrutable, dangerous.

Not long afterwards Machiavelli had an opportunity to observe Cesare Borgia in action at the time of his greatest triumph. Cesare was not much of a general: he never learned the rudiments of tactics or strategy, logistics or supply. He was not even a good combat leader, and though he has been praised as a disciplinarian, the only available instance seems to be that once he quelled an incipient riot among some of his brawling soldiers by the terror of his presence. Similarly, if he ever gave any proof of ability as a statesman or ruler, no evidence survives. But he was a ruthless gangster and an expert confidence man, and the revolt of some of the smaller gangsters, his captains, gave him an opportunity to display his talents. Machiavelli watched, fascinated, while Cesare, all mildness and goodwill, lured his mutinous subordinates into a peace conference, lulled their fears, invited them to a banquet to celebrate their renewed friendship, and when they arrived unarmed and unescorted at a rendezvous where Cesare had hidden his bodyguards, had them seized and murdered. Machiavelli was delighted at the virtuosity of the performance and set it all down in detail for the edification of his countrymen and of posterity.

Machiavelli had a third opportunity to observe the Duke. He arrived in Rome on the business of the republic some months after the death of Alexander VI and just at the moment when Cesare, with incredible stupidity, had helped swing the election of his most implacable enemy. It was plain to see that Cesare was finished. Everything really had depended on his father's being Pope, and as soon as his father died, his allies deserted him, his people rose against him, and his army fell apart as his captains scrambled for the service of some luckier master. Machiavelli assessed the emptiness of the man at a glance, avoided him when he could, wrote of him and no doubt looked at him with cold contempt. But later Machiavelli seems to have preferred to forget the cringing, whimpering, blustering, dithering creature his hero had become. The picture is spread out in detail in his dispatches, but Machiavelli never openly alluded to this aspect of Cesare again.

One thing Machiavelli admired about Cesare was that he raised his soldiers in his own domain instead of hiring foreign mercenaries. It was not, in fact, a great departure. The Romagna was the great source of mercenary troops, and for years its petty despots had enrolled their subjects and farmed them out to fight other people's wars. But Cesare's action was like a project very close to Machiavelli's heart, one which after years of urging he finally got the Florentine government to adopt. They not only adopted it, they put him in charge of it, so that for the last six years of the republic he had added to his other duties most of those of minister of defence. Instead of the cut-rate mercenaries who had prolonged the Pisan war for twelve years (being a republic in which the taxpayers held the purse-strings, Florence hired only the cheapest mercenaries), Machiavelli persuaded the government to raise a militia in its own territory. Since the militia were not Florentine citizens, but conscripts from the wretched peasants of the *contado*, a folk without political rights or any material stake in the success of their bourgeois masters, the scheme had an obvious weakness, but it did not work badly at first. In 1509 Pisa fell, and Machiavelli's militia could claim a share in the long-delayed triumph. Three years later the militia failed a harder test. When the veteran Spanish infantry moved in to attack Prato, the militia ran like rabbits, and the Medici epigoni came back behind a column of Spanish pikes to rule once more in Florence. Machiavelli's active career in politics was over. But not his interest in politics. The next year he wrote that he could think about, talk about, nothing else, and from then on until he died in 1527, only a few weeks after the Florentines had again expelled the Medici, most of the writings with which he sought to allay the

67

boredom of his exclusion from office were concerned, one way and another, with statecraft. He also wrote some verses – pretty wretched verses – and a not unamusing version of an old smutty joke, and comedies, one of which is a masterpiece. But mostly he wrote about politics. Had he been asked to name his political writings in an ascending order of importance, surely the top three would have been his *History of Florence*, his *Art of War*, and his *Discourses on the First Ten Books of Livy*. Into these writings, and particularly into the last, Machiavelli had poured, or so he thought, all his practical experience of government and diplomacy and all his wide reading of ancient and modern history. However surprised some of the successful statesmen of his day might have been to find the little Florentine secretary the political spokesman of their age, Machiavelli himself would not have been too surprised. He would have regarded the reputation accrued as a poor compensation for the fame as a statesman which fate had denied him, but he had often said that he was the first modern man to look at politics with a clear and open eye, and he would certainly have taken the recognition of posterity as no more than due to the merit of his books.

Only, of course, the recognition of posterity has nothing to do with the books Machiavelli would have named. When people speak of the Age of Machiavelli, they are not thinking of any of them, but of one little pamphlet apparently dashed off at white heat in 1513 just after the fall of the Florentine republic. It is called *The Prince* and it bears only an ambiguous, tangential relationship to Machiavelli's big, serious works or, some people think, to the actual history of the time and place over which its fame casts such a lurid and sinister light. The discrepancy between the impression of Renaissance Italy to be gathered from *The Prince* and that given by the rest of Machiavelli's writings, to say nothing of the writings of his contemporaries, who often turn out to be more reliable about matters of fact, is sufficient to raise doubts about the appropriateness of letting *The Prince* describe the political atmosphere of its time.

Perhaps our doubts about letting Machiavelli speak for the age which bears his name ought not to be increased by our knowledge of his private life. But among his contemporaries, surely Niccolò Machiavelli was one of the least Machiavellian. It is true that he often preferred drastic methods and sweeping all-or-nothing solutions, and despised delay and improvisation and compromise, attitudes usually more characteristic of academic theorists than of practical men of affairs. But though this quirk of temperament sometimes misled him into a temporary enthusiasm for a mountebank like Cesare Borgia, it does not seem otherwise to have affected his own behaviour. If the discipline of the Florentine militia had been harsher, they might not have run so soon at Prato. Machiavelli often praised the efficacy of hypocrisy and smooth deceit, but in his dealings both with his own government and with foreign potentates, he was usually inept at concealing his feelings, likely to show his hand, and, in negotiation, blunt to the point of tactlessness. He often spoke of the value of clear-eyed, dispassionate observation and seems rather to have prided himself on the possession of this faculty, but, in fact, his views were usually clouded by wish and prejudice, he was easily deceived, and he was not, in the things that really mattered – those affecting the daily course of politics – a very acute, discriminating, or even very accurate observer. This judgment, suggested by comparing his dispatches with those of his contemporaries, is reinforced by the fact that his employers, the Florentine Signory, never gave him responsibility for any important mission.

Niccolò not only lacked the virtues he praised, he possessed others even more incompatible with our picture of Old Nick. He was as anti-clerical as most literate adult male Italians of the last six centuries have always been, and, in spite of his pious mother's teaching, no more zealously practising a Catholic than one would expect. But as he had been baptized, confirmed, and married, so he died in the arms of the Church, having seen to it that his children followed the same conventional course. Nor – and this is farther from the popular picture of his age – is there any evidence that he indulged in any fantastic crimes or vices. He was probably no more faithful to his wife than most middle-class husbands in any age or clime, but he seems to have been a kind, affectionate, considerate husband and father, as he was a warm and true friend, a man of his word in money matters, and an admired and respected citizen.

A digression may be called for here about the handful of pornographic letters which shocked the Victorian sensibilities of J. A. Symonds. The fifteenth-century humanists had made fantastic obscenities a normal epistolary ornament. Certainly no Anglo-Saxon in the last two centuries would have written down such anecdotes about himself as Machiavelli wrote to his friends, though they are not much different from what one may hear in any changing-room or thoroughly masculine bar. But they are responses, all of them, to anecdotes which his friends wrote him, and they differ from them not in essential subject matter but in elaboration and intensification. They are clearly meant to top his friends' stories, and do top them so successfully that one is led to wonder whether literary artifice and imagination have not been called in to supply the defects of experience. Machiavelli himself would have been the first to resent the implication that he was a saint. But there is not the slightest evidence that he was anything but the most conventional, commonplace, and prudent kind of sinner.

One inappropriate virtue is particularly surprising. It even surprised Machiavelli himself. The man who wrote that men are moved so predominantly by self-interest that princes need take account of no other motives, that 'a man will resent the loss of his patrimony more than the murder of his father', was himself the devoted, unselfish servant of his ungrateful state. He lived in an age when the use of public office for private gain was perfectly customary. He had during most of his fourteen years as a servant of the Florentine republic unrivalled opportunities to enrich himself at the expense of the condottieri and other contractors with whom as

secretary to the Ten of War he had to deal. Yet he quitted the
Florentine service as poor as the day he had entered it. His whole
public career was a testimony to the inaccuracy of his own cynical
maxims. It is hard to reconcile it with the trend of his major serious
books. It is impossible to square it with the lurid picture which we
have drawn from his one famous little book, *The Prince*.

Drawn, in part, quite unjustifiably. Most people, whether they
have read *The Prince* or not, retain the conviction that somewhere,
they cannot say quite where, Machiavelli commends the famous
(quite mythical) poison of the Borgia and justifies the pagan de-
bauchery which, ever since the Reformation, Protestant countries
have associated with the Italian Renaissance.

Most of these false imputations are quite old and go back to a
book called *Anti-Machiavel* which a Huguenot pamphleteer wrote
against Catherine de' Medici and her Italian entourage just after
the Massacre of St Bartholomew's. But even after these old vulgar
errors have been cleared out of the way, *The Prince* remains a
shocking book, shocking both for what it says and for the deliberately provocative way it says it, and for the discord between a part
of its contents and the life and other writings of its author.

As for its contents: *The Prince* lays it down as a major premise that
men in general are selfish, treacherous, cowardly, greedy, and,
above all, gullible and stupid. It therefore advises a prince, and
particularly a new prince who hopes to destroy the liberties of those
he rules, to employ hypocrisy, cruelty, and deceit, to make himself
feared even at the risk of making himself hated, to divide the people
and destroy their natural leaders, and to keep faith with no one,
since no one will keep faith with him. It views the world of politics
as a jungle in which moral laws and standards of ethical conduct are
merely snares for fools, a jungle in which there is no reality but
power, and power is the reward of ruthlessness, ferocity, and
cunning. In such a jungle, not the actual Cesare Borgia, but the
picture of himself which Cesare succeeded in conveying at the

height of his fame, a savage beast – half lion and half fox – would be the natural king. To a society which regarded the relations between its parts as ruled by justice and equity and sanctified by religion, all this was more shocking than we can quite imagine.

It was shocking, too, to find a man of staunch republican principles and flawless republican antecedents, a man who had served the Florentine republic with selfless devotion and suffered for it more than most, turning, within months of his country's fall, to writing a handbook for tyrants, a book meant to teach the Medici, the enemies of his country's liberties, how to hold his fellow countrymen in thrall, and writing it all for the mean object of helping himself to wriggle back into some minor government post. If Machiavelli behaved so, he earned, for the only time in his life, the epithet Machiavellian. That his behaviour seems to have been a momentary aberration, that when it was over Machiavelli returned to the defence of republican principles and the society of republican friends, makes his defection not less shocking but only more puzzling.

From the first there were at least two explanations of the puzzle. One was that Machiavelli had been inspired by the Evil One to write a plausible book of advice for princes, meant to damn the souls and ruin the fortunes of princes who followed it, and to destroy the prosperity of their subjects. This was the official view, shared by the cardinals and popes who placed and kept *The Prince* on the Index and by the Protestant pamphleteers who pointed to it as the manual of the Jesuits and the political inspiration of the Counter-reformation. Meanwhile a second view was expressed openly by some of Machiavelli's fellow countrymen (those in exile) and hinted at by some who remained in Italy, where the banned book continued clandestinely to circulate. This was that *The Prince*, under the guise of giving advice to princes, was meant to warn all free men of the dangers of tyranny. One wonders whether the originators of this explanation of the puzzle may not have been the ardent Florentine republicans who always remained Machiavelli's friends. From this second view sprang the judgment, popular in the eighteenth century, that *The Prince* was, in fact, a satire on absolute monarchy, and that all its epigrams were deliberately double-edged. The nineteenth century offered other solutions to the puzzle. The one which gained ascendancy as the cause of national self-determination triumphed in Western Europe was that, ardent republican though he was, Machiavelli made up his mind that only a strong prince could liberate Italy from the barbarians, and so chose to sacrifice the freedom of his city to the unity of Italy. Just before the First World War this solution began to be questioned by those who said that Machiavelli was not a chauvinistic patriot but a dispassionate political scientist who described political behaviour as it actually was. After about 1920 this view took the lead over all its competitors, and among orthodox Machiavelli scholars it still dominates the field.

Obviously none of these answers is entirely satisfactory. It is possible that Machiavelli was mean enough to sell his birthright of republican ideals for the chance of some third-rate post under a petty tyrant; but that he was at the same time stupid enough to believe that a book like *The Prince* was the best way into Medici favour, and to let advice which, if it was seriously meant, should have been highly secret escape into general circulation, seems much less credible. Both the notion that *The Prince* was inspired by the devil and the counter-notion that it was the subtle weapon of republican idealism seem equally oversimplified. And, of course, the proposal that *The Prince* was conceived as a satire is the kind of anachronism which only the eighteenth century could have perpetrated. Machiavelli knew perfectly well that satires were compositions in verse after the manner of Horace and Juvenal, such as his friend Luigi Alamanni wrote. He would have failed completely to understand the proposition that *The Prince* was a satire. As for the theory that Machiavelli was willing to accept a tyrant prince in order to effect the unification of Italy, there is no sign anywhere in his writings that he would have grasped the idea if anybody had put it to

73

him. There is nothing about unifying Italy anywhere in *The Prince*, only about driving out the barbarians, a commonplace of Italian rhetoric from Petrarch to Paul IV. But Machiavelli the Italian patriot is a little easier to swallow than Machiavelli the dispassionate scientist, unless someone can explain how the scientific temper can accord with facts and generalizations equally distorted by emotion and prejudice.

It is probably hopeless to try to explain the whole puzzle of *The Prince*. How do you reconstruct the motives at a particular moment of a man more than four hundred years in his grave who has left only the scantiest and most ambiguous clues to what they might be? How do you tell, in the case of a man like Machiavelli, how much of the demonstrable distortion in *The Prince* was due to faulty observation (he was a passionate man) and how much to the deliberate irony which he certainly sometimes practised? How do you probe the bitterness and agony of spirit which must certainly have been his on the collapse of all his hopes, and decide which wild statements come from anger, which from despair, and which from a calculated will to undermine his enemies by indirection?

Probably, like most insoluble problems about men of genius, this one has taken up more time and energy than it deserves. The real importance of Machiavelli, his claim to give his name to a whole period of history, lies elsewhere, not in the points in which *The Prince* differs from his other writings, but in those in which it agrees. Here the transformation of his legendary figure from a diabolist or a rebel, a spirit who says 'No', to a major culture hero, offers the clue. What had happened, in almost three centuries between the time when Machiavelli was either praised as a daring rebel or denounced as an emissary of Satan and the time when he began to be acclaimed as a prophet, was that all Europe had become what Italy in Machiavelli's lifetime already was, a congeries of autonomous, purely temporal sovereign states, without any common end to bind them into a single society or any interest higher than their own egotistical drives for survival and expansion.

To pretend that the relations between such states were governed by Christian ethics seemed to Machiavelli a contemptible hypocrisy. Many Italians since Dante had lamented that the nearer one came to Rome the wider the gap between Christian teaching and Christian practice, and charged that the Papacy had corrupted the morals of Italy. Indeed, the major assumption of the stern reformers of what we call the Counter-reformation was not much different. But Machiavelli went further. He compared his own embittered picture of the degeneracy of his countrymen with Livy's of the virtues of republican Rome, and without asking how much exaggeration there might be in either, he leapt to one of his drastic all-or-nothing conclusions. Christianity, whatever its value as a guide in private life, was not a viable fountain for the good society. So for the religion of Christ he proposed to substitute the religion of patriotism. In politics the Christian ethic was worse than valueless, it was positively harmful. It might serve to keep the masses more law-abiding in their private lives, but when it came to public actions the only test of good or bad was what best served the safety and aggrandizement of the state. Since every state was an autonomous entity, recognizing no superior and no interest higher than its own, no rules of ethics whatever applied to relations between states. The only test was success. This was Machiavelli's consistent position. It appears in his earliest state papers and is as firmly held in his writings in praise of republics as it is in *The Prince*. In 1513 it was a desperate paradox. By 1813 it was an axiom of statecraft. By 1914 it was the tritest of platitudes. Machiavelli did not invent it. It was apparent in the behaviour of the Italian states of his time and more or less openly acknowledged in the memoranda of statesmen and diplomats. But Niccolò Machiavelli first gave the fresh attitude of his age towards statecraft a permanent literary form, and the progress of history compelled general recognition of his insight. For that reason, perhaps he does deserve to be accepted as the voice of the Rennaissance State. Perhaps his age should be called 'The Age of Machiavelli'.

THE ARTS

I N 1546 a young, successful painter, Giorgio Vasari, was at a small
supper party in Cardinal Farnese's palace in Rome. The conversation turned to the extraordinary flowering of Italian art in
the previous century and to the exceptional artists who had revolutionized painting and sculpture since the far-off days of Giotto
and Pisano. Yet Vasari's presence was even more remarkable still,
for even a hundred years earlier it would have been unthinkable for
a young painter to have been a frequent guest at a cardinal's table.
The social position of the artist had changed as much as art itself.
To the men at that supper party, the age of heroes was passing; only
the formidable genius of old Michelangelo could challenge, Vasari
thought, the giants of the past. Encouraged and helped by the others,
Vasari determined to collect all that men knew about these remarkable artists of the recent past; to immortalize, above all, the painters
of Florence, which, for Vasari, was the cradle of the arts. Florence
had nurtured what Rome had used. There had been a time when
Milan, with Leonardo da Vinci at the court of Lodovico Sforza, had
seemed about to be the leading city of the Renaissance. The great
invasions cut that short. And it was Venice, secure and rich, that
became the heir of Florence and the rival of Rome. Yet it was these
four cities – Florence, Milan, Rome, and Venice – in which the
practice and patronage of art had become a civic virtue; it was these
cities that witnessed the triumphs of painting and sculpture and the
emergence of the artist from the confines of a craft to the lonely
pursuit of his genius.

In the early fifteenth century the artists had been as certain as

Apollo and Daphne, by A. and P. Pollaiuolo   77
National Gallery, London

Vasari that they were heralding a new age; behind them stretched dark and barren times. They acknowledged the genius of Giotto and Cimabue, but few others. Their admiration was kept for antiquity, which they yearned to equal, if not surpass, but certainly the modern age began with them: painting with Masaccio, sculpture with Ghiberti, architecture with Brunelleschi. And this was not idle boasting. Donatello's statues possess exceptional originality. In painting the break is, perhaps, less vivid than in Donatello's free-standing statues, but it is remarkable enough. In architecture success came more slowly. In literature and in music men were equally confident of their own originality and in the superiority of their age: between their own time and antiquity stretched the 'barbarous Middle Ages'. Seen against the broad sweep of modern history, their claims seem wholly justified. The language of Renaissance art is the language of the modern world – at least until recent times – whereas the art of the Middle Ages possesses some of the same difficulties as the art of Islam or India or China. Its beauty can be recognized, its contents discerned, but its impact on the feelings rarely immediate.

And yet, as soon as one considers individual works of Renaissance art or considers the purpose for which they were painted or modelled or built, one is immediately aware how entangled the artists of fifteenth-century Italy were in the traditions not only of Gothic art but also of Byzantium. They were also deeply indebted to the imaginative originality and technical skill of the great Flemish and Burgundian schools of painting and illumination. These strands of tradition and of foreign influence give an added richness of texture to the achievement of the Renaissance painters; but when all debts and obligations are acknowledged, what a fabulous achievement in painting and sculpture remains! Great artists are as common as peaks in the Himalayas, leading one to believe that the ability to draw or to carve is no rarer in man than mathematical skill and only requires the appropriate social circumstances to call it forth in abundance.

And certainly the social circumstances were exceptionally favourable for artists and craftsmen. Firstly there was a strong, deep-rooted tradition, which went back to the earliest days of Christian Europe, that men whom God had prospered should give thanks for their good fortune by embellishing the churches and monasteries in which He was worshipped. Building for God and the adornment of God's buildings were a part of the Christian life – sanctioned by time and anchored in belief. After all, it was the most vivid, the most dramatic way of reaching the illiterate. Therefore, it was inevitable that as the men of affairs flourished in Venice, in Florence, in Milan, or in Naples, they should wish their wealth to be reflected in their parish churches, in the monasteries and nunneries which they founded or patronized, and in the cathedrals of their cities. And in this exercise of artistic benevolence in the service of God, they had a supreme mentor in the Pope. At Avignon, and afterwards at Rome, the popes had fostered a visual splendour that was the envy of the kings of Europe as well as the princes of Italy. The sense of merit in the visual expression of piety was universally held even by such naturally puritanical characters as Bernardino of Siena or Savonarola. Although they called for the burning of vanities, that did not include pictures of sacred subjects. To all men, even the most ascetic, these were a part of religion as old as the Church itself.

Furthermore, it had long been the custom of princes to adorn their palaces; to encourage the skilled crafts of metalwork and jewellery; to take delight in tapestries and frescoes that told them a well-loved story such as the Virgin and the Unicorn or reminded them of the pursuits – hunting or the art of love – in which they took delight. It satisfied their senses, as well as enhanced their pride, to read their prayers from costly books, illuminated with exquisite skill. By 1400, however, there were hundreds of merchants in Italy and in Burgundy who could afford the artistic elegance that had once been the prerogative of the country's aristocracy. And these merchants were city-born; often their families had risen to greatness with their towns, and their civic pride was as strong as chivalry, stronger perhaps than a knight's loyalty to his prince. And they wished their city to mirror their own greatness, to reflect in its buildings and their adornment the wealth in which they took such sturdy delight. The competitive state system of Renaissance Italy was not merely concerned with power; it flourished equally strongly in the arts. It added to the stature of kings to have a world-renowned artist attached to their courts; and the republics – particularly

Mars From the MS. De Sphaera *Biblioteca Estense, Modena*

Florence and Venice – were as jealous of their geniuses as any king.

Into the pursuit of art, therefore, both money and social energy were poured, and the effect was as dramatic as the investment of capital during the nineteenth century in technology and invention – and in many ways similar in its results. Naturally, the need for artists drew some men into a career which they might otherwise have ignored. Any poor peasant boy who showed some natural skill was likely to find a sponsor among the neighbouring gentry or local merchants, as did Mantegna, who had herded sheep in the fields near Padua until discovered by Squarcione. Of course, the greatest source was the families of craftsmen – the jewellers, goldsmiths, metal-workers, and decorative painters – in which there was a tradition of design and the opportunity for early apprenticeship. Yet probably only the religious life had before drawn its practitioners from such a wide social background or caught in its orbit such a rich variety of human temperament. And this in itself had a fertilizing effect on artistic expression.

To the competition for artists was added the competition by artists. In early centuries, the craftsman could spend a lifetime beautifying one cathedral or monastery, adding, perhaps, a personal variation to the traditional themes and colours in which he worked, but unconcerned with public reputation or rivalry with his fellow artists. By 1450 personal vendettas and public rivalry between artists had become a commonplace of Florentine and Venetian life, and again to the advantage of art, for they led men to attempt to exploit their techniques to the fullest, to give their imagination free rein, to emphasize the singularity of their personal vision. It needs the skilled eye of a connoisseur to distinguish between one Burgundian master of illumination and another; a child can tell the difference between a Botticelli and an Uccello. Of course, this does not mean that attribution is easy or absolute. A successful painter of the Renaissance was the head of a workshop – often, as with the Bellini or Tintoretto, a large-scale family affair in which brothers, sons, and even daughters joined. And, furthermore, apprentices abounded, and so did journey-men who were skilled in hands or costumes or backgrounds or *putti*. And, as ever, the works of the second-rate emulated slavishly the genius of a few.

The circumstances of the Renaissance encouraged the cultivation of individual style. And the rewards of the successful creation of a deeply personal idiom were so large that artists took risks which craftsmen in earlier days would never have dared take. Some men followed their daemons wherever they might lead, and painters committed themselves to their artistic vision with the fervour of a saint following his calling. The stories that Vasari tells may or may not be true, but they reveal what Italian society expected of the lives of its artists – Andrea del Castagno killing Domenico out of envy; Piero di Cosimo boiling the eggs that he lived on, fifty at a time, with his varnishes to save time; Paolo Uccello loving perspec-tive so much more than his wife. What is common to all is the acceptance of dedication and the acceptance of self. This swarming crowd of painters, sculptors, goldsmiths, decorators, jewellers, con-tained men of widely differing gifts and most varied temperaments: men of profound curiosity such as Leonardo, of soaring imagination

Chalice, by Uccello
Uffizi, Florence

such as Michelangelo, of highly intellectual powers such as Piero
della Francesca, of exquisite sensitivity such as Giorgione, and of
supreme technical accomplishment such as Raphael.

The three great arts – painting, sculpture, architecture – changed
most profoundly between 1400 and 1500. Indications that change
might come had not been infrequent in the fourteenth century.
Painting in the thirteenth century had been largely dominated by
Greek (that is, Byzantine) influence – indeed, many of the artists
were themselves Greek; the olive-skinned, slant-eyed, ikon-like
madonnas of Cimabue and Duccio di Buoninsegna are refined expressions, with a hint of personal involvement, of established traditions. In comparison, Giotto towers like a giant, even if by fifteenth-
century standards he is naïve and primitive. His figures have, to use
Berenson's excellent phrase, 'tactile values'; you feel that you could
touch them, walk round them, and that they could walk round you.
He used with great economy light, shade, colour, and strongly-
featured men and women to give this sense of solid form and
three-dimensional space. Yet for a hundred years there was little or
no advance from his innovating skill, only imitation. Florentine art
was, apart from Orcagna, less imaginative, less technically dexterous
than the achievement of the great painters and illuminators of Burgundy, Flanders, and Avignon, whose skills were steadily to seep
through the Alps to enrich Italy. Certainly Florence lacked the
achievement of Siena, where strong Byzantine and weaker Gothic
influences blended to create a school of painters – Lorenzetti,
Martini, Duccio – of great charm and some originality, particularly
in landscape.

Then, suddenly, as Italian art seemed to be drifting gently and
skilfully into its own version of the Gothic, the promise of Giotto
was fulfilled in one of the greatest of all Florentine painters – Masaccio. His frescoes in the Brancacci Chapel of the Carmine were
revered by generations of artists, who subjected them to the closest
study. His great abilities were not, however, like Giotto's, exercised

The Tribute Money. Detail, by Masaccio
Brancacci Chapel, Sta Maria del Carmine, Florence

in isolation. From 1400 onwards two artists of outstanding ability – one a sculptor, Donatello, and the other an architect, Brunelleschi – also helped to create a totally new attitude to art. Both were entranced by perspective, by human nature, and by reality as they saw it – not through symbol or myth but directly and clear-sightedly. Donatello's *David* was a piece of amazing originality; the beauty of a boy's naked body displayed frankly for the first time since antiquity. It marks as emphatically as Watt's invention of a modern steam engine the birth of a new age. Brunelleschi contributed as much, perhaps, by his ardent proselytism of the rules of perspective as by the soaring dome that he built for Florence's cathedral. And in addition to these three great Florentines there were others – Ghiberti, Uccello, Luca dell Robbia, Fra Angelico – painters and sculptors of exceptional talent, perhaps even touched with genius, who were deeply moved by the new technical triumphs which the

Unloading wheat, by Fra Angelico
Detail from Scene from the Life of St Nicholas *Pinacoteca Vaticana*

study of perspective had brought; indeed, Uccello painted with
scarcely any other object in view than to demonstrate his skill in
handling perspective in the most unlikely circumstances. Naturally,
those men who in more recent times would have turned to the
career of a scientist or a mathematician were deeply stirred by the
complex harmonies that could be achieved by following the strict
rules of perspective. The greatest of these was undoubtedly Piero
della Francesca of Borgo San Sepolcro, an artist of genius who in
the end preferred his mathematics to his art and painted nothing for
the last fourteen years of his life. He combined an exceptional control of linear relationships with a sense of life that was both grave
and serene. A preoccupation with, as it were, the density of things,
combined with a tragic view of life, became the dominant theme in
Florentine art. A further preoccupation was a sense of movement
which infuses the reliefs, the statues, the pictures of this extraordinary
city, and was to culminate in the writhing nudes of Michelangelo,
locked forever in their struggle with Fate. Power of intellect, gravity
of feeling, a sense of Time, these qualities artists were able to express
visually.

Both Donatello and Brunelleschi, who were devoted friends,
were concerned with other intellectual preoccupations apart from
perspective. They searched deliberately and consciously for the
antique. They went off together to Rome. Brunelleschi measured
and drew ruin after ruin; Donatello studied the few Roman and
fewer Greek bronzes and statues that men were beginning to collect
at this time. And both men felt that they were the heirs of Rome,
that between them and the fifth century there was a great gulf of
barbarism.

And yet the art of the early fifteenth century was deeply entangled
in its past. The scenes which painters were called upon to paint were
the traditional scenes of Christian mythology – Nativities, Circum-
cisions, Crucifixions – the miracles of saints, the Stations of the
Cross – and they were expected to execute them in traditional places,

on the walls of churches and monasteries and on panels for altars. And skill in the control of perspective, or even a delight in the antique as absolute as Mantegna's, did not abolish the old symbols or the traditional iconography: four or five jagged rocks, realistically drawn, still represented mountains, as they had done for centuries in Byzantine art. The egg, hanging in the apse in Piero della Francesca's great picture of the Madonna and Child with saints, in the Brera, Milan, represents the four elements of the universe – a purely medieval symbol – as well as being a perfect conic section and the central point of a complex composition, requiring superlative skill in perspective. And although Uccello might gently mock the traditions of chivalry in his *Saint George and the Dragon*, nevertheless they absorbed his imagination; and Gozzoli's *Journey of the Magi* is as Gothic in feeling and intention as a fifteenth-century tapestry from Burgundy. Indeed, the new art of Donatello and Masaccio had no easy victory except in technique, for the Gothic feeling from the North seeped like an estuarine tide through the brushes and canvases of Italian artists of the fifteenth century: they were no more conscious of it than children playing with new toys in the sunshine, yet it caught them inexorably.

The other great triumphs of Renaissance art – the painting of landscape, the exploration of space and light through colour, the full acceptance of the nude, and the development of the portrait – came only slowly.

And again they were partly due to foreign influence. Landscape in early Renaissance art was mainly the landscape of symbol, such as the paradisal gardens derived probably from Persia – containing sometimes delicately observed flowers and plants and animals, but painted for their value as symbols, not to stir feeling, not to evoke mood deliberately, except in a formalized and quasi-theological sense – or the terrible mountains, rocks and forests which were the age-old symbols of hell and horror. But as individuality began to creep out from traditional expression, and as the control of technique became more certain, painters and illustrators could not resist the challenge of the outward-seeing eye. In the *Très Riches Heures* of the Duc de Berry, ordinary life is revealed – peasants cut the crops, the children swim, the sheep feed on the mountainside. About the time that these were being painted by the Limbourg brothers, a Flemish artist, Jan van Eyck, began to give small background landscapes to his great altarpieces, which influenced Italian art as profoundly as his discovery of oil painting. Both his feeling for landscape and his knowledge of oils were taken back to Italy, where Antonello da Messina was one of the first to employ the new technique. The exploration of colour, of light and shade, of the intimate relation of man and nature, became dominant themes in Venetian art. Actually, Florentine artists had not been entirely indifferent to landscape; its study was partially involved in their preoccupation with perspective. Also, feeling inspired by natural objects was an integral part of their Neo-platonism. Brunelleschi made an optical device for viewing the city, and Alberti told how nature stirred him to tears and to joy. The intellectual problem of drawing figures against a distant background was bound to preoccupy Piero della Francesca, and he solved it about 1465, when he painted his great Urbino diptych. And realistic landscapes, particularly of the Val d'Arno, were painted shortly afterwards by Pollaiuolo. But neither painter responded with such a deep sense of personal discovery as did Giovanni Bellini, although the stimulus for his preoccupation may have come as much from della Francesca as from van Eyck. Bellini loved light, loved the first clear light of morning that touches the mountain tops and leaves the plain in shadow, and the golden light of the last hours of day, the time that Leonardo was to love so deeply, a time that gives depth to shadow and softness and glow to colour. Even the full light of midday in all its hardness and brilliance did not repel Bellini. He could drink in its heat and intensity, as his Saint Francis does with his outstretched arms, raised as much to the sun as to God. Although his delight in light and its

Flagellation of Christ, by Piero della Francesca
Palazzo Ducale, Urbino

effects on colour passed into the Venetian tradition, his almost
Brueghel-like concern with the detail of landscape did not.

Landscape was used by Giorgione, by Titian, by Tintoretto, to
interpret mood, to reflect the emotion felt by the painter and to
stimulate it in the beholder. In Giorgione and in the early works of
Titian, landscape painting reached hallucinatory heights of feeling,
reflecting mystery, horror, fear, tenderness, security, bliss, and love.
As with perspective, so with landscape, a new world of artistic
expression had been created.

The Venetians, of course, were not the only artists in the early
sixteenth century to take delight in the painting of landscape. True,
Michelangelo largely ignored it, and Botticelli used it merely as
decoration or to emphasize his flowing, vibrant movement, but the
Umbrian painters – Perugino and Pinturicchio – drew much from
the tradition of Piero della Francesca; a tradition that was absorbed
with masterful ease by Raphael. And, naturally, Leonardo da Vinci's
sense of beauty as well as his avid curiosity were stirred by nature.
The geological structure of mountains as well as their evocation of
emotion caught his imagination, as did the turbulence of water as
well as the mechanics of its flow; as did the flight of birds or the
botany of flowers as well as their beauty; and, as in so many other
aspects of Renaissance art, the scientific spirit and the delight in the
eye were combined in one aesthetic pleasure, for in Leonardo the
creative imagination was as multi-dimensional as geometry.

Throughout the Renaissance, artists were working for a small
public. They were well known in their cities, they were familiar to
popes and princes. The atmosphere in which they worked was
intimate. Also their art served a civic as well as a religious purpose.
The Venetians realized early that narrative paintings about their
heroic moments could have a public function, could impress both
citizen and stranger with the republic's greatness. For the same
reason artists were paid to paint the vast pageants that gave drama
and colour and pomp to the Venetian year. In such pictures Vene-

tians as well as Venice appeared, citizens as recognizable as the Piazzetta itself. The princes, too, helped to domesticate art. Their profiles had long adorned medals – indeed the only claim to fame of some of them is that Pisanello made a cast of their features. They hungered, as princes will, for eternity, and they needed not only to patronize painting, or to construct huge palaces, but also to see themselves immortalized by one in order to adorn the other. They appeared, as the Medici did, in the retinue of kings making their offerings to the infant Christ, or in symbolic pageant, as Federigo da Montefeltro and his wife, Battista, did in the Urbino diptych. And, of course, the preoccupation with the nature of man must of itself lead to the attempt to interpret character through portraiture; and for this the treatment of the face in profile was insufficient. Although there were brilliant portraits elsewhere – Pollaiuolo's *Portrait of a Man*, Botticelli's *Giovanni di Pierfrancesco de' Medici*, and many others – Venice was the true home of the portrait. A great series of doges, unhappily destroyed by fire in 1577, was painted by Bellini for the Doge's Palace. And the portrait rapidly became fashionable. Procurators and merchants quickly followed in the steps of the doges, and the walls of private palaces were adorned with the portraits of their owners, many of them masterpieces of human interpretation by Titian.

Through perspective, through the introduction of oils, through the exploitation of landscape and the human body, Renaissance Italy created the traditions of Western art, in which it was to remain embedded for centuries. Sculpture and architecture had flourished in like manner. Donatello's *David* remained an isolated phenomenon only for a generation. Verrocchio, Leonardo, and, above all, Michelangelo created statues of a beauty that equalled the best that the ancient world had to offer; and Michelangelo infused his statues with an emotional force that none have equalled since. The tragic nature of man – his immense loneliness and his inevitable end – gripped him like a vice. His tension and suffering, generalized for

Ideal City, attrib. to Piero della Francesca, Palazzo Ducale, Urbino

mankind, passed into stone or paint. Social circumstance and technical change allowed such supreme artists to flourish. And the distance travelled in a little over a hundred years – from Lorenzo Monaco, Gentile dá Fabriano, or Lorenzetti to Leonardo, Michelangelo, or Raphael – is stupendous. Such a leap was only possible because art had become the expression of complex social forces.

By the High Renaissance, art had come to pervade all aspects of life. From the arrangement of sweetmeats to the construction of fortifications – all were matters of moment upon which an artist's opinion might be needed or offered. And most of the great artists, too, regarded themselves as Jacks-of-all-trades. Leonardo did not think it beneath his dignity to design the costumes for the masques which his patrons loved or to fix the heating for a duchess's bath. And most of the great figures of the Renaissance displayed exceptional versatility. Michelangelo felt himself to be a man wholly dedicated to sculpture, yet after his reluctance had been overcome, he could paint the frescoes of the Sistine Chapel. And, of course, he could, and did, turn to architecture with equal facility and, when the mood was upon him, express his deepest feelings in poetry. The versatility of a Leonardo or a Michelangelo was far from being unusual. Princes and patrons wished their lives to be embellished richly, ostentatiously, beautifully, and they were willing to pour out their ducats and florins on all the arts and crafts that adorn the

93

lite of man. They pursued physical beauty like a drug. Their heightened sensibilities, due to the sudden turns of chance which threaded their days with light and shadow, lusted for colour, richness, wanton display. This aristocratic spirit at large in a world of bourgeois delights had no use for pewter dishes, sober costume, modest feasting, or chaste jewellery. It revelled in gold, in silver, in bronze, in gaudy dishes of majolica, and in silks, in satins, and in damasks, in cunningly wrought pearls, in sapphires, in rubies, and in emeralds. And the pageantry, the masquerades, the feasts, the dancing, and the music provided the background to this peacock world. This pride, this ostentation could find expression in the intellectual world as well as in the senses, and collections of antique bronzes, marble statues, splendidly illuminated manuscripts, beautifully bound books from the new presses, ancient rings and seals, became a prince as much as his palace or his pictures. The mania for collecting, as a reflection of social grandeur, emerges during the Renaissance. This delight in the eye, this desire to impress, created a constant demand for the services of the great masters, even for the most trivial and most ephemeral commissions – the moulding of pastry, the decoration of a table, the casting of a candlestick, the cutting of an intaglio, the design of a dagger – almost all of which have disappeared into limbo. The works of a few craftsmen of genius – the terracottas of della Robbia, the metalwork of Cellini, the bronzes of Riccio – survive. Those of nameless craftsmen who achieved high excellence are more plentiful. Their ornate *cassoni*, their haunting bronzes, their brightly patterned majolicas, and, above all, their exquisite jewellery, scattered about the museums of America and Western Europe, give a glimpse of the sumptuous world for which they worked.

This was the way, they thought, the great Romans had lived. They loved to act the parts of classical mythology, to be Jupiter or Hebe or Apollo or Diana for a day. And although, of course, they never gave up their Christian roots, they were drawn increasingly closer to the pretence of a pagan world. It gave them what all aristocracies need, a sense of separateness, as certainly and as completely as chivalry and feudalism had given a sense of caste to the warrior knights of the Middle Ages. Classical mythology, Neo-platonism, the mysteries of the pagan world, became chic. The education of a gentleman took on the strong classical bias which it was not to lose until modern times. The popular philosophers – Ficino, Pico della Mirandola, the friends of painters as well as their patrons – encouraged the revival of these ancient allegories. But they were not to be shared with the vulgar. Taste, sensibility, were to be linked with esoteric, almost private, knowledge. Poets, philosophers, painters, should speak in the language of riddles, of mysteries, which the *cognoscenti* alone could read. Such an attitude bred a sense of singularity, of exclusiveness, which courts and courtiers found as seductive as sin. Even Leonardo jotted down in commonplace books the trivial riddles of the Sforza, and Pico boasted in a philosophical essay, 'If I am not mistaken it will be intelligible only to a few, for it is filled with many mysteries from the secret philosophies of the ancients.' The esoteric, the mysterious, developed a fashionable cachet, and its cult opened the floodgates not only to much of the nonsense of late Neo-platonism, but also to astrology, to the language of emblems, and to the absurdities of late medieval bestiaries, and in the revival of learning was intermingled a great deal of hocus-pocus. Much, however, of this is germane to the image that Renaissance man created of himself and will be dealt with later, but this delight in an exclusive world of myth and mystery also influenced artistic expression profoundly. A naked Mars and Venus, tired but happy from their wanton sport, might shock the uninitiated, but the cultivated knew better. Mars, of course, was War, and Venus Love, so Love could conquer War and bring forth Peace. And if by chance Venus was wearing a bit of the armour, that merely illustrated that Love itself involved Strife. Such were simple allegories which even the fringe of the élite could read, but the theology as well as the mythology of poetic virtue grew ever more complex in its expression. Bellini's *Feast of the Gods* is the subject of a monograph, and all the iconographic scholarship of the Western world has failed to probe the hidden meanings of Giorgione's *Tempest*. For those artists who felt keenly the mystery of things, the way of allegory often proved enriching. It enabled them to explore feeling, to describe atmosphere, to hint at hidden presences, and to still in one luminous moment the fever and the fret of life and give its transience significance. So the *Virgin of the Rocks*, or even the *Mona Lisa*, possesses a sense of depth, of the abiding value of individual life, of eternal knowledge, that is both nostalgic and humane.

Giorgione responded to this sense of awareness as well as to Leonardo's mastery of light and shade. In Giorgione's paintings, and in many of Titian's, the value of earthly life is increased and given

Fête Champêtre, by Giorgione
Louvre

a significance that is as remote from the Middle Ages as it is from China.

A great artist like Giorgione could give universality to a private and exclusive myth, indeed deepen his genius by indulging in it, but many lesser artists could not. In their hands the mysteries became hollow, the allegories obvious and banal. Also, this cult of a private language of art marks the drift of the tide. The great masterpieces of the Renaissance had been, and many of them even in the first quarter of the sixteenth century still were, great public performances, even if they were created for popes or princes. But increasingly the direction of art was towards private enjoyment, and its style both more aristocratic and more exclusive. This was bound to be, as the heroic age of the city-state waned; as power and wealth and the sense of opportunity passed to the sea-borne nations of the West. Yet the achievement was so fabulously great that the traditions created in four or five generations proved far too strong for the creative imagination to wither quickly, and for the next four hundred years the arts of Italy continued to entrance the mind of Europe.

THE YOUNG MICHELANGELO

by Kenneth Clark

MICHELANGELO belongs to that small company of poets, artists, and musicians whose greatness has never been seriously questioned; but he differs from his companions – Dante, Shakespeare, Goethe, Titian, Mozart – in one important way. All of them have maintained this hold on our admiration by appealing to a wide range of human experience, so that each generation may extract from their works what suits it best. But Michelangelo has made his own terms with posterity, just as he did with his employers. He is the most concentrated and undeviating of great artists. We come to him for one particular revelation, communicated by one particular means. And the revelation is so important to us, and the mastery of means so absolute, that having once experienced it we, like his contemporaries, can never get it out of our systems. It makes everything else seem small and tame and worldly.

When we speak of an artist's greatness, as opposed to his talent or even his genius, we are usually referring to an aspect of his personality, and this is particularly true of Michelangelo. We know about him from many contemporary records, including the two *Lives* of Condivi and Vasari, men who knew him well, and every one of these records gives us the impression of an awe-inspiring character. Leaving aside the great religious teachers, I cannot think of any other man in history who has commanded such respect.

Our visual image of Michelangelo is of an old man, his face deeply marked by spiritual struggles. But there is a quantity of

Michelangelo in later years, from his atelier
Louvre

99

evidence that as a young man his force of character was equally apparent. The following episode recorded by Condivi will serve as an example. In 1506 Michelangelo had left Rome in a huff because he had been debarred from immediate access to Pope Julius II. Seven months later Michelangelo was brought into the papal presence. Julius asked him why he had walked out. Michelangelo answered, 'Not from ill will, but from disdain' (*ma per isdegno*). A bishop who was present nervously intervened, 'Pay no attention, Your Holiness; he speaks out of ignorance. Artists are all like that.' But before the wretched bishop could finish his apology he was hustled out of the room with blows; and Michelangelo resumed his former relationship with the Pope. Julius was then the most formidable figure in Christendom; Michelangelo was thirty-two.

Michelangelo used this transcendent force of character, which was like the spiritual power of a medieval saint, to transform the physical perfection of antiquity. He appeared at the moment when Graeco-Roman sculpture was a new and compelling discovery accepted by artists and patrons alike as an ultimate model. But in fact the bland materialism of antique art could not alone have expressed the crisis of the human spirit which took place during the years between Luther and Galileo. Michelangelo, by changing and twisting the forms of antique sculpture, created an instrument through which the spiritual turmoil of the sixteenth century could be made visible.

He was born in Florentine territory on 6 March 1475, and was one of the very few artists to come of aristocratic stock, although by his time the family fortunes had declined. His father, who claimed descent from the counts of Canossa, strongly objected to his son becoming an artist, which at that date meant an artisan; and when Michelangelo was one of the most famous men in Italy, his father still regarded the whole affair with bewildered incredulity. He was, as Condivi says, 'somewhat old-fashioned'; but Michelangelo treated him with patience and respect, asked for his prayers and sent him money, and often said that his sole aim in life had been to help the family regain its former status.

From the very first no one had any doubt that he was supremely gifted in the arts of design. After a short apprenticeship with Ghirlandaio, the most successful Florentine painter of the period, he is said by his biographers to have joined the privileged youths who were drawing antiques in the Medici gardens of the Via Larga, under the direction of the sculptor Bertoldo, and where he attracted the attention of Lorenzo the Magnificent. I see no adequate reason for disbelieving this tradition, and Michelangelo's earliest carvings seem to confirm it, for they consist largely of imitations of the antique, of a kind which he would have learned only in this particular school. Bertoldo's own masterpiece was a bronze relief of a battle, done in imitation of an antique sarcophagus in Pisa; and Michelangelo's earliest carving is also an imitation of a battle sarcophagus, although the nominal subject is the *Rape of Dejanira*. Although it was surely begun in the Medicean academy (and was perhaps left unfinished on Lorenzo's death in 1492) it looks out of this enchanted garden, both backwards and forwards: back to the charged and passionate Last Judgments of the Pisani and forward to the achievements of Michelangelo's maturity. There is no more striking example of Proust's saying, '*Les grands artistes n'ont jamais fait qu'une seule oeuvre.*' Michelangelo's first great carving foreshadows not only the classical style of his Florentine period, but the anti-classical expressiveness of his later works. In many respects it is closer to the *Last Judgment* of the Sistine than to the cartoon of the *Battle of Cascina*. And the affinity with the Dantesque spirit of Giovanni Pisano is also very revealing, for Michelangelo's heroic seriousness was, perhaps unconsciously, a reaction away from the daintiness of the *quattrocento*, back to the passion and gravity of the first founders of Tuscan art. His earliest drawings were copies of Giotto, and the poems of Dante were his continual inspiration.

But the Dejanira relief is exceptional. During his years in the garden of the Via Larga, and for some time afterwards, Michelangelo's whole conscious effort was directed towards the imitation of the classical style, and he succeeded so well that one of his works, a sleeping cupid, was actually sold as an antique, having been buried in a vineyard by a Roman dealer. When the fraud was discovered, Michelangelo, unlike modern imitators of antiquity, derived nothing but credit for his skill, and the cupid was afterwards purchased by that most pedantic of collectors, Isabella d'Este. It has now disappeared, and the *Bacchus*, which survives from about the same epoch, suggests that the loss is not a serious one. For the *Bacchus* is an all too successful imitation of Hellenistic sculpture at its least attractive. The swaying, dreamy movement of the body and a certain Dionysiac beauty in the head do not compensate for the lack of tension in the modelling, and one is left wondering how Michelangelo, even in a technical exercise, has contrived to suppress his energy of hand.

The *Bacchus* was executed in Rome, soon after Michelangelo's arrival there in 1496. After the death of Lorenzo de' Medici in 1492 he had remained two years in Florence, and it was at this time that he is supposed to have begun a scientific study of anatomy, under the protection of the Prior of Santo Spirito. These were the years when Savonarola was the virtual ruler of Florence, and although Michelangelo was never a direct follower, he read Savonarola's books throughout his life, and told Condivi that he could still hear the *frate*'s voice ringing in his ears. So two essential ingredients of Michelangelo's art, a passion for anatomy, and a consciousness of sin, were, so to say, poured into his mind at the same moment. But he was not happy in the Florence of Piero de' Medici; and in October 1494 there occurred the first of those panic flights which were to be repeated three times in the course of his life. Psychologists have occupied themselves with the question why this man of immense moral courage, who was utterly indifferent to physical hardship, should have suffered from these recurrences of irrational fear; and perhaps it is true that continuous inner tension led to an occasional snapping of the spirit, which expressed itself in a sudden need to escape. Or perhaps in each case there really was some ground for running away, and Michelangelo, who recognized his own genius, felt that he must preserve his life at any cost. In 1494 he fled to Bologna, where, as usual, his gifts were immediately recognized and he was commissioned to work on the chief sculptural project of the town, the ark of Saint Dominic; but fifteenth-century Bologna offered no scope to a youth of Michelangelo's genius, and as soon as possible he returned to Florence, and thence to Rome.

He arrived in Rome in the summer of 1496, having a letter of introduction from Lorenzo di Pierfrancesco de' Medici, the pupil of Marsilio Ficino and friend of Botticelli; and a week after his arrival he wrote back to Lorenzo, 'There are many beautiful things here.' Medieval Rome, the city of vineyards and cow pastures, with its stranded basilicas and aggressive watch-towers, was just beginning to give up its buried treasure; and Michelangelo's chief patron at this epoch, Jacopo Galli, had already a considerable collection of antiquities, amongst which Michelangelo's *Bacchus* was given a place of honour. However, the outstanding work during this first visit to Rome was of an entirely different character, the *Pietà* in St Peter's. It was commissioned by a French cardinal, Jean Bilheres, and this may account for the fact that Michelangelo accepted a Gothic motif in which the full-grown Christ lies on Our Lady's knees. This was originally a wood-carving motif, and the difficulty of adapting it to the crystalline character of marble has led Michelangelo to a marvellous feat of technical skill. This is the first work in which he shows that consummate mastery of his craft which his contemporaries, both artists and patrons, valued so highly. It has also involved a new stretch of the imagination, for he has achieved what theorists tell us is impossible, a perfect fusion of Gothic and Classic art. The motif and sentiment are northern, the physical beauty of the nude Christ is Greek; and Michelangelo has given the Virgin's head, so painfully distorted in Gothic Pietàs, a union of physical and spiritual beauty which is entirely his own. Ever since the *Pietà* was put in place, people have asked how the mother of a grown man, in the depths of grief, could appear so young and beautiful; and Michelangelo's reply is recorded in both Vasari and Condivi. It expresses in vivid, colloquial form the doctrines of Neo-platonism, which he had absorbed from the Medicean philosophers of his boyhood: that physical perfection is the mirror and emblem of a pure and noble spirit. This is the belief that had led his friend Lorenzo di Pierfrancesco to commission Botticelli's *Venus*; and we know, from Michelangelo's sonnets, that it justified to his mind his passionate admiration of the naked beauty of young men. Our scientific modern way of thinking, with its reliance on experience and psychology, may reject Neo-platonism as a compound of myth and self-deception. But there is no question of the sincerity with which Michelangelo believed (in Spenser's words) that 'soule is form, and doth the bodie make'.

In 1501 Michelangelo returned to Florence. These were the years in which the Florentine republic was able to assert some of the heroic virtues which had made it great a century before, and Michelangelo must have found the atmosphere of his native city a sharp contrast to the Medicean *douceur de vivre* of his youth, or the parasitic, anti-quarian Rome of his more recent experience. It was an atmosphere which suited him perfectly, and he was immediately called upon by the city magistrates to carry out commissions which should express the pride, vigour, and austere idealism of their regime; and the results were the *David* and the cartoon of the *Battle of Cascina*.

The *David* was carved out of a gigantic block of marble from which, seventy years earlier, the sculptor Agostino di Duccio had begun to carve the figure of a prophet. Agostino had completed little more than a knot of drapery, and when at last the derelict block was given to Michelangelo, his first symbolic act was to cut this drapery away. In his austere and uncompromising nudity the *David* states for the first time the essence of Michelangelo's ideal. As a piece of modelling the torso is equal to the finest work of antiquity, both in science and plastic vitality. Cut out the head and the hands, and you have one of the most perfect classical works of the Renaissance. Put them back and you put back the rough Tuscan accent, which was part of his birthright. It is possible to feel that there is a certain lack of harmony between the two elements: the *David* is in many respects an imperfect work. The marble block was too thin, and apart from this material shortcoming, Michelangelo has made a mistake common at the time; he has taken a motif from a relief as the basis for a figure in the round. But if the whole is unsatisfactory, the *David*, taken part by part, is a work of overwhelming power and magnificence, and it is Michelangelo's first great assertion of that quality which is so often in our minds when we think of him – the heroic. I suppose that the heroic in life or art is based on the consciousness that life is a struggle; and that in this struggle it is courage, strength of will, and determination which are decisive, not intelligence nor sensibility. The heroic involves a contempt of convenience and a sacrifice of all those pleasures which contribute to what we call a civilized life. It is the enemy of happiness. But we recognize that it is man's supreme achievement. For the heroic is not merely a struggle with material obstacles; it is a struggle with Fate. In so far as it magnifies the individual in his conflict with the blind forces of destiny it is the highest expression of a humanist ideal, and was recognized as such in antiquity. But the heroic stands on the borders of humanism, and looks beyond it. For to struggle with Fate man must become more than man; he must aspire to be a god. Now apotheosis announced the end of humanist art. If there is a single point at which the art of classical antiquity turns towards the Middle Ages, it is when the emperor is accepted as a god. The first great medieval work of art is the statue of Constantine at Barletta: and like the *David* it is of heroic size.

So on the perfectly antique body of the *David* is set a head which looks, with proud and conscious heroism, away from the happy, concrete world of the *quattrocento*. Like other great revolutions in history, we may wish that it had never happened, but once it has taken place we must accept it with all its potency for good or evil.

The mere size of the *David* (the statue stands over sixteen feet high), which is embarrassing to us, impressed Michelangelo's contemporaries. As a technical achievement alone it was a source of civic pride, like a space rocket. Significantly, the committee of artists who considered its site took it away from the cathedral and placed it in front of the Palazzo della Signoria, the centre of democratic government. A few months later Michelangelo began, in this building, the other great composition of these heroic Florentine years, the *Battle of Cascina*. It was executed in rivalry with Leonardo da Vinci, but unlike his *Battle of Anghiari*, it was never carried out as a painting, and the cartoon on which it was drawn proved so irresistible to artists that it was soon cut up and lost. Vasari called it 'the school of all the world', and Benvenuto Cellini was certainly voicing the professional verdict when he said that Michelangelo never did better. What gave it this immense authority? We can see from copies and from Michelangelo's original studies that it consisted of a number of naked men grouped in such a way as to show off the human body in action. Each body was not only an admirable human specimen modelled with scientific knowledge, but was in a pose selected for its completeness and nobility. Such poses were the legacy of antique art, surviving almost like symbols, through four hundred years of attrition; and in fact some of Michelangelo's drawings for the *Battle* are not done from nature, but from wax models he had made of antiques. So the *Battle of Cascina* was the foundation of the academic ideal, that strange, compelling approach to form which dominated art education until the present century; and the fact that Michelangelo himself transcended this ideal has always been a source of confusion to his more academic admirers.

For Michelangelo's vision of antique art was not bounded by the firm and finished outlines of the Cascina drawings. Throughout his life he had two ideals of antiquity which were in a sense complementary to each other. One of these was the ideal of perfection, the belief that what gave antique art its durability was the unflinching firmness with which every detail was realized. This had inspired the *Bacchus* and the *David*, and was to be realized, in later life, in those curious labours of love, the drawings executed for his friend Tommaso de' Cavalieri. For these the source of his inspiration was chiefly cameos and gems. But parallel with this admiration for its completeness, Michelangelo was fascinated by the fragmentary character of ancient sculpture; and the appeal of these weather-worn survivors of a mightier age was all the stronger because they gave a free play to the imagination. This attitude to ruins and fragments became common in what we call the Romantic Movement. Michelangelo was not the first man to feel it – Mantegna had already made evocative use of ruins – but he was the first to let it influence his style. Like the half lines in Virgil, the rough and unfinished state of Michelangelo's sculpture has evoked a whole literature of explanation, and no doubt the cause lies deep in his temperament. But I am certain that he was encouraged in this means of expression by the suggestive decay of antique sculpture. A proof of this dates from the very period of the *Battle* cartoon, the unfinished figure of St Matthew, commissioned by the Duomo in 1503 and executed a year or two later. It is imitated from a battered Roman figure, the so-called *Pasquino*, which had already inspired Donatello; and I doubt if this rather grotesque work would have had so compelling an appeal to the imaginations of two great artists had it been better preserved. In decay only the large lines of movement were perceptible, and gave the effect of a giant struggling out of the mists of antiquity.

This sense of titanic struggle was an aspect of Michelangelo's character which had appeared already in the Dejanira relief, and came more and more to dominate his art; and the crumbling magnificence of antique sculpture showed him that he could express it by leaving a great deal to the spectator's imagination. This also involved two other advantages which, although not consonant with the artistic principles of Michelangelo's time, appeal most strongly to our own: it allowed him to preserve the character of his material with the vivid mark of his own hand upon it; and it allowed him to dispense with those parts of a figure which did not fit into the main rhythm of his design, just as time has lopped off such excrescences as the arms of the *Torso Belvedere*.

This titanic struggle of form to emerge from matter reaches its climax in the marble figures destined for the tomb of Julius II. Michelangelo had been summoned to Rome in March 1505, and commanded to design and execute the greatest tomb in Christendom. His new master was a formidable man of action, with a powerful mind and boundless ambition. He was also as proud and wilful as Michelangelo himself. Gorki once said of Tolstoy, 'His relations with God are very uneasy: like two old bears in a den'; and such were Michelangelo's relations with God's vicar on earth. Yet it was one of those momentous conjunctions for which posterity must be grateful, for without Julius II, Michelangelo might never have had the opportunity of developing the full power of his imagination.

In the summer he went to Carrara to superintend the quarrying of blocks of marble big enough for the tomb, and for eight months he remained inaccessible in that awe-inspiring landscape, surrounded by stone. These long sojourns in Carrara, repeated several times in his life, were to Michelangelo like religious retreats, and were the prelude to spells of his greatest activity. He returned to Rome in the winter of 1505–06, ready to concentrate all his force on executing his grandiose ideas. Then there occurred the first catastrophe in what, since Condivi, all writers on Michelangelo have called the tragedy of the tomb. Pope Julius refused to see him. It was Michelangelo's first experience of court intrigue and of the readiness with

108

which princes allow themselves to be swayed by rival coteries. Later in life he accepted such intrigues with a firm and melancholy stoicism. But to the young man of thirty-one, his mind charged with colossal images, his spirit burning like a fire, this treachery was intolerable; and in April 1506 he left Rome without a word and returned to Florence. For seven months the Pope tried to lure him back to Rome, but Michelangelo was suspicious and the Florentine government protected him. Finally, when the Pope conquered Bologna in November, Michelangelo felt bound to go there and ask for forgiveness, and there follows the scene I have already described. I should add that although Condivi says that he had this account from Michelangelo's own lips, contemporary documents suggest that the artist was considerably more penitent. Almost as a penance, he was commissioned to make a gigantic bronze statue of the Pope to go over the door of San Petronio in Bologna. It cost him one of the most miserable and unproductive years of his life; and shortly after it had been put in place, was broken up and melted down for the bronze.

At the beginning of March 1508 he left Bologna for Florence, intending to settle down in his native town and complete the commissions that he had left unfinished there. He thought that he was 'free of Rome'; but within two months his terrible old master had forced him to return there. What was worse, Julius did not allow him to finish the tomb, but gave him a new and in many ways unsuitable commission, to paint the ceiling of the papal chapel in the Vatican, known as the Sistine. Michelangelo's early biographers believed that the proposal was put forward by his enemy, Bramante, in order to discredit him; and it is true that Michelangelo accepted the commission under protest, complaining that painting was not his art. Documents show, however, that the proposal had been discussed two years earlier; and there is no doubt that Michelangelo had practised painting. The *Holy Family* in the Uffizi, known as the Doni *tondo*, dates from 1504; and as an apprentice to Ghirlandaio he seems to have had a hand in the frescoes of Santa Maria Novella.

It was not as a technical, but as an intellectual feat that the Sistine ceiling involved such a vast extension of his faculties. Hitherto his sculptures had been concerned with single figures or traditional themes, and in the *Battle of Cascina*, the subject had been only a pretext for a pictorial exercise. Now he had to illustrate the first phase of human destiny, and what theologians called the world *ante legem*. He was no longer concerned with problems of form alone, but with problems of philosophy.

In the chief history paintings of the Renaissance, the artist was usually given a 'programme' by his patron or some attendant poet or philosopher. But Michelangelo, in a well-known letter, explains that he was told to work out his subject for himself. Even he could not conceive the whole theme in a single flash of inspiration. Both in subject and style it developed prodigiously as the work continued. Yet at some early point, Michelangelo recognized that the story of the Creation could be transformed from a fanciful narrative into a profound philosophy. He did so by compelling us to read his 'histories' in a reverse order. Over our head, as we enter the chapel, is the *Drunkenness of Noah*; at the far end, over the altar, is the *Creation*. Thus the ceiling illustrates the Neo-platonic doctrine, so dear to Michelangelo, and so often expressed in his sonnets, that life must be a progression from the servitude of the body to the liberation of the soul. It begins with the inert figure of Noah, where the body has taken complete possession, and ends with the figure of the Almighty dividing light from darkness, in which the body has been completely transformed into a symbol of the spirit, and even the head, with its too evident human associations, has become indistinct.

The same evolution, both of spirit and style, can be seen in the so-called athletes, those deeply personal creations which come first to most people's minds at the mention of Michelangelo. They are not, as used to be supposed, mere decoration, but symbolize the thoughts of the prophets and seers in the spandrels and are a link between them and the histories. But because this subject is limited to the representation of a single naked youth, we are made more conscious of changes in style. At first they are classical in the narrow sense. They are symmetrical, bound by a firm outline, forming a closed rhythm, and several are actually derived from antique gems. The athletes on the middle of the ceiling, beside the Creation of Eve, are already less symmetrical and the unity of planes has been abandoned. In the last pair of athletes, those beside the Creation of Light, a balanced and reciprocal movement is entirely abandoned, and Michelangelo has created a continuous movement which twists round the central scene.

In the use of this twisting rhythm he is realizing an experience which he had stored away in his mind almost five years earlier, the impact of the famous antique group known as the *Laocoön*. It had been discovered in January 1506, and Michelangelo had been one of the first to identify and admire it. No doubt he recognized immediately that it confirmed his own feelings about the potential expressiveness of the nude. But like most great poets and artists he had a long period of gestation, and it was not till about 1510 that a reminiscence of the *Laocoön* is perceptible in his work. Then, finally, in the corner spandrels depicting the *Crucifixion of Hamar* and the *Brazen Serpent*, this new system of form, in which tormented rhythms and violent fore-shortening are used to express mental and physical agony, is pushed to a limit never surpassed. By 1511 Michelangelo had anticipated almost every extremity of style which would engage the ingenuity of mannerist and baroque artists in the next hundred years.

Two years before the ceiling was completed it had begun to make itself felt by premonitory rumblings, like those which anticipate the theme in the last movement of Beethoven's Ninth Symphony. Raphael himself had been smuggled in by Bramante, and had immediately added a Michelangelesque figure to the already complete design of his fresco of the *School of Athens*.

When, on 31 October 1512, the frescoes were officially unveiled, artists and connoisseurs were prepared for something which should change the course of painting; and that, in fact, is what it did; and not only painting, but the whole mode of feeling. The freshness and wonder of the early Renaissance, the delight in living things unburdened with a conscience, birds, children, flowers – all this was crushed by the oppressive awareness of human destiny. And instead of a natural ease of arrangement in which flower was set beside flower and face beside face, there came into being the new unity of struggle, the unity of Hercules grappling with the lion.

When the ceiling was finally unveiled, Michelangelo was thirty-seven. He lived to be eighty-nine. In this half century he executed some of his greatest works – the marble prisoners, the Medici tombs, the *Last Judgment*, the marvellous and tragic Pietàs of his old age. The mood becomes graver; the confidence in physical beauty diminishes, and is at last rejected with a kind of horror. But fundamentally there is an unvarying aim; to use the human body as an instrument with which to reveal the ascent of the human soul. The body must perish: and Michelangelo became increasingly preoccupied with death; the soul must be judged: and he became more and more burdened by the consciousness of sin. But in his imagination body and soul remain indivisible, fatally united in their struggle; and out of this involvement he creates movements, gestures, limbs, proportions which allow us poor worldlings, with our sordid material interests, to become, through the contemplation of form, momentarily capable of spiritual life.

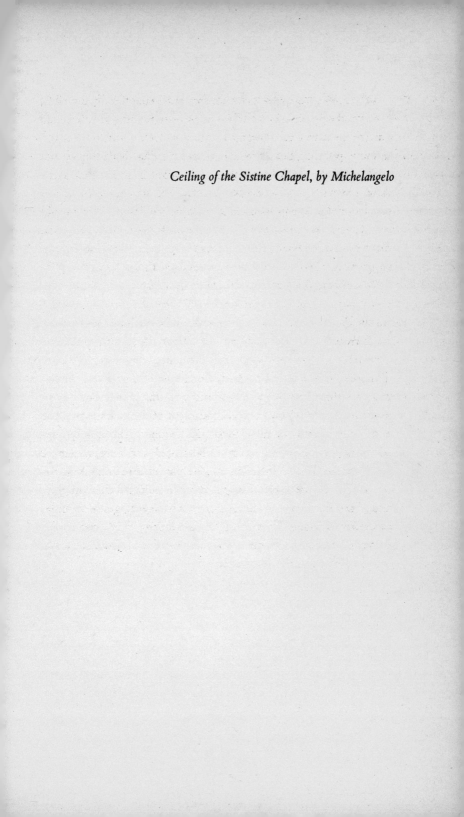

Ceiling of the Sistine Chapel, by Michelangelo

'IN a few hours they were burnt, their legs and arms gradually dropping off; part of their bodies remaining hanging to the chains, a quantity of stones were thrown to make them fall, as there was a fear of the people getting hold of them; and then the hangman and those whose business it was, hacked down the post and burnt it on the ground, bringing a lot of brushwood, and stirring the fire up over the dead bodies, so that the very least piece was consumed. Then they fetched carts, and accompanied by the mace-bearers, carried the last bit of dust to the Arno, by the Ponte Vecchio, in order that no remains should be found,' wrote Landucci in his diary after watching the execution of Savonarola and his disciples. So ended the strange, doom-haunted Dominican monk from Ferrara, whose bitter tirades against luxury, greed, extortion, and tyranny had torn Florentine society apart.

The Piazza in which Savonarola met his end was adorned with some of the most profoundly moving works of Renaissance art. He had given the apocalyptic sermons for which he was condemned under the vaulting dome of the cathedral, itself a triumph of the new architecture. Among his audience had sat the flower of Italian humanism – Pico della Mirandola, Poliziano, and Marsilio Ficino, the president of the Platonic Academy – and he told them roughly that an old woman knew more of faith than their Plato. Even Lorenzo de' Medici, the greatest of all Florentine patrons, had sought his friendship, only to be spurned. Savonarola rejected the Renaissance. He would have none of it, ignoring the fact that for a hundred years Florence had led Italy in painting, in sculpture, in philosophy, in sophistication. Of all Italian cities, Florence had been the cradle of the Renaissance, but curiously, except in its very earliest days, the spirit of Savonarola had always been abroad. Florence was a city of violent contrasts, a city of the light and the dark.

Physically Florence deceives: the golden Tuscan landscape, so rich, so fertile, so gentle in climate, bespeaks a pastoral, idyllic, Virgilian life in which the rhythms of living achieve a harmony with nature. Here, if anywhere, is a countryside made for a Giorgione or a Titian, yet Florence produced neither, nor indeed any painter who sought to immortalize the poetry of nature. The facts of Florentine life were brutal, not gentle. Rich and beautiful its situation might be; economically and strategically its position was always desperate. To the west, controlling its only outlet to the sea, lay Pisa, prosperous and powerful, linked by its commerce with the four corners of the Mediterranean world. Athwart the route to Pisa, Florence had an unbeatable enemy in Lucca. To the north, the peril was worse – Milan, ravenous for land and rich in men and money. To the south, almost on Florence's doorstep, Siena controlled the road to Rome, and the Sienese were as fiercely proud and warlike as the Florentines. To the east were the wolves, the ravagers, the petty tyrants of the Papal Patrimony who lived by war and violence; for these despots the rich lands of Tuscany were sweet to plunder. To survive, therefore, let alone expand, Florence required from its citizens both courage and resourcefulness, a willingness to practise the arts of diplomacy as well as war. Both needed money, and, in the last analysis, wealth, and wealth alone, enabled Florence to survive and to triumph over the disadvantages of its geographical situation. The realities of Florentine life were the sword and the florin. The use of both was improved by skill in reading human nature, and it is not surprising that a preoccupation with man and his destiny lies at the heart of the Florentine Renaissance.

Despite all its perils, Florence triumphed. The prime source of its strength and wealth lay in its *arti* – the guilds which drew together its merchants and skilled craftsmen. One of the earliest to be organized was the *arte di Calimala*, and throughout the golden age of Florence it held its dominating position. It was a company of merchants who traded with England, Flanders, and France, bringing undressed cloths to Florence, where they were reworked into fine materials and dyed in the splendid, vivid colours that the Renaissance painters have made so memorable – the blues and crimsons and reds in which they dressed their saints and madonnas. They exported the finished goods throughout Europe, and the stamp of the guild became a guarantee of worth and workmanship. The guild was meticulously ruled and its members subjected to a close discipline not only in their public, but also in their moral life. The *Calimala* became a model for the other great guilds that began to dominate Florentine economic and political life in the late twelfth and early thirteenth centuries. Including the *Calimala* there were seven of them – the wool merchants, the silk weavers, the bankers, the notaries, the druggists (Dante was a member of this guild, which also dealt in spices and precious stones), and the furriers. These seven included all the great merchants of Florence, who formed the heart of its economic life. But Florence was a large town, and it served a populous hinterland, and its shopkeepers were numerous enough, and powerful enough, to form their own guilds, which were known as the lesser arts – the innkeepers, shoemakers, carpenters, blacksmiths, grocers, bakers, and the like – fourteen in all. Each guild had its officers of state – its consuls, its notaries, and its

Woodcut of Florence, ca 1486 Staatliche Museen, Berlin

banner-bearer (*gonfaloniere*) – who carried the heraldic symbols in the great processions which were held on the day of their patron saint. Each guild, too, had its church which it patronized and in which were held its special masses, for these merchants were as deeply steeped in religion as in trade. (At the head of each page of one of their surviving account books is the sign of the cross, made to make forgery hell-worthy.) The Florentine guilds were small worlds unto themselves, closely regulated, self-conscious, jealous of their rights and customs, and fully aware of their power.

Naturally, relations between the greater and lesser guilds were often uneasy. The lesser guilds felt their numbers gave them a right to power; the greater knew that, in the last resort, it was their money which sustained the government of Florence both in peace and in war. Yet there were never more than three or four thousand men in these twenty-one guilds, and Florence embraced nearly a hundred thousand souls. The bulk of the population was proletarian – workers for a day wage: spinning, dyeing, weaving, carding, or hauling the great bales of wool and cloth and silk – the citizens who, in the very beginning, had fought for the liberties within the city and for its rich territories without, the people into whose hearts Savonarola's words burned like fire. They were organized into four districts, each with four quarters led by a gonfalon – the Unicorn, the Viper, the Lion – under which each citizen was enrolled to fight, if need be, for his city's liberty. From these quarters were drawn the governors of the city who made up the Signory which ruled Florence, made peace or war, and levied the taxes. Naturally, the Signory was attended with immense ceremonial and its chief officers, the priors, lived in grandeur, but their tenure was as brief as a butterfly's, for they ruled for two months only. To control this complex governmental machine, men fought in the streets, assassinated, exiled, pillaged, and destroyed each other generation after generation, so that one Florentine gloomily remarked that there were enough citizens in exile to populate another city. The main strife revolved about who should or who should not be prior-worthy – whether, in fact, power should be widely distributed or kept close – and whether the major arts or the minor arts should dominate the institutions of government. There was factional strife not only within the ranks of the guilds but among the restless proletariat, often made politically conscious by the hunger of their bellies, for Florence suffered the sharp economic storms of an uncontrolled capitalism. So over the centuries power in Florence swayed like sea-weed in a tide, drifting into the hands of oligarchs only to be snatched out, but never for long, by a great upsurging wave of popular feeling.

During most of the Renaissance, political power in Florence was in the hands of a group of very rich merchants, led by the Medici family. This closely knit oligarchy controlled all the elections to office with the sureness of a Tammany electioneering machine. Better still for them, they handled the city's taxes. And, of course, they were the inheritors of the vast wealth which the far-flung trade of Florence had drawn from the four quarters of Europe.

Suspicious, guarded, rich, the oligarchs clung tenaciously to their power, willing to serve the Medici only as long as the Medici served them. Their greed and envy occasionally drew them close to conspiracy, and the plot of the Pazzi family to kill the Medici in the Duomo toppled some of them into disastrous treason. Politically and financially these men had little foresight: they exploited their power to siphon the city's riches into their own pockets. Yet they had one saving grace: they had been born into a tradition of civic patronage. Their fathers, and their fathers before them, had endowed monasteries, beautified churches, and established charities. A sense of sin still clung to usury and to the banker's trade, and they had felt a need to return a tithe of their profits. Naturally, they were stirred by particular acts of God's goodness to them, and then their piety turned more quickly into patronage. Yet about 1400 this tradition began to change, both in its nature and its expression.

This change was wrought by a desperate war, working on the

literary and artistic movements which had already seeded themselves in Florence, and the result was a remarkable leap forward in painting, in sculpture, in architecture, in philosophy, and in the countless arts and crafts that adorn the life of man. The change was as dramatic as water turning into ice.

After its failure by 1343 to secure dominion of Tuscany by force of arms, Florence had resolved to ally, whenever possible, with neighbouring city-states, to protect rather than absorb. As Coluccio Salutati, the chancellor of Florence and one of its first great humanists, wrote, the Florentines who hated tyranny at home were willing to defend the liberties of others. The feeling was strong in the city's governing circles that Florentines were the true heirs of republican Rome: Salutati, Bruni, and Poggio studied Cicero in their leisure from running Florence's diplomacy and collecting its taxes. His ideas, which lie at the heart of humanism, struck them with the force of a new discovery, and they began to weave afresh the belief that the full life, indeed, the good life, could only be lived if a man dedicated himself to civic virtues. It was about Rome, about Cicero, about Plato, that they talked when they lingered in the sun in the Piazza or gathered together in each other's houses. Nor did they disdain to discuss their ideas with the sculptors and artists – Ghiberti, Donatello, Brunelleschi – whom they and their friends patronized. And how right they seemed in their interpretation of the past and the present when Florence withstood alone the might of Gian Galeazzo Visconti, who, in 1402, stood poised to overwhelm the city and so bring the whole of Lombardy and Tuscany under his sway. Then, as in some Athenian tragedy, the Fates took up their shears. Gian Galeazzo, in the prime of life, with the cup of success at his lips, sickened and died. So the threat to Florence passed, but, in passing, fused a mood into an attitude to life.

The Florentines did not consider themselves saved by chance. For them it was a triumph of civic virtue, of steadfast republicans thwarting tyrants. The ancient Roman virtues of which Cicero spoke and of which old Cato was the ideal, had been, they felt, reborn in Florence, which gave the city an identity with the past. The year 1402 represented a triumph and a liberation, and this sense of freedom renewed, of the breaking of the shackles of the immediate past, invigorated not only philosophy and history but also the plastic arts. It is not surprising that Masaccio's grave saints should wear their cloaks like togas.

Interest in classics, interest in ancient art, delight in new techniques of painting, sculpture, and architecture, existed before the cataclysmic struggle with Milan, but none can doubt that it gave an immense impetus to the peculiar qualities of the Florentine Renaissance. Symbolically, at the height of the struggle the city appointed Chrysoloras, the first and most deeply influential teacher of Greek, a public lecturer. A belief in the value of classical learning as the moulder of a citizen's character, a conviction that great moral value could be derived from a study of its philosophy, became as deeply embedded in the Florentine tradition as it did in nineteenth-century England. And when the Medici founded and encouraged a Platonic academy, and patronized handsomely the great philosophers – Ficino, Pico, and the rest – they were no innovators, and the purpose of their patronage was widely understood. It would strengthen an attitude to human life that was thought to be singularly Florentine. Although humanistic study had its roots in civic life, naturally it developed rapidly within the terms of its own disciplines and needs. Scholars dedicated themselves to the textual and philological problems inherent in the study of the classics – and as scholars will, became obsessed with their own techniques. Yet even if preoccupation with style, grammar, emendation, and the minutiae of criticism often took the place of creative imagination, there was nevertheless a great deal of fine poetry and fine prose, written in a Latin that would have been no disgrace to the age of Augustus. And the encouragement to classical studies given by the humanistic Renaissance in Florence was in harmony with scholarly activity scattered throughout the courts and cities of Italy.

Yet the greatest gains from this self-identification with the antique were in the arts, particularly sculpture. As in ancient Athens, statues taught citizens the lessons of their public life. The mysterious David of Donatello and the vast David of Michelangelo both told the Florentines that their city had always been a giant-killer, proud of its liberty: the citizens themselves dragged Holofernes and Judith from the Medici palace and set them up in front of the Palazzo della Signoria to underline what should be the fate of tyrants. In no other place were sculptors so handsomely patronized or so deeply admired. Florence, in consequence, produced the greatest masters of the fifteenth century, whose work graced Rome, Venice, Milan, and the lesser cities of Italy. So, too, in architecture: while Milan and Venice still lingered in the grip of the Gothic, and Rome lay in ruins, Brunelleschi began recreating the austere harmonies of the classical world and giving to the Florentines a proper setting for their intense civic consciousness. In painting there was the same sense of *gravitas*, of weight of human character, of the power of human destiny, particularly before the sophistication and self-indulgence of the High Renaissance produced in some artists a more esoteric cultivation of art. Even so, the last great artist of Florence, Michelangelo, still recalls the tradition of his city, created by Giotto and Masaccio.

The struggle with Milan did more than render humanism fashionable, or encourage a cult of the antique, or stimulate the arts, or make a study of Cicero an essential part of the education of a gentleman. It consolidated the power of the oligarchy, and peculiarly so, as the lucky death of Gian Galeazzo not only plucked them from the jaws of destruction, but set them on a course of military success. Surging economic prosperity was linked with the triumph of their arms. Florence, still free, still republican, enjoyed a prosperity, a fame, a serenity unparalleled in her annals – giving further point, if point were needed, to the antique virtue of her government and its citizens. Oligarchies, however, are rarely stable for long; after the first difficulties, criticism is quickly followed by intrigue. The death in 1417 of Maso degli Albizzi, the most powerful member of the ruling oligarchy, unleashed a struggle for power in which the old class and guild antagonisms once more erupted to the surface. By dexterous exploitation of these jealousies, Giovanni de' Medici and, after his death in 1429, his son Cosimo were able to establish their family so securely in power that Cosimo's grandson Lorenzo enjoyed the power if not the title of a prince. Yet even at the height of the family's greatness respect was always paid to the letter of the republican constitution. The survival of the Medici and the ease with which they defeated the conspiracies of the Neroni and, afterwards, of the Pazzi, were due to the loyal support of their fellow merchants as well as their dependants.

During this half-century of Medicean rule, Florence dominated the intellectual and artistic life of Italy: Cosimo poured out a torrent of wealth on buildings – palaces, monasteries, churches – on sculpture, and on paintings. Feeling himself to be God's debtor, he did his best to make restitution – reconstructing and embellishing his favourite monastery of San Marco, as well as his parish church of San Lorenzo. Following in his footsteps, his son Piero ordered a sumptuous tabernacle for the miraculous crucifix in San Miniato al Monte, and another for the wonder-working image at Santissima Anunziata, which bears the proud boast that the marble alone cost four thousand florins. Cosimo built his own palace modestly but strictly according to the new style; he patronized Donatello for as long as he lived, and sculpture, as might be expected from so dedicated a Florentine, was his greatest passion after architecture. He preferred his sons to deal with mere painters and decorators, but *he* paid. And many superb frescoes of Fra Angelico, Filippo Lippi, and Benozzo Gozzoli were the fruits of Medicean gold, of their sense of the usurer's sin, of a need to return the riches that one man had acquired, in beauty that all could enjoy.

Lorenzo the Magnificent, his grandson, amazed by the staggering sums that his grandfather had spent, preferred the cheaper patronage of philosophers. Nevertheless, he maintained the tradition of his ancestors, and the beauty and splendour of Florence steadily grew. The citizens were continuously regaled with pageants, tournaments, and carnivals. It proved to be a reckless world in which capital was too easily squandered on military manoeuvres, diplomatic activity, and Lorenzo's anxiety to cut a figure in Italy whatever the cost.

As the fame of Florence reached new heights, so did its public debt (not that the debt worried the oligarchy overmuch, for they lent the money on excellent security and at a splendid interest). The world was a rich man's oyster: the tentacles of Florentine trade stretched from Cairo to the Cotswolds, and even the shocks and disasters in the eastern Mediterranean – the spread of the Ottoman Turks and the fall of Constantinople – seemed, for a time at least, to be turned to Florence's advantage by a benign Providence. The loss of Byzantine alum, so vital to the luxury cloth trade, was immediately countered by the discovery of huge deposits at Tolfa in the Papal States, for which, naturally, the Medici secured the concession. Wandering Greeks with manuscripts to sell and an ancient tongue to teach were welcome as a further adornment to a refined household. Secure and self-indulgent, the leaders of Florentine society tried to evade present disasters and future cataclysms, while the Florentine government sought to survive by the use of mercenaries, diplomacy, subsidies, and bribes. The call to civic virtue, the mobilization of the city's wealth and the city's men, no longer appealed to a bourgeois aristocracy. Their exclusive world possessed too much delight to be foolishly risked. In the soft elegance of Lorenzo di Pierfrancesco de' Medici's villa, in the golden glow of the Tuscan evening, young men might listen to Ficino's subtle explanations of the hidden meanings in Botticelli's *Primavera*, which adorned its walls; for them the bales of wool, rolls of cloth, stacked hides, and piled spices were a necessity, not a way of life, and although they could use the dagger and the sword, they felt no compulsion to sweat in arms amid the horrors of war for the future of their city. All the authority, all the skill, of Lorenzo were used to avoid such bleak necessities. This elegant world was perched precariously, however, on the edge of turbulence, and it depended on the subtlety and statesmanship of Lorenzo not only to prevent the system from collapsing in internecine strife, of which the Pazzi conspiracy was a clear enough warning, but also to still the dangerous antipathy of a restless population whose fears and hopes were already being played upon by a master demagogue, some years before Lorenzo's death.

The Florentine Renaissance has entranced generations of men by the astonishing range of its artistic and scholarly achievements – from the serene perfection of Leonardo to the tragic realism of Machiavelli – and all too often the endless toil of the labouring men and women, whose grievous lives made it possible, is forgotten. It was the tragic situation of the common man that stirred deeply the creative imagination not only of Michelangelo, but also of Botticelli, who reflected the bright elegance and exclusive charm of the Florentine world more faithfully than any other painter. The compulsive rantings of Savonarola haunted them both.

The last decades of the fifteenth century brought a sharp contraction of Florentine trade. Englishmen were beginning to make their own cloth, the Flemish were showing a more than Italian skill in dressing and dyeing it. In 1478 the London bank of the Medici was closed; in 1483 the Tolfa alum concession had to be abandoned; for a time the merchants of Florence even lost their traditional role as papal bankers. Trade with the eastern Mediterranean steadily wasted away. Renewed wars, with expensive alliances, and even more costly condottieri, added further strain to an economy which had already accumulated far too many obligations. The Florentines had been dealing in futures for too many generations, and, skilful as their financiers were, they could not conjure increased wealth from diminishing trade. For centuries urban poverty had helped to breed epidemic diseases that raged with the ferocity of a prairie fire through the dirt-encrusted slums. Plagues, fevers, and consumption made

Famine
Miniature from Il Biadajolo
Biblioteca Laurenziana, Florence

death a constant visitor at the houses of the poor, who, to exorcize horror, fortify their courage, and set their hopes on future blessedness, pleaded for the intercession of the Virgin and the saints. Religion – ecstatic, even apocalyptic – assuaged the wounds of their poverty and its pain. For them the elegant, exclusive domain of the scarlet-wearing burghers who exercised authority in their city was a bright, elusive world as impossible to understand as dreams in a language they could never comprehend. The sufferings of Christ and the pity of God lay closer to their knowledge, and in their lives the priest was as necessary as bread. This contradiction – poverty, suffering, and pain amid a world of profusion, extravagance, and delight – stirred the consciences of deeply sensitive men. It was this that made Pico della Mirandola seek the solace of Savonarola's mysticism, that led him, at his death, to adopt the habit of a Dominican; it was this that brought about that stranger conversion which drew Botticelli away from the gaieties and urbane moralities of the antique to an acceptance of Savonarola's prophecies; it was this that fused Michelangelo's tragic sense of human destiny with Savonarola's apocalyptic vision.

The story of Savonarola is a mixture of tragedy and hysteria, in which a genuine pity for man's condition became enravelled in hate and muddled by political intrigue. His denunciation of worldliness, his childish burning of vanities, his fiery condemnation of a lazy and corrupt clergy, were a part of the threnody of the life of Europe, frequently heard, frequently forgotten; but Savonarola spoke at a time when the young Piero de' Medici was displaying a singular lack of his family's genius. Behind Savonarola loomed the discontented poor, eager for a chance, eager for secular as well as religious hope. Those families whom the Medici had excluded and despised knew how to manipulate this superlative demagogue, whose wild sermons could inflame a multitude. So what started in evangelism finished in political revolution.

The little people, the *piagnoni* (snivellers) as the old oligarchs called them, became a power in the land. *Popolo e Libertà* frequently echoed

in the Piazza – a cry which Pisa promptly adopted as it threw aside
the Florentine yoke and claimed the protection of the French, when
invasion of Italy had triggered the revolution against Piero. Savonarola combined a dependence on the French that was quite unrealistic
with a hatred of the Papacy that bordered on insanity. His loud denunciations of papal sins (interlarded from time to time with stagger-
ingly sane bits of hard-headed diplomacy) grew more shrill as the
French left him in the lurch. Alexander VI – aware of, and tolerantly
amused by, his own shortcomings – bore with the fulminations so
long as his diplomacy required it. Time, of course, favoured the Pope.
The French were content to use Florence, but naturally disinclined
to save it from the consequences of its own folly, or to restore its
Tuscan empire. And in Florence itself, the oligarchs disliked both the
rantings of Savonarola and the government of the people; in the
wings lurked the exiled Medici – *they* were powerful in Rome. The
inevitable end came: the rack and the faggot for Savonarola; the
defeat of his *piagnoni*; and in the fullness of time, the return of the
Medici.

The whole Savonarola episode is a curious mixture of idealism,
ineptitude, and iniquity. Certainly Savonarola wanted a Florentine
government that represented more fully the whole citizenship – the
poor and the dispossessed as well as the rich and the powerful. He
also hated life, grew drunk on his own megalomaniac visions, preferred prophecy to policy, and welcomed the disasters he had done
so much to promote. Ignorance married to prejudice, blind hatred
linked with a disgust for life, proved an unsatisfactory basis for statesmanship, even when practised by a saint.

Never again was the republic the same; the power of Florence was
greatly diminished. For a decade after the burning of Savonarola in
1498 for heresy, and after the failure of her mercenaries, Florence's
blood and treasure were poured out in the Pisan war. In 1509 Pisa
was captured, but the expense was far beyond the weakened resources
of Florence's dwindling trade. Indeed, three years later a refusal to

The Burning of Savonarola
Anon., Museo San Marco, Florence

act in concert with the Papacy was treated by Julius II as an impertinence. His professional Spanish troops scattered the Florentine militia. The papal-inspired revolution followed, and the Medici returned. They lacked the ability of their ancestors, and proved little better than pawns in the hands of the Medici Pope Leo X, and it required further rebellions and plots, another brief republic haunted by the puritanism and religiosity of Savonarola, as well as the sack of Rome by Charles V, before Florence was finally subjected to the rule of the Medici as dukes of Tuscany. In the first three decades of the sixteenth century the greatness of Florence faded. Economically – and the splendour of the Florentine Renaissance was based on its wealth – Florence lacked a future. The heart of its trade – cloth – was lost to England and to Flanders, and banking followed trade. Florence was far more vulnerable than Venice, or even Milan, to the great decline in Mediterranean prosperity which followed the discoveries of the New World and the sea-route to the Indies.

Artists lived uneasy lives in post-Medicean Florence, for patronage grew scarce. Art and humanism no longer reflected the civic virtues – these were adequately exercised by private prayer and public repentance. During the middle decades of the sixteenth century the cult of sensitivity, or elegance, and of learning as the peculiar attributes of a gentleman had also narrowed the social basis of art and, to some extent, limited its appeal. In the wanderings of Leonardo and of Michelangelo, in the frustrations that marred their lives and marked their art, there is a reflection of the growing impotence and decay of the society in which they were born and grew to manhood.

Yet that tradition of individual destiny, of the worth of man, which the Florentines had cultivated so carefully in their heroic days, remained strong enough not only to sustain them in spite of the tribulations of their age, but also to buoy up a number of artists of lesser genius – Bronzino, Pontormo, del Sarto, and Fra Bartolommeo. And to one art, namely history, the decay of Florence provided a greater stimulus than its climb to greatness. The cataclysms of Florentine experience opened the same creative vistas for Machiavelli and Guicciardini as neuroses in individuals were to do for Dostoyevsky or Proust. Indeed, even in its last, sad days, republican Florence still produced an astonishing array of genius, and no city of so small a compass has ever, before or since, made a greater contribution to art and letters within the brief span of a hundred and fifty years.

LORENZO DE' MEDICI

by Ralph Roeder

LORENZO DE' MEDICI was, first and last, a financier; he was much more besides – politician, statesman, patron of art and letters – but these were merely functions of the financier developed by his forefathers, which he inherited together with the fortune of his family, and in each of these roles his performance was the consummation of theirs. His biography begins before he was born, and he sits for his portrait under his family tree.

His great-grandfather, Giovanni di Bicci de' Medici, was the first millionaire of the family. Of plebeian origin, the Medici had risen by prosperous trade to the front rank of the *nobili popolani* – the merchant princes of the major guilds – but they had not abandoned the class from which they sprang, and it served them steadily in their subsequent ascent to power. The banking business which Giovanni built up with branches in sixteen European capitals entitled him to a leading position among the eighty banking firms of Florence, and would have assured him a corresponding influence in the government had he chosen to claim it, since the bankers' guild supplied the capital and the connexions for the enterprises of the state; but Giovanni was prudent and avoided politics. Retiring by nature, modest and unassuming, he spent his money on the construction of churches, the encouragement of art, and works of charity (the Foundling Hospital built for him by Brunelleschi, and the church of San Lorenzo rebuilt for him by the great architect as a family temple, were his monuments), and as long as he confined his public spirit to such modest activities, he passed for a safe man and honours came to him unsought. Summoned to the Signory, he revealed a different form of public spirit, however, by supporting against powerful opposition a tax reform, which substituted for the universal poll tax and the arbitrary assessments of the past a $1\frac{1}{2}$ per cent levy on capital. This innovation was a boon for the poor, who reckoned it among his major charities; and since it was enacted when an unsuccessful war was about to be resumed and the tax rate raised, it won him high favour with the little people; but it incensed the rich. 'Since the burden was to be distributed by law and not by men,' Machiavelli, the official biographer of the family observed, 'it weighed heavily on the powerful citizens and was received with extreme displeasure by the mighty.' Their anger rose and turned to alarm when the little people proposed to make the reform retroactive to compensate the losses they had suffered in the past; but Giovanni dissuaded them from this abuse of his bounty, and having done his duty impartially by both sides, retired to private life and the practice of his private charities. When he retired to the grave in 1429, he was widely missed and mourned by those whom he benefited.

The eldest son of this model Medici followed closely in his footsteps. Equally modest and unassuming and no less charitable, Cosimo also minded his own business carefully; but that business was constantly growing, and with it the motives to ruin it. The rich had not forgotten the tax reform imposed on them by his benevolent father, nor the fund of goodwill he won with his churches and his charities. For four years Cosimo was not molested, but in 1433 the blow fell. The Albizzi, a rival family which had long been conspiring with the former nobles to uproot the upstart Medici, judged the moment ripe to strike. Before a Signory predisposed in their favour and a *gonfaloniere* in their debt, they preferred charges against the opulent family as a danger to the state because of their wealth and ambition. Among other proof, they cited a new mansion which Cosimo was building on a scale and in a style unbefitting a private citizen. The evidence, based on prejudice and suspicion, prospered; Cosimo was arrested and imprisoned. The Albizzi, bent on obtaining the death penalty,

summoned a popular assembly to appoint by acclamation a *balia* –
a commission created in emergencies and entrusted with absolute
power for a limited length of time – and the *balia*, composed of two
hundred citizens, deliberated without reaching a decision. Many
were for death, many for banishment, many more, moved by com-
passion or fear, were silent. For four days the prisoner refused food
until a friendly jailer shared it with him; with his jailer's help he
smuggled a substantial bribe to the *gonfaloniere*, and the sentence was
commuted to banishment for himself and his family for ten years. A
year later, a friendly Signory cancelled the decree and recalled him.
'Seldom,' said Machiavelli, 'has a citizen returning from a great
victory been greeted by such a concourse of people and with such
demonstrations of affection as Cosimo on his return from exile.' The
Albizzi, after failing to seize the government by force before his
return, fled, two hundred of their partisans were banished or fled,
and when Cosimo was reproached for so drastic a purge of prominent citizens, he replied that new nobles could be made with two
lengths of crimson cloth and that states were not ruled by Pater-
nosters. 'Better a city destroyed than lost,' he added.

As a result of this experience, and to prevent its recurrence, Cosimo
sought and secured a controlling influence in the government. The
forms of the republic were respected and adapted to his purpose.
Profiting by the reaction in his favour, he served a brief term as *gonfaloniere*, but soon abandoned public office in favour of a less con-
spicuous but far more permanent and powerful position as banker to
the republic and confidential adviser to the government. His foes
having fled, his friends assumed office, and he kept them there by the
customary methods of the politician. One was purely Florentine –
the *balia* – employed whenever a direct appeal to the people was
needed to support his authority, but discarded when he was so firmly
established that he could afford to restore normal elections and
humour his enemies by the free play of Florentine democracy. The
other was money, universally valid in all times and places. Reviving

the famous tax reform of his father, which had fallen into disuse, and enforcing it in favour of his friends and against his foes, he wielded it as a defensive and offensive weapon more deadly than daggers.

Neither of these methods would have availed him long, however – and they served him for thirty years – had he not identified his interests completely with those of the state and guided and guarded them wisely and well. As banker to the commonwealth, he put the republic in his pocket by liberal loans and assumed many public expenses himself to lend it lustre and prestige. He entertained distinguished visitors at his own expense and went out of his way to attract them to Florence when they were worth it. On one such occasion he travelled to Ferrara where a council of the Pope, the Primate of the Eastern Church, and one of the last Byzantine emperors was sitting, and induced them to transfer their deliberations to Florence, where he lodged them magnificently and converted the city for a season into a brilliant political, religious, cultural, and commercial convention town. The council accomplished nothing, but it left a lasting impression on Florence, where the painter Benozzo Gozzoli commemorated the sumptuous exotic costumes of the Eastern dignitaries on the walls of the Medici chapel.

In foreign affairs Cosimo took the same risks as a statesman. Like his father, he loved peace and avoided war, and with a single exception he made war to secure peace. Reversing the traditional alliance with Venice against their mutual enemy, the aggressive duchy of Milan, he supplied a soldier of fortune, Francesco Sforza, with money and means to overthrow the Visconti dynasty, and won an equally peace-loving friend in their place; and when Venice and Naples turned against him, he paralysed their military operations by calling in his loans.

Again like his father, he was a great builder of churches and a liberal patron of art. Architects of the stature of Brunelleschi and Michelozzo, sculptors of the grace of Donatello and Luca della Robbia, painters of the demure splendour of Fra Angelico, Filippo Lippi, and Benozzo Gozzoli, worked for him building or adorning his monuments – the monastery of San Marco, the church of San Lorenzo, the Medici palace, among others – and he added to his laurels by the encouragement of learning. Learning he encouraged with the curiosity of close acquaintance, for he was uncommonly well educated. He maintained agents abroad searching for rare prizes to fill his library and found the best at home: the Bishop of Bologna, a fellow collector who borrowed from his purse to satisfy his passion for books, repaid his debt by cataloguing his library and later, when he became Pope Nicholas v, by awarding the management of the papal finances to the Medici bank in Rome, whose books showed a fair profit in the Jubilee year of 1450.

But it was in the art of politics that Cosimo shone. Studiously effacing himself and remaining in the background of government, he was recognized, nevertheless, both at home and abroad as the real Head of State – *Capo della Repubblica* – by virtue of financial sovereignty and adroit brainwork without the support of armed force. Living simply and soberly, he reached the ripe old age of seventy-five, but as he aged he was crippled by gout, his grip on the government weakened, and his last days were darkened by fear for the future of his family. Of his two sons, one was a chronic invalid and the other died before he did; and he was heard to murmur as he was borne through the rooms of that mansion which almost cost him his life, 'Too large a house for so small a family.' His fears were well founded, for his grandsons were mere boys; and his party, loyal and obedient while it was curbed by opposition, became unruly and insolent as soon as resistance subsided, and outraged Florence by unbridled oppression, corruption, and excesses which, weary, old, and infirm, he could no longer control and which threatened to wreck his lifework. It was a tribute to his own moderation and political tact that he preserved public respect to the end, and when he was laid to rest with his father in 1464, his countrymen inscribed on the tomb of the man who had given them thirty years of domestic peace and external stability the title PATER PATRIAE.

The second model Medici left a son, Piero, hampered by gout, the indolence of an invalid, a mild disposition, and perfidious advisers. Finding that his father's liberality had left his financial affairs in confusion and disorder, he consulted a trusted friend of his father's, who advised him to call in his loans, counting on a panic to wrest the state from his hands. Piero fell into the trap, many business failures followed, and he was denounced by his debtors as an ungrateful miser and accused of jeopardizing the prosperity of Florence to protect his capital; but he survived this blow as well as two attempts to overthrow him by force of arms.

His five brief years as head of state, marred by civil dissension, saw one event which was to set the reputation of his son and successor. So well had Cosimo gilded the Florentine lily that Louis XI of France conferred on Piero the right to add the French fleur-de-lis to the five red balls of the Medici coat of arms, and Piero took advantage of the favour. He married his nineteen-year-old son Lorenzo into the house of Orsini, one of the great feudal families of Rome, but as this was a departure from custom (Cosimo had made it a rule to marry the Medici at home), the match was unpopular in Florence. Malcontents complained that the ambition of the rising bourgeois was unbounded, that the city was no longer big enough for the citizen, that the Medici were satisfied with nothing less than a foreign and baronial alliance, and that they would soon be assuming the style of princes themselves. The betrothal was celebrated by a tournament, an aristocratic spectacle so foreign and unfamiliar in Florence that Machiavelli felt it necessary to explain it: '. . . a scuffle of men on horseback in which the leading young men of the city contended with the most renowned cavaliers of Italy; and among the Florentine youth the most famous was Lorenzo, who carried off the prize not by favour but by his own valour.' Gorgeously accoutered in ornate armour, bearing the French fleur-de-lis on his shield and the Medici device on his banner, the powerful young athlete unhorsed all his opponents easily, and the pride which his countrymen took in his prowess reconciled them to his marriage. It was celebrated splendidly, and his father, who had once been called a miser, made ample amends with the wedding feast. As Machiavelli added slyly, 'Piero decided to celebrate the nuptials of his son Lorenzo with Clarice of the house of Orsini magnificently, and they were held with the pomp of apparel and all other manner of magnificence befitting such a man.' Long before he earned the title of Magnificent, Lorenzo learned its political value and developed an appetite for it.

Such was the heritage of Lorenzo de' Medici. 'Two days after the death of my father,' he wrote in later life, 'although I, Lorenzo, was very young, being only in my twenty-first year, the principal men of the city and the state came to our house to condole on our loss and encourage me to take on myself the care of the city and the state, as my father and grandfather had done. This proposal being contrary to the instincts of my youthful age and considering that the burden and danger were great, I consented unwillingly, but I did so to protect our friends and our property, for it fares ill in Florence with anyone who possesses great wealth without any control in the government.' I, Lorenzo! How lonely, how isolated the identification! More fortunate than his father, however, he found faithful friends who rallied to him loyally, and it was due to their devotion that he succeeded him peacefully. With the backing of a body of eminent citizens bent on banishing civil dissension from Florence, he began governing under singularly favourable conditions, and the first years were fairly easy – peaceful at home and only briefly disturbed abroad.

For nine years Lorenzo was indeed the most fortunate of his family. His father had been called the most mediocre of the Medici, because of his mild disposition; but no one could cast that slur on his son. Sheltered by his family tree and with no opposition to overcome, Lorenzo encountered only critics. Guicciardini was one of them, and he echoed many others. Lorenzo, he said 'desired glory and excellence above all other men and can be criticized for having had too much ambition even in minor things; he did not want to be equalled or imitated even in verses or games or exercises and turned angrily on anyone who did so'. Unlike his father and grandfather, who were mature men when they became heads of the house, he was in the first flush of youth, and youth claimed its privileges of pleasure and the carefree enjoyment of life. Besides his other accomplishments, he was a poet – another variation from his breed, for though his ancestors took many risks they never ventured to write verses – and he composed fluently for festive occasions. Improving on his father, he entertained Florence continually with masquerades and revels, pageants and processions, engaging the best artists to design the masks and decorate the floats, and taking part in them himself; for these he wrote his *Trionfi*, his *Canzoni a Ballo*, and best of all, his famous carnival songs. Later historians were scandalized by the obscenity of these songs and lamented that Lorenzo catered to the taste of the common people, forgetting that Lorenzo was young, virile, and lusty. The tournament was an aristocratic entertainment; these spectacles preserved his ties with the people. A more serious charge was raised by his elders, who professed to see in these light-hearted frolics a profound political design to beguile the people and divert them from public affairs, as his father had done; but this was to credit him with sagacity beyond his years and needless guile, for these were untroubled times of peace and plenty, and public affairs went well. If ever history could be happy, it was then, and wisely he made the most of life while he could sing:

> How passing fair is youth,
> Forever fleeting away;
> Who happy would be, let him be;
> Of tomorrow who can say?

It was as if an uneasy premonition of doom prompted the haunting refrain; for, in fact, the triumph of time was approaching.

In every generation plots had been laid to ruin his family; they were part of his heritage; and his turn came, long belated, in 1478, with the most formidable threat of all – the Pazzi conspiracy. The Pazzi were an old and numerous family with aristocratic pretensions superior to those of the Medici, and they had old scores to settle with Lorenzo.

Wealthy and proud, the Pazzi had been denied public office and the honours to which they were entitled, and they bore discrimination and abuse bitterly. The most sensitive of the family, Francesco, unable to suffer any longer, fled to Rome, where he fell in with a nephew of one of the most grasping and turbulent of the popes, and between them they hatched a plot for their mutual benefit. As ambitious as he was low-born, Pope Sixtus IV was burdened with six covetous nephews, three of whom he placed profitably in the Church and a fourth in Imola, one of the poorest and smallest of the papal fiefs. When Francesco proposed to create a vacancy in Florence, Sixtus fell in with the scheme and consented to second the Pazzi in ousting the Medici. Thus encouraged, Francesco returned to Florence to enlist his family. Jacopo de' Pazzi, the head of the house, hesitated until he was convinced that the scheme had the blessing and the backing of the Pope.

The scheme was senseless on the face of it. A foreign potentate aiming to add Florence to the papal domain and impose a papal curb on a fiercely freedom-loving people, and relying on a Florentine family ambitious to fill the vacancy themselves – the plot was a patchwork of cross-purposes perfectly calculated to fail. Yet it nearly succeeded.

The Pope opened hostilities by cancelling the concession of the Medici bank in Rome and transferring it to the Pazzi; then he lent a helping hand to the plot by appointing as Archbishop of Pisa a member of another family hostile to the Medici, the Salviati. Notwithstanding these unfriendly acts, Lorenzo seems to have suspected nothing, although he refused Salviati admission to his see. In April 1478 the conspirators assembled in Florence and were hospitably entertained in Lorenzo's villa at Fiesole, where they planned to kill him during a banquet. However, his brother Giuliano was absent, and since the murder of both was essential to success, they postponed the blow until the following morning, during the celebration of High Mass in the Duomo, where both were bound to appear for the celebration of Easter Sunday. The change created an unforeseen difficulty; the hired assassin suffered an attack of conscientious scruples and shrank from committing sacrilege as well as murder in the cathedral; Francesco de' Pazzi, a priest, and an accomplice assumed his duties, but still another hitch developed. Giuliano was missing when the service began, and they were forced to fetch him to the slaughter, coaxing him out of bed, where he was nursing a bad knee. They braced him between them, embracing him fondly and feeling his body to make sure that he was unarmed, and brought the laggard limping to the altar; then, having finally united the victims, they struck. The church was crowded; the signal for attack was the solemn moment when the Cardinal who was officiating (another papal curb but not privy to the plot) raised the Host and hundreds of heads bowed devoutly. Giuliano bent obediently, the priest behind his back struck the first blow, and Francesco finished him off with eighteen more – so furiously that he hacked himself in the leg and in the confusion was mistaken for one of the victims. Lorenzo defended himself, escaped with a gash in the neck, and ran into the sacristy, where his friends bolted the doors and waited for help. In the meanwhile Archbishop Salviati, entrusted with the most difficult part of the undertaking, entered the palace to seize the government. His confederates waited below in the chancery, where they locked themselves in by mistake, while he mounted to the upper floor to parley with the Signory, but his agitation betrayed him and aroused their suspicion, and before he could summon assistance the *gonfaloniere* hanged him, stammering, from the window. The city was now in an uproar. Francesco de' Pazzi, weak from loss of blood, took to his bed and begged his uncle to rally the people to their cause. Sallying forth with a hundred armed men, Jacopo de' Pazzi roamed the streets raising the cry of *Liberty*! without arousing a response, and running into a mob acclaiming the Balls, abandoned the attempt and fled. Lorenzo, escorted by his friends, returned home.

The mob avenged him loyally. Francesco de' Pazzi, dragged from his bed, was hanged beside the body of the Archbishop, dangling limply with a cluster of comrades overhead. A furious man-hunt followed: everyone even remotely connected with the conspiracy or suspected of sympathizing with it was brought to justice or mobbed; seventy perished in the first four days and two hundred more before the tumult subsided. Jacopo de' Pazzi, caught and killed, was not allowed to rest in his grave: a horde of scavenging boys unearthed his body, dragged it through the streets, and flung it naked into the Arno. Of his ten sons and nephews, two were beheaded; one was saved by Lorenzo, who was his brother-in-law; the survivors were sentenced to imprisonment or exile, and even the name Pazzi was wiped out by proscription.

Infuriated by the failure of the plot, the Pope demanded that Lorenzo surrender and that the Florentine government answer before an ecclesiastical court for the crime of sacrilege committed on the person of the Archbishop. Lorenzo protested that his only crime was that he had not allowed himself to be murdered; the Signory seconded him, circulated the confession of one of the conspirators exposing the complicity of the Pope, and appealed to the sovereigns of Europe for support. The sovereigns of Europe sided with the Medici; the Pope excommunicated the Florentine state; the Florentine clergy outlawed him in turn; the Pope declared war. Brandishing both his spiritual and temporal arms, he forbade the faithful to trade with the rebellious republic, broke their previous alliances, prohibited any state from forming new ones or any soldier from taking service with them, and summoned to his assistance the Sienese republic and his feudal ally the King of Naples; and their troops invaded Tuscany. The fortunes of war ran against the Florentines, and Lorenzo, unwilling to tax the loyalty of his people, volunteered to surrender himself, but the issue had long since outgrown a personal sacrifice and the Signory refused to abandon him. He insisted, however, slipped off to Pisa, and sailed for Naples to treat with King Ferrante. Ferrante was a notoriously treacherous monarch, but, impressed by Lorenzo's daring, he detained him less as a prisoner than as a guest, listened to his arguments, and consented to abandon the Pope. The Pope fumed, but an incursion of the Turks in Calabria compelled him, like Ferrante, to make peace.

The Pazzi conspiracy, formidable in its folly, failed; but it created a crisis and marked a turning-point in Lorenzo's political career. To prevent its recurrence, he surrounded himself with an armed guard and adopted those precautions which his enemies denounced as a tyranny. He tightened his grip on the government, subordinated the Signory and the councils to a self-perpetuating privy council responsible to himself alone, and converted the controlling influence created by Cosimo into absolute personal rule. Before the Pazzi conspiracy, he was the most fortunate of the Medici; after it, the most masterful; and *I, Lorenzo* now assumed its full meaning for Florence. But the crisis had a further effect: it stimulated his powers as a statesman, and he devoted them diligently to preserving the balance of power and keeping the peace in Italy.

No sooner was the crisis over than his critics found fault with his conduct. The expedition to Naples was blamed as a rash, foolhardy, and unnecessary adventure. It was argued that he could have attained the same success sitting safely at home, instead of risking his life in the hands of a faithless enemy and returning to Florence as a hero. Also, instead of antagonizing the Pope and playing the injured party, if he had concealed his grievance and handled him gently he might

Medal, by Bertoldo di Giovanni,
to commemorate the Pazzi conspiracy
against the Medici
National Gallery of Art, Washington

have averted a war that caused the greatest damage to the city, especially in trade and taxes. Also his punishment of the Pazzi was excessively cruel. By some he was considered unnaturally vindictive and heartless for imprisoning the innocent young men of the family and preventing the Pazzi girls from marrying and breeding more of their kind; although Guicciardini admitted that 'the event was so bitter that it is no wonder that he was extraordinarily angered by it. And it was seen later that, softened by time, he gave permission for the maidens to marry and was willing to release the Pazzi from prison and let them go and live outside of Florentine territory. And also it was seen that he did not employ cruelty in other matters and was not a bloodthirsty person.' But while suspicion lingered, and it lingered long, he intervened vigilantly in domestic affairs, preventing powerful families from intermarrying, arranging matches to suit himself, and permitting no important marriage in Florence without his intervention and consent.

No sooner was peace restored than he returned to his pleasures and won his final and most undeniable triumphs in their pursuit – the patronage of art and letters and the pursuit of women. In both he was resolved to excel. The lover of art and letters more than maintained the fame of his family – he increased it by his boundless liberality. Under his enlightened lead Florence became the mother of arts and the cultural capital of Italy, imitated but unsurpassed by rival states. He set the pace, and other princes were compelled to compete; but he was the highest bidder for the services of scholars and artists and carried off all the prizes for the glory of Florence and the greater glory of the Medici. In Pisa he founded a superfluous branch of the University of Florence for the sheer pleasure of surpassing rival schools, paying the highest salaries and sparing neither trouble nor expense to secure the most famous teachers in Italy. In Florence the Platonic Academy formed part of his household and boasted the best philosophers he could find. Sharing the craze for ancient learning which was widening the mental horizon of his age, he introduced it even into his home and made philosophy a household word, collecting intellectuals at his table to discuss it and teach Florence that no one could live without it. He could not. 'When my mind is disturbed by the tumult of public affairs and my ears are stunned by the clamour of turbulent citizens,' he confessed to a friend, 'how could I bear such dissensions unless I found relief in learning?' Study was a refuge from politics and an escape from statecraft. Educated as a boy by humanists, he was one of them and collected them to preserve the most precious of his treasures, his peace of mind. His Poggio, his Poliziano, his Pico della Mirandola, his Marsilio Ficino, were bosom friends who formed his intellectual family. On books alone he spent more than half the annual income of the state, and for art his bounty was unbounded. Ambitious to be the most universal as well as the most glorious of the Medici, he befriended all the arts, and they flourished abundantly at his bidding. 'For vernacular poetry, music, architecture, painting, sculpture, and all the fine and mechanical arts he showed the same favour, so that the city overflowed with all these graces,' Guicciardini acknowledged. Artists flocked to Florence from far and near, attracted by the magnetic name of Lorenzo de' Medici. Not merely for pecuniary reward, either, for he was a connoisseur who appreciated their gifts, understood their problems, and defended them against fools. (When someone found fault with the music of Squarcialupi, he scolded the critic as sensitively as if he were the composer himself.) 'If only you knew how difficult it is to attain perfection in any art!' he admonished.

When it came to his other ruling passion, Guicciardini found it difficult to forgive his fidelity to it: 'He was licentious and very amorous and constant in his loves, which usually lasted several years. In the opinion of many, this so weakened his body that it caused him to die comparatively young. His last love, which endured many years, was for Bartolomea de' Nasi, wife of Donato Benci, who was by no means beautiful but with a style and grace of her own. . . . What folly that a man of such great reputation and prudence, forty years old, should be so infatuated with a woman who was not beautiful and already well along in years, that he was led to do what would be disgraceful in any boy!' Physically, also, he found fault with him: 'Lorenzo was of medium height, his countenance coarse and dark in colour, yet with an air of dignity; his voice and pronunciation harsh and unpleasing, because he spoke through his nose.' But the fact remains that he was attractive to women; neither his nasal voice nor his coarse features nor his swarthy complexion nor the natural blemishes with which he was born were displeasing to them.

As he matured he mellowed and became as tolerant of his critics as they expected him to be. Though Guicciardini was one of them, he was the most indulgent and judicious of his judges, and his final verdict was fair. 'Though the city was not free under him, it would have been impossible to find a better or more pleasing tyrant. From his natural goodness and inclination came infinite advantages, but through the necessity of tyranny some evils although they were restrained and limited as much as necessity permitted . . .'

Twelve uneventful years followed the Pazzi conspiracy, cloudless and carefree until Lorenzo succumbed to gout and to another, graver affliction. He neglected his financial affairs, which fell into confusion and disorder, and the fall was fatal. Machiavelli blamed his misfortunes on mismanagement by his banking agents abroad, stating that

Lorenzo, to avoid further reverses, abandoned his mercantile enterprises and turned instead to 'possessions, as a more stable and firm form of wealth'. Among his possessions was the state, and his forays into the public coffers played havoc with the public finances. Insolvency became so acute that in 1490 a commission was created to reform the fiscal administration of Florence; the currency, hitherto the most stable in Europe, was depreciated to a fifth of its face value; and the government was driven to desperate measures to avoid bankruptcy. Lorenzo was just enough of a financier to save his private fortune by withdrawing it from commerce and investing in real estate, but at the cost of his good name. Financial acumen was the foundation of the Medici political fortunes, and he who lacked it was exposed to the ruin which the enemies of his house had tried in vain to bring about for three generations.

Under these gathering clouds, his last days were also darkened by a new adversary. An alien agitator raised his voice in Florence to echo the complaints of his enemies and disturb his peace of mind; the sermons of Savonarola kindled contention anew and in an unexpected quarter. From the pulpit of San Marco – a Medici foundation – a foreign reformer called Lorenzo to account for his political sins. The festivities with which Lorenzo entertained Florence were denounced as political snares: 'The tyrant is wont to busy his people with spectacles and festivities, that they may think of their pastimes and not of his designs, and becoming unaccustomed to the conduct of the commonwealth, leave the reins of government in his hands.' The charge, old and familiar though it was, could no longer be ignored in the gloom of changing times, and it was followed by graver ones. Summoned to preach before the Signory, Savonarola said: 'Tyrants are incorrigible because they are proud, because they love flattery, because they will not restore their ill-gotten gains. They allow bad officials to have their way; they yield to adulation; they neither heed the poor nor condemn the rich; they expect peasants and paupers to work for them gratis or they tolerate officials who do

so; they farm out the taxes to aggravate the people more and more ...
The people are oppressed by taxes, and when they come to pay unbearable sums, the rich cry: Give me the rest ... When widows come
weeping, they are told: Go to sleep. When the poor complain, they
are told: Pay, pay.' The preacher was popular, his following grew,
and in the Lent of 1491 he moved into the Duomo, where, before a
congregation packed to the doors, he preached inflammatory sermons which terrified his hearers, predicting a coming calamity,
ordained by divine wrath, which would sweep away the princes of
Italy, including the Medici and all their iniquities. Lorenzo was
tolerant, but he was troubled: what the Pazzi failed to accomplish,
the prophet promised to perform. He made advances to mollify him,
but he was rebuffed. He sent a delegation to reason with him. They
hinted at banishment. 'Tell Lorenzo to do penance for his sins,'
Savonarola replied, 'for God will punish him and his. I do not fear
your banishments. Though I am a stranger here and he a citizen, and
the foremost in the city, I shall remain and he will go. I shall remain,'
he repeated proudly, 'and he will go.' And he foretold the death of
Lorenzo within a year.

A year later Lorenzo lay dying in his villa at Careggi. He was in
great pain, suffering from an abdominal disorder aggravated by his
physicians, who fed him powdered pearls, and he sent for Savonarola
to relieve his soul. Savonarola came. According to a popular but
probably apocryphal account of the scene, the priest's price of salvation included the restoration of all ill-gotten gains and the restitution
of liberty to Florence; to the first Lorenzo agreed, but he gave up the
ghost and expired unabsolved before he could consent to the second.

Machiavelli was kinder. He acquitted Lorenzo of his political
sins for the sake of the statesman whom Florence had lost, and
acquitted him in a bountiful obituary. 'Of Fortune and of God he
was supremely loved, wherefore all his enterprises ended well and
those of his enemies ill ... All the citizens mourned his death and all
the princes of Italy ... and that they had good reason to grieve the

153

result soon showed; for Italy being deprived of his counsels, none of those who remained found any means of curbing or satisfying the ambition of Lodovico Sforza, the governor of the Duke of Milan ... as soon as Lorenzo died, all those bad seeds began to sprout which not long after, he who could quell them being no longer alive, ruined and are still ruining Italy.'

And so it proved. Lorenzo was the pivot of Italian politics, and his eldest son, Piero, was born to be unfortunate – for himself, for his family, and for Florence. Two years after the death of Lorenzo, a revolt broke out, the Medici were driven into exile, and their palace sacked by a mob of vandals. Of Lorenzo nothing was left but the memory. The financier was a failure, the politician and the statesman were ephemeral, and of all the titles to fame which he left on deposit for posterity, only the patron of culture was remembered as Lorenzo the Magnificent.

MILAN: CITY OF STRIFE

MILAN seemed singularly favoured by nature; to the south, over an easy pass in the Apennines, lay the great seaport of Genoa, a city of such majesty that the Venetians feared its power and envied its wealth; to the west and north swept the great arc of the Alps, as natural a frontier as a statesman could wish for; the few mountain passes that led to France or southern Germany gave Milan control of the routes from the great Genoese emporium to the markets of the North. Seen spread across an atlas of physical geography, the great, fertile valley of the Po seems one of the more natural places in Europe for the development of a strong unified state. Between the fall of the Roman Empire and the unification of Italy in the nineteenth century this was achieved only once – by Napoleon. The history of the Lombard plain is a history of invasion and war. For more than a thousand years some of Europe's bloodiest battles were fought on it. If Florence belonged to Minerva, Milan belonged to Mars.

The trouble lay partly in the fertility of the alluvial plain: the great walls of the Alps and the Apennines gave it some of the forcing quality of a hothouse. Crops grew with ease; heavy crops meant a large and prosperous population; and the whole of Lombardy was studded with thriving cities – Turin, Pavia, Lodi, Brecia, Bergamo, Vicenza, Verona, Padua, Ferrara, Bologna, Mantua, Parma, Piacenza, and Alessandria, among others. Only in times of desperation were these cities capable of acting in unity, as when the Emperor Frederick Barbarossa attempted to extend his power over them; otherwise they were content to intrigue and plot and fight among themselves. From time to time a city or a family arose like a bubble in this boiling cauldron, and, like a bubble, burst. Furthermore, the Holy Roman Emperor often found it advantageous to strengthen his natural aristocratic allies at the expense of the communes, for the Emperor preserved the legal right of overlordship, even if he failed often enough to exercise it in fact. What he never failed to do, once he possessed the strength, was to angle for greater power in these troubled but fish-laden waters. In this he was not alone. The princes of Savoy found morsels of the Lombard plain far sweeter than the granite wastes of the Alps which their country bestrode. Beyond Savoy were the French, whose king was willing to try to hold Savoy in check – at a price – or urge him forward if they were unpaid. And naturally the two great parties, the Guelphs and the Ghibellines, which polarized so many ancient feuds, thought they could manipulate the great European powers to their advantage.

Milan and its satellite cities had failed to do what Florence and the Tuscan towns had succeeded in doing – they had never subjected the feudal nobility to the authority of the merchant class. In this bullring of Europe, it is not surprising that men harassed by invasion, ruined by petty strife, and hamstrung by vendettas should dream of a 'natural' state in which princes – powerful, all-wise, and intensely patriotic – should succeed generation after generation, wielding an iron authority that brought peace and fame. At times the imagination of poet and panegyrist soared in a wilder flight and saw the princes of Milan, whether Visconti or Sforza, adding to the duchy of Lombardy the kingship of all Italy. There were three dukes of Milan – Gian Galeazzo Visconti, Francesco Sforza, and Lodovico Il Moro – who, for the brief periods of their rule, removed, at least, all absurdity from this vision, although they were far too realistic ever to indulge themselves in such fantasies. Nevertheless, they did between them what no other rulers did: they created a state equal in power and wealth to Florence and to Venice.

Milan, which became the epitome of the Renaissance state, is best seen reflected in the lives of its three greatest dukes.

The Visconti's emblem was a viper, and they had needed all the serpent's cunning not only to survive the vicissitudes of a fickle and bloody fortune but also to grow in riches and in authority. By the time Gian Galeazzo Visconti was born in 1351, his family had played a leading part in Lombardic affairs for over two hundred years. They had resolutely defended the interests of the merchants, acquired increasing judicial authority from the Holy Roman Emperor to provide a legal basis for their power, and arranged their marriages with dynastic prudence. Nevertheless, his father had been forced to fight for his inheritance, for the death of a Visconti ruler, followed as it was by the division of his lands among his heirs, always provided an opening to rebels and exiles in the discontented cities on the fringes of their lands. Galeazzo II shared the Visconti territories with his brother Bernabò, who ruled in Milan, while he remained at Pavia. Bernabò struggled to regain Bologna, Galeazzo to push westward to the Alps; in so doing they aroused a hornets' nest, and in 1373 they were nearly overwhelmed. It was a typical story of treachery, turbulence, and violence that fed the darker side of Galeazzo's nature – his suspicion, his avarice, his hate. His son Gian Galeazzo, born of his diplomatic marriage with Blanche of Savoy, was turned as quickly as possible to dynastic ends. At the age of nine he was married off to Isabelle of Valois, a princess of France, and by the time he was fourteen she had produced him a son. Both in battle and in diplomacy he proved equally precocious; but when he inherited his father's lands in 1378, his position was far from enviable. His uncle Bernabò, with a reputation for brutality and violence even in his own age, still ruled in Milan, and he had five sons, all ambitious, all land-hungry.

Gian Galeazzo was already known for his resource and cunning, but the latter got the better of his discretion. He suddenly made a wild bid for greatness. He secretly negotiated his own betrothal (his first wife had died at twenty-three) to the heiress of Sicily – a bargain that stood if he consummated the marriage within twelve months. The news outraged the particularist sentiments of the Italian princes, and they made certain that the bride never got within five hundred miles of her groom. And while Gian Galeazzo was wrestling with his strange problem of logistics, his uncle Bernabò extorted concession after concession from him, to make certain that the Visconti of Pavia should never be linked with the power of Sicily to the discomfiture of the Visconti of Milan. When the year had passed, Gian Galeazzo found himself without a wife and tied dynastically far tighter than he had ever been to his uncle, for the latter insisted that, having failed with the heiress of Sicily, Gian Galeazzo's bride should be his daughter Caterina, and no obstruction was placed before the immediate consummation of this marriage.

Gian Galeazzo complied, and brooded. He cultivated his garden. He devoted his considerable intelligence and remarkable concentration to the problems of government. He reduced taxation, reformed administration, weeded out corruption, and what leisure he had from the cares of government he spent on the adornment of his palace, the conversation of scholars, and consultation with astrologers. Although he enjoyed a reputation for piety, he placed his trust in the efficacy of the zodiac rather than of prayer, and when the stars were truly propitious, he set out on a pilgrimage to the Madonna del Monte at Varese. His timidity was known, and his entourage therefore surprised no one by its size; he hesitated (it was assumed through fear) to enter Milan, so his uncle and his cousin rode out to meet him. After an affectionate greeting they were taken prisoner, and Gian Galeazzo entered Milan to cries of 'Long live the Count, and down with the taxes!' Gian Galeazzo's wife seems to have taken the destruction of her father and brothers with the phlegm usual in a Renaissance princess. The boldness of his enterprise was widely admired, and even Geoffrey Chaucer in far-off London turned a few verses on the event in his *Canterbury Tales*.

This success naturally gave Gian Galeazzo confidence, and since he was highly intelligent, he learned from it. More important than the timing of the plot, in the proper conjunction of the stars, was the fact that the Milanese did not close their gates but welcomed him as a liberator – a sentiment which he quickly turned to an article of faith by distributing some of Bernabò's treasure to the great financial relief of those whom he needed as allies. For the next seventeen years he exploited the paternalism of his government so that he might realize his almost insatiable dynastic ambitions. In order to impose his iron despotism, he posed as the liberator of cities and men. His success was the result of unwearying application, aided by good fortune and blended with a nice sense of contingencies. 'He was wont,' wrote his chronicler, Giovio, 'to give himself up to meditation during solitary walks, to hold discussions with those who were most experienced in every branch of affairs, to quote instances from the annals of the past. He found relaxation for his mind in the conversation of scholars and in constant reading.' Not for him, it would seem, 'the delights of hunting or hawking, nor games of dice, nor the allurements of women, nor the tales of buffoons and jesters'. He thought, he planned, he acted. In two swift campaigns, having made certain that treachery was rife in the cities he wished to conquer, he had absorbed all of eastern Lombardy save Mantua and Ferrara.

The Florentines, of course, were deeply disturbed to see one tyrant control all the Alpine passes on which so much of their trade depended, and they used their powers of persuasion, of which the florin proved the most efficacious, to raise a league against Gian Galeazzo. This merely succeeded in enlarging Gian Galeazzo's ambitions, for he was quick to realize that his gains could never be consolidated so long as Florence remained unsubjected. To do this he proceeded with skill and caution; each city-state had its party that hated Florence or the powers that ruled it. He fought wars when he had to, but he adroitly avoided a head-on collision with the combined powers of Florence and Venice. By 1402 he had acquired control of

Pisa, Siena, Perugia, and Bologna, and it was within his power to strangle Florence politically and economically. The foundation of a great northern Italian kingdom seemed within his grasp, when he caught a fever and died.

By that time Gian Galeazzo had done more than enlarge the boundaries of his dukedom, for he had created a state as well as a despotism. He centralized government, reformed administration, and removed inequalities and special rights and privileges. Where possible he weakened the feudal nobility and encouraged the merchant class. He tried to fulfil the ideal which his humanists at Pavia had delineated – that of a 'natural prince' whose state was serenely based on justice and equality. And by these means he had created the duchy of Milan, a coherent state that was to last until Napoleon swept it away. In many ways he is the prototype of the Renaissance prince – unscrupulous in diplomacy, yet deeply concerned for the welfare of the state; passionately ambitious for his dynasty, yet aware of the needs of his country; scholarly, remote, and dedicated to the pursuit of power.

Gian Galeazzo's death broke up his empire. His captains of war thought no opportunity better for taking their pickings; the Tuscan and Umbrian cities, mindful now of the power of Florence, threw off their allegiance. The Venetians' indifference to Gian Galeazzo's success turned to alarm; his demise brought about a fundamental change in their policy. They decided to be a Lombard power – to secure territorial control of the Alpine passes which they needed for their trade, and of sufficient territory to give them ground for manoeuvre against a resurgent Milan. Once again the great feudal families whose power Gian Galeazzo had attempted to reduce flourished their standards. The Colleoni, Anguisola, Cavalcabò, and Correggio demanded their pounds of flesh, and the plain of Lombardy once more reeked of blood and slaughter, pillage and rape. In the midst of this desolation the Milanese core of the Visconti state held firm. It is a measure of Gian Galeazzo's success that it did so, for in some ways his heir was a greater disaster than the conflagrations of war that consumed Lombardy. Although it is certainly untrue that he fed his hounds on human flesh, such were his tyrannies that the Milanese had no difficulty in believing the story. His assassination in church in 1412 caused no surprise. Perhaps as a tribute to his brother's memory, his successor, Filippo Maria, had the murderers put to death by the most refined tortures. By nature Filippo Maria was not excessively cruel, merely neurotic. He was obese to the point of ridicule, and ugly to the point of embarrassment. His portrait was never painted, his marriage never consummated, and his appearance in public rare. Nevertheless, he ruled with skill if without *panache*. He maintained the machinery of the state and kept his head above the turbulent waters of Italian politics. Precluded by nature from the pursuit of martial glory, he was content to employ one of the best condottieri for this duty – Francesco Sforza – at least from time to time, for Filippo could never trust anyone for long.

Sforza, the son of one of the first great Italian condottieri – Muzio Sforza – came, as most condottieri did, from the Romagna, which had little to sell but the strength of its men. Sforza proved himself a great captain. His direct manner, tough physique, and aggressive nature made him an excellent general; his attention to detail, ferocious discipline, and deep personal loyalty gave him a band of soldiers of passionate devotion and exemplary technique. His personal magnetism was such that he won the enduring friendship of the two most outstanding men of his day – the highly sophisticated and cultivated banker Cosimo de' Medici, and the equally highly cultivated condottiere Federigo da Montefeltro. In the hard, tough school of war he won himself a vast reputation and a small territory, too small either for his purse or his ambition. And the situation in Milan was as clear to him as to his friends. Cosimo de' Medici did not relish the steady advance of Venetian power across the Lombard plain (the Alpine passes were vital to Florentine trade, and the Venetians were traders first and republicans second). A powerful, friendly Milan had become a necessity to Florence, so Cosimo provided Francesco with good advice and handsome loans. Federigo, as generous a condottiere as ever lived, admired Francesco's prowess as only a professional could, but he preferred, naturally enough, that Francesco should win his kingdom in Lombardy and not on *his* doorstep in the Romagna, where the Sforza had their patrimony.

Filippo Maria did not need to be instructed in the drift of their thoughts, for he was as subtle as his father if less ambitious. It proved toil enough for him to weld together the Visconti lands, bring the recalcitrant nobles and cities to a proper subjection, and withstand the encroachments of Venice. For these projects he needed Francesco, and to stay alive for his natural span in his castle of Milan, it was necessary to keep Sforza both expectant and dependent. So Francesco rattled his sword, and Filippo Maria dangled his daughter – not a legitimate daughter, of course, but a mistress had been more skilful than a wife, and Bianca was the result. The long wrangle ended in a betrothal; a longer engagement ended in a wedding; the wedding ended in a son and heir. Before, however, his succession had been determined, Filippo died, when Francesco was away from Visconti territory.

The Milanese erupted with republican sentiment, abolished the dukedom, and created chaos. Neither Venice nor Florence was amused by the advent of a sister republic and gave no help as its troubles multiplied. Sforza moved cautiously until the republic crumbled, and when he finally entered Milan, the citizens went wild with delight, rushed him and his horse into the Duomo, and acclaimed him duke. For many years that was the sole right the Sforza had to their dukedom – that and the sharp edge of their swords – for the emperors refused to acknowledge them. The powers of Italy, however, lacked the prejudice of the Germans, and while Francesco consolidated his power with military precision, the Medici got a bank in Milan, and alliances were formed with France, Savoy, Naples, and Florence. The Sforza went bull-headed for peace and stability. Wars there could not fail to be, but Sforza wanted them local, petty, and circumscribed.

The dukes of Milan became an accepted fact in the major state-system of Italy as Francesco Sforza completed the work Gian Galeazzo Visconti had begun. No condottiere had won such a prize as Francesco; and the tough captain who had once stood amazed by the luxury of Pavia and the splendour of its library now enjoyed the prosperity his sword had brought him. War or no war, the Milanese throve. Francesco settled his court at Milan, the heart of his dukedom, ruling his subjects until his death in 1466 as he had once led his troops – wisely, directly, decisively – always keeping within the limits of the possible. About him there was something of the inexorable single-mindedness of the long-distance runner. Unhappily, his children proved more devious, more extravagant, more brutal even than their Visconti ancestors. The Sforza brood would have done honour to the pages of the most bloodthirsty of Elizabethan dramatists. And the story of Milan and its Renaissance reaches a climax in the rule of Lodovico Sforza.

Francesco was a great warrior – in love as well as in war – and his brood of Sforza, legitimate and illegitimate (the difference in Renaissance Italy was scarcely remarked – Francesco himself was a bastard), numbered twenty. Lodovico was number six (legitimate), so his prospects of the throne of Milan were remote enough. He possessed, however, one card, spurious perhaps, but not without value: he was the first legitimate child to be born *after* Francesco had been acclaimed Duke of Milan. Its use, however, lay in the future, for his brother Galeazzo Maria Sforza had every intention of enjoying to the full the power and the riches which his father had bequeathed him. Indeed, his court left no doubt that the Sforza had arrived, that the wealth of Milan was vast, that neither the Doge in Venice, the Pope in Rome, the Medici in Florence, nor the Aragonese kings in Naples could outvie them in magnificence. The great Castello Sforzesco, built like the

Tower of London on the verge of the city – a convenience which fulfilled both the needs of strategy and sport – witnessed some of the
most remarkable spectacles of the fifteenth century. Galeazzo loved
shows. He made St George's Day the great military spectacle of the
year; tournaments, pageants, processions gave his mania full rein,
and he thought nothing of ordering a thousand or more special
liveries in costly velvet to put on his servants' backs. A greater pleasure still was to take a visiting prince or ambassador to his jewel
house, Galeazzo's special pride and joy, where rubies, emeralds, sapphires, and diamonds lay in heaps – a treasure which King Christian
of Denmark somewhat churlishly called 'unbefitting a true and
generous prince'. Galeazzo, however, possessed a taste for more
refined delights: his interest in music led him to comb Flanders, let
alone Italy, for the singers who were almost the dominating passion
of his life. Almost, but not quite: undoubtedly Galeazzo's greatest
pleasures were drawn from the enjoyment of his courtiers' wives and
the exercise of his personal power; and neither endeared him to his
subjects. The latter, in fact, was his undoing. Rumours of his cruelty
were inflated to the heights of a Gothic fairy tale, and rendered just
as macabre by the Duke's pious, almost morbid, insistence on the
strictest observance of religious ritual. So perhaps it was not entirely
unfitting that his assassins should have dispatched him in church.
They were a typical Renaissance bunch – a penniless noble adventurer, a cousin who resented the rape of his sister, an old, very dis-
reputable master of rhetoric who had preached too ardently, and
practised too publicly, the Greek way of life, and a youthful republican intoxicated by the concept of tyrannicide, who, as he was slowly
and carefully torn to pieces, murmured, '*Mors acerba fama perpetua est.*'

Galeazzo's wife was deeply troubled that her husband, whom she
knew so well, should have been dispatched unconfessed. She made a
list of his sins and was appalled. He was, she wrote, 'Versed in warfare, both lawful and unlawful; in pillage, robbery, and devastation
of the country; in extortion of subjects; in negligence of justice; in

injustice knowingly committed; in the imposition of new taxes which even included the clergy; in carnal vices; in notorious and scandalous simony and innumerable other crimes.' Obviously the torments of Galeazzo in Purgatory would be long and grievous, so the Duchess implored the aid of the Pope. The Pope, moved by the distress of the widow, granted absolution in return for a considerable subsidy for the papal army.

Galeazzo left a child and five brothers; so the years after his death proved dramatic enough for Milan and Italy. Conspiracies in Genoa and Parma linked themselves with greater conspiracies, engineered by the Pope and the King of Naples, in Florence. Lodovico tried his utmost to kidnap the child Duke, but he failed until the ructions in Florence gave him the backing of the Holy Father and King Ferrante. With luck and good judgment, aided by the silliness of the Duke's mother and the misguided cunning of her lover, Lodovico became regent of Milan. He imprisoned the Duchess, ousted her favourite, and chopped off the head of Cecco Simonetta, the brilliant ducal secretary who throughout his long life had devotedly served the Sforza, for the crime of attempting to secure an undivided inheritance for the legitimate heir. Fortunately for Lodovico, his most active and ambitious brothers had died during the struggle for power, and his nephew proved so weak in intellect and character that it was unnecessary to dispatch him. As soon as this internecine struggle was over, Milan settled down to such spectacular festivities that they pushed the memories of Galeazzo's junketings to the commonplace. The child Duke was betrothed to Isabella of Aragon, and Lodovico himself took Beatrice d'Este, the daughter of the Duke of Ferrara and granddaughter of the King of Naples, for his bride. Although their marriages were long delayed, the festivities celebrating their nuptials provided the hired chroniclers of the court of Milan, a subject worthy of their hyperbole. Men and women were dressed, or rather undressed, as pagan gods and goddeses; fabulous animals were wondrously contrived; knights jousted in Moorish costumes; wild men, dressed by Leonardo da Vinci, scared the ladies; dwarfs, giants, hunchbacks provided robust fun; sycophantic poets produced verse by the ream to give a sense of immortal occasion; the best musicians of Italy played and sang through the day and night; masques with elaborate scenery and ingenious fireworks linked the intervals between gargantuan banquets. The prodigious munificence of Lodovico naturally stirred the interest of painters, sculptors, engineers, historians, philosophers, and poets. Leonardo, frustrated and restless in Florence, was one of the first to seek his patronage.

Lodovico's extravagance was not mere self-indulgence. He wished to demonstrate not only the wealth and power of the Milanese state but also his own supreme control. He was a highly intelligent man with a deep sense of cunning, who realized acutely the insecurity of his realm as well as of his dynasty. Prosperity, he thought, would cure the former, diplomacy the latter. He cultivated the rich Lombard plain assiduously. He promoted canals. He encouraged new crops, particularly rice. He fostered trade and manufacture. And his interest in Leonardo da Vinci owed as much to the artist's inventive genius in mechanics and fortifications as to his ability as a sculptor and painter. By such means he created the sinews of power, but its exploitation depended on his wit.

Milan's dangers were these: first Venice, secondly France, thirdly the Holy Roman Emperor, and fourthly the Swiss, who could be manipulated by the others. Milan had been intermittently at war with Venice since the Venetians decided to become a mainland power at the beginning of the fifteenth century. The problems represented by the Emperor and France were interrelated. For Lodovico's Visconti ancestors, the Emperor had been a safety factor, since they were his legal representatives in Lombardy. The Sforza were not, however, and the legal basis of their power had to rest on popular acclamation. To complicate the matter further, the Visconti had intermarried with the junior branches of the French royal family, and this had given the French certain dynastic claims on Milan. Furthermore, the

French had always coveted Genoa, which was a linchpin of the Milanese economy; and they supported the Anjou pretensions to the throne of Naples. To create some stability in this world fraught with danger, Lodovico, Lorenzo de' Medici, and Ferrante, the King of Naples, had enacted the Triple Alliance. Together they had been able to present the threat of sufficient force to make external or internal powers hesitate to attack them. War had not been abolished, but certainly the Triple Alliance diminished it, and Lodovico was the beneficiary. Milan had other reasons than the Triple Alliance for friendship with Naples. Ties between the two cities had been strengthened by the marriage of the young Duke and Ferrante's granddaughter, Isabella of Aragon. Or so it would seem. Reasons of state and reasons of strategy were at variance, however, with Lodovico's personal ambition. He wished to be Duke of Milan, *de jure* as well as *de facto*. That meant setting aside, or killing, the young Duke, whose wife already bitterly resented the anomaly of her position and the slights, real and imagined, from Lodovico's wife – the intelligent, formidable, and far from discreet Beatrice d'Este. Behind the wronged wife, Naples could be arrayed; so might France, for the Duke of Orléans had better dynastic claims than Lodovico; so might the Emperor, who could bestow his Vicariate on whomsoever he wished. In so complex a situation Lodovico worked his astrologers hard, and the conjunction and combination of the stars became his daily concern. The point of desperation was reached when his nephew came of age and fathered an heir before Beatrice d'Este produced a son for Lodovico. The arrival of an heir to the dukedom was received with modest celebrations, and much to Isabella's fury the banquets, jousts, pageants, and *Te Deums* that celebrated the birth of Lodovico's son were as splendiferous as they were prolonged. No doubt remained as to how the Regent's mind was working.

Lodovico's opportunity came when Charles VIII of France, who had acquired the Anjou claims to the Neapolitan throne, having settled his quarrel with the Emperor, thought that he might exercise his nobility and seek honour and reward by invading Naples. This seeming act of folly Lodovico encouraged; and in return for his benevolent neutrality Charles supported Lodovico's claim to the Emperor to be appointed Imperial Vicar of Milan – a legitimization of power never yet won by a Sforza. A further piece of luck – as no doubt the stars had foretold – took place. His nephew, the Duke, died. Lodovico proclaimed the infant Francesco duke. Not surprisingly, the Council would not have him; they begged Lodovico, at such a time of peril for the state, to assume the title with the power. Lodovico complied; the populace cheered. So Lodovico achieved his *coup d'état* – a bloodless one and timed to perfection. In his campaign against Naples, Charles VIII proved almost miraculously successful (as is common with military miracles, it was based on superior armament, particularly cannon). With Charles thus occupied and the imperial edict safe in his pocket, Lodovico suddenly changed sides, and when Charles began to withdraw from Italy, Sforza was one of those who harried and hurried him on his way. Then, sensing the possible benefits, he seized the opportune moment to switch allegiance to Charles once again.

So Lodovico had his years of triumph. He could boast that the Pope was his chaplain, the Emperor his condottiere, Venice his chamberlain, and the King of France his courier. For a time Milan was prosperous, the court brilliant, the prince magnificent. And then death took a hand. Beatrice, who had done so much to bring Lodovico's subtleties to decisive action, died in childbed. Charles VIII of France also died; his successor, Louis XII claimed Milan and regarded Charles VIII's failure to take it for him as a disgrace. Apart from Naples, which feared a fresh invasion, the powers of Italy leapt as rapidly as possible on to the French bandwagon (Venice alone bargaining hard for its ticket) and were overjoyed that the victim beneath the juggernaut's wheels should be Lodovico. The French won; Lodovico retreated to the Tirol; the French puppet outraged the Milanese; Lodovico returned; so did the French, and won again with consummate ease. This time they packed Lodovico off to France, where his imprisonment was strict enough to titillate the most morbid humanist, obsessed with the fate of tyrants. He finally died in a tiny, lightless, underground cell in the dungeon of Loches.

It was not the end of the Sforza. They had become pawns in the battle between the great European powers who used Lombardy as their tilting ground. Sforza's son, Massimiliano, was brought back by the lances of the Swiss, and after a brief and extravagant career he was removed, after the Battle of Marignano, by Francis I and pensioned, not imprisoned, in France. These two wars, which devastated Milan, were soon followed by a third, when Charles V, who combined the formidable power of his Holy Roman Empire with that of Spain, decided to expel the French from Lombardy. This he did in 1525 outside the great Visconti capital of Pavia. It was a fitting place, for with that battle the last gleams of Milanese independence disappeared. The reason for this tale of blood is not far to seek. Although Milan possessed natural frontiers and great wealth and an able ruling house, as a state it never acquired the stability of Florence or Venice or even Naples, simply because its class struggles went unresolved. The feudal nobility were never uprooted; they constantly quarrelled with each other and provided a ready support for any adventurer, internal or external, who would favour their personal ambitions. This powerful aristocracy also thrived on the divisions and jealousies of the merchant class which hated it. Finally, Milan was hemmed about with cities almost as great as itself, all possessing rich, ambitious, jealous guilds of merchants who see-sawed between wanting the stability which the leadership of Milan alone could bring and the gain that might accrue from its humiliation. In such an unstable world the abilities of the Visconti and the Sforza were largely wasted. The great horse designed by Leonardo for Lodovico in memory of his father seems curiously symbolic of their destiny – conceived in grandeur, executed in clay, never cast, ruined by the French, and destroyed by time.

LEONARDO DA VINCI

by J. Bronowski

LEONARDO was born outside the small town of Vinci, near Florence in 1452; the traditional date of his birthday is 15 April. The birthday is hardly worth remembering, but the year is, for its remoteness remains a constant surprise. Leonardo's gifts speak so directly, his imagination is so immediate to us, that we have to remind ourselves with an effort that he was born more than five hundred years ago. He lived long before William Shakespeare and Rembrandt and Isaac Newton. Leonardo was dead before Nicolaus Copernicus felt sure that the earth goes around the sun; he was an old man, unhappy and full of regrets, when Martin Luther began the Reformation; and he had already passed the turning point of middle life when Christopher Columbus discovered America.

Leonardo was the illegitimate son of a lawyer and a woman who may have been a servant in the house of Leonardo's grandparents. The boy's father did take several wives – each a member of a good Florentine family – but not for over twenty years were there any more children. Leonardo was thus his father's only child during those formative years.

Italians in the Renaissance were not outraged by the thought that a bright child had been conceived out of wedlock. Illegitimacy was a commonplace of the time; men were proud of making their own way; and churchmen and condottieri, artists and statesmen, boasted that they were born out of wedlock. This was no stigma among the thrusting, self-made men of the Renaissance; indeed, as the historian Jakob Burckhardt wrote, 'The fitness of the individual, his worth and capacity, were of more weight than all the laws and usages which prevailed elsewhere in the West.'

Nevertheless, we get the feeling that Leonardo never walked easily in the houses of the great, and that this wariness goes back to his childhood. There is something hooded and withdrawn about his character which calls up a picture of a child made much of and yet not at home in the house of his birth. All his life he hated to see suffering. The story is told of Leonardo buying birds in the market place, holding them in his hand for a moment, and then setting them free. It is evident that in that rough, insensitive time he was one of the few men who could not bear to give pain to animals.

When Leonardo was about fourteen, his father apprenticed him to Andrea del Verrocchio, one of the foremost artists in Florence. The time was 1466 or thereabouts; Florence was aflower with wealth and splendour; its tone was set, its taste was led, by the great family of the Medici. Here the display of riches was more than a reward for success – it was almost a ritual, a public announcement of status and authority.

The *botteghe*, or workshops of Verrocchio and other artists supplied this society with its beautiful treasures and trinkets. Verrocchio was a painter and sculptor, and was also a goldsmith and a decorator. His studio was, in an exact sense, a workshop, and it was Verrocchio's business to supply from it a picture or a chair, a statue or a goblet, a golden chafing dish or a ceremonial suit of armour. Verrocchio himself could turn his hand to all these things; however, he was a rather wooden painter, and he seems therefore to have turned more and more to sculpture.

One reason why Verrocchio could turn from painting was that his apprentice Leonardo was so good at it. The artist who ran his studio as a workshop had to conserve and to divide its labour intelligently and expediently; and when he had an apprentice who could paint, he gave him his head – and did something else himself. Tradition has it that Leonardo was still a boy when he painted an angel in one of

Verocchio's religious commissions, and made it more life-like than his master could.

The story of the boy painter who outdoes his master is characteristic of the Renaissance; it is also told of Raphael and others. For this was an age in love with surprises, eager to discover genius, native and untaught. Yet the evidence is that the story is true of Leonardo. There is at least one picture by Verrocchio, *The Baptism of Christ*, in which one of the angels is unlike the rest, and has clearly been painted by a more sensitive and subtler hand. Moreover, the landscape of the *Baptism*, the detail of trees and grasses, has a vivid intimacy and an absorbed lucidity of vision which belong to no painter before Leonardo. There is at least one other painting by Verrocchio whose landscape shows the hand of Leonardo in the same way. Verrocchio must have known that the young Leonardo was not merely a better painter: he was a new painter.

Leonardo finished his training with Verrocchio about 1472, when he was twenty or so, and then went on working in Florence for another nine or ten years. He was good at other things beside painting. He is described as tall and handsome, graceful in all his actions, and apparently he had a fine singing voice, and the official records show that he was accused once of some homosexual scrape. (The evidence is that he lacked the usual sensual feelings for women, and tended rather to admire strong men.) He was interested in mathematics and mechanics, and particularly in the mechanics by which living things move: he constantly drew birds in flight, and he also made his first studies of human anatomy then.

These are odd interests in a painter, in the traditional sense; and yet they are inseparable from that desire to enter into the very structure of natural things which to Leonardo was the essence of painting. Later in life he wrote very simply about this:

And you who say that it is better to look at an anatomical demonstration than to see these drawings, you would be right, if it were possible to observe all the details shown in these drawings in a single figure, in which, with all your ability, you will not see nor acquire a knowledge of more than some few veins, while, in order to obtain an exact and complete knowledge of these, I have dissected more than ten human bodies, destroying all the various members, and removing even the very smallest particles of the flesh which surrounded these veins without causing any effusion of blood other than the imperceptible bleeding of the capillary veins. And, as one single body did not suffice for so long a time, it was necessary to proceed by stages with so many bodies as would render my knowledge complete; and this I repeated twice over in order to discover the differences.

This is an account of work in anatomy, but it carries no hint of a medical interest. For Leonardo did not want to cure men: he wanted to know how their bodies are made and work. He distrusted the doctors of his time, and indeed the whole of medical and chemical science then, which saw nature as an interplay of occult qualities. Leonardo looked at nature directly, not through the mind but through the eye. And his was a wonderful eye, sharp and abrupt as a camera, which could stop a bird in flight and fix the muscled movement of its wing. He wanted no speculation about the soul of the bird, which scholars were still repeating from Pythagoras; he wanted to understand the harsh mechanics of its flight:

A bird is an instrument working according to mathematical law, which instrument it is within the capacity of man to reproduce with all its movements, but not with a corresponding degree of strength, though it is deficient only in the power of maintaining equilibrium. We may therefore say that such an instrument constructed by man is lacking in nothing except the life of the bird, and this life must needs be supplied from that of man.

These preoccupations with the structure of things, with the muscle under the skin and the bone under the muscle, seem to have grown on Leonardo from the time that he began to work for himself. They made him uninterested in, and perhaps unhappy with, the opportunities which Florence in the 1470s held out to artists who could display the warm beauty of the surface of things.

At this time Verrocchio was working on a statue of the great condottiere of Venice, Colleoni, and he left Florence to finish the work in Venice. Perhaps Leonardo felt that Florence was no longer the centre of art it had once been. Or perhaps he could not resist the urge to create a statue better than Verrocchio's, for although he was not a sculptor, he wrote a long letter in 1482 to Lodovico Sforza in Milan, offering among many other things, to make a statue of his father, the condottiere Francesco. In that same letter he described in detail his talents as a military engineer and inventor (two abilities likely to appeal to a Sforza), and soon after, at the age of thirty, he left Florence, carrying with him a silver lute that he had made in the shape of a horse's head, to spend nearly twenty years at the turbulent court of Milan.

Leonardo was in many respects self-taught, a self-willed man who did things almost truculently at times. Some of his paintings have perished as a result of ordinary bad luck, but others because of his insistence on mixing pigments with curious ingredients or on drying them in new and different ways. He was an innovator, an experimenter, a man never satisfied with the accepted or acceptable, and his decision to leave Florence was taken because Florence was a city of tradition, living on its golden dreams of the past.

We can only guess at the reasons for Leonardo's move from Florence to Milan. Yet if his reasons, intellectual and emotional, had any psychological coherence, it is clear enough what was the common strand in them. When Leonardo chose between Florence and Milan, he was not merely choosing between different cities: in a profound sense he was choosing between different cultures – between two different aspects of the Renaissance.

The Renaissance had begun, as its name implies, as a rebirth of a culture which had already been born once. It was, in the first place, a recovery of ancient learning, and the early Renaissance was not a revolution, but a revival.

Florence was above all the home of this classical revival. The medieval Church had leaned heavily on Aristotle, and had elevated him almost to the status of an honorary saint; now the Medici, in opposition, praised the work and the outlook of Plato. The pride of Florence was the Medici library of ancient manuscripts and commentaries on them, and the Platonic Academy. Florence in the 1470s, when Leonardo worked there, was dominated by the taste of the greatest of the Medici, Lorenzo the Magnificent, which was wholly classical and luxurious.

By contrast, Leonardo was one of the first men in whom the Renaissance expressed itself in a new way, not as a recovery but as a discovery. By the standards of Lorenzo, Leonardo was an unscholarly, unlettered painter: he did not even know Latin (he learned it later in Milan) and he never aspired to Greek. This is a subject to which he returned often and with heat in his notebooks:

I am fully aware that the fact of my not being a man of letters may cause certain arrogant persons to think that they may with reason censure me, alleging that I am a man ignorant of book-learning. Foolish folk! Do they not know that I might retort by saying, as did Marius to the Roman patricians, ' They who themselves go about adorned in the labour of others will not permit me of my own.' They will say that because of my lack of book-learning, I cannot properly express what I desire to treat of. Do they not know that my subjects require for their exposition experience rather than the words of others? And since experience has been the mistress of whoever has written well, I take her as my mistress, and to her in all points make my appeal.

In this and other passages Leonardo is making two points. First, he is expressing his contempt for the new aristocracy of Florence, the moneyed men who lean on the talents of others, and whose taste, however authoritative, shows no mind of its own: 'Whoever in discussion adduces authority uses not his intellect but rather memory.' And second, Leonardo is setting up a new standard for the creation of works of art: the standard of the original mind that goes directly to nature, without intermediaries:

The painter will produce pictures of little merit if he takes the works of others as his standard; but if he will apply himself to learn from the objects of nature he will produce good results. This we see was the case with the painters who came after the time of the Romans, for they continually imitated each other, and from age to age their art steadily declined. . . . it is safer to go direct to the works of nature than to those which have been imitated from her originals with great determination and thereby to acquire a bad method, for he who has access to the fountain does not go to the water-pot.

In those quotations we have the crux of principle which divided Leonardo from his predecessors in the Renaissance. The medieval Church had taught that the universe can be understood only spiritually, as a God-given and abstract order; that the beauty of man and of nature is a snare which tempts us away from that stark understanding. The Renaissance denied these morose dogmas, holding instead that fleshy and natural beauty is not sinful, that it is, on the contrary, an expression of the divine order. Yet the form which this humanistic belief took was different at different times. The pioneers of the Renaissance found their ideal of man and nature in the splendid texts of the classics and in the works of art of antiquity. But the new men of the Renaissance, the self-taught and self-willed men like Leonardo, were not content with anything at second hand. They wanted to see, to understand, to enter into nature for themselves. Leonardo above all wanted not to recover, but to discover, his own humanity.

When Leonardo left Florence, he was, therefore, turning his back on the classical Renaissance, and looking for the kinship of other men who shared his thirst for a more popular Renaissance. It was natural

177

that he should look for such men in Milan. Here was a city larger than Florence, less dependent on its rich men, less self-satisfied, and with a more cosmopolitan outlook towards the rest of Europe – particularly towards France and towards Germany. Printing had been invented before Leonardo was born, but hitherto had spread little into Italy; now in the 1480s it became important in Milan. Mathematics and mechanics, too, were more highly regarded in Milan than they were in the Platonic climate of Florence. Leonardo all his life was deeply drawn towards mathematics, and in Milan he drew the pictures for a book, *The Divine Proportion*, which the mathematician Luca Pacioli wrote and later printed. The divine proportion is that geometrical ration which we now call the golden section, and it may be that this modern name was in fact first used for it by Leonardo da Vinci.

Intellectually, Leonardo was drawn to Milan because he was seeking a more downright and popular expression of Renaissance humanism than Florence offered. Emotionally, also, we sense that there was something about the brutal power of the court of Milan which attracted him more than the classical air of Florence. Lodovico Sforza was hardly a gracious man; yet something in the sinister directness of such a man, his naked drive to power, his simple and single will, plainly fascinated Leonardo. Like other sensitive men of the mind, he seems to have found a satisfaction in watching other men impose themselves ruthlessly on a world in which he himself was so ill at ease. We catch a hint of the same regard for male power in Leonardo's feelings for his model Giacomo Salai, whom he picked up in the streets of Milan, and whose endless misdeeds he forgave year in and year out with a tender and tolerant contempt.

This is another side of the search for the simplest, most rudimentary forces in man and in nature which took Leonardo to Milan. It made him accept the whims of Lodovico in a way in which he would not have accepted those of Lorenzo. Whatever his other faults may have been, Lodovico was an admirable patron. The fact that his patronage lacked the literary overtones of the Medici made it more attractive to Leonardo, and the variety of the work which Leonardo was called upon to perform at once appealed to his ingenuity, his curiosity, and his interest in experiment. In Milan, Leonardo became a busybody bending his great powers of invention to the trivial mechanics of court entertainment. He painted portraits of Lodovico's mistresses. He designed the costumes and devised the trick surprises of scenery for the court masques. To celebrate a visit of the King of France, he made an automaton shaped like a lion, which spilled a shower of lilies from its breast. He drew maps and proposed schemes of irrigation, he founded cannon and installed central heating, he planned engines of war and palaces, he designed a dozen schemes that Lodovico disregarded. And he went on making countless sketches of the most stupendous surprise of all, the statue of a rearing horse on which should sit Francesco Sforza, the soldier who had created the Milan that Lodovico now ruled. (It is interesting that he considered the animal the centre of the monument, and that he should have referred to the statue simply as 'the horse'.) But like everything that Leonardo did for his patron, this also came to nothing.

Yet the years that Leonardo spent in Milan were not wasted. In an odd way, he could follow his bent here. The pageants and the plans that were expected of him can hardly have filled his time, and Lodovico was too busy with his ambitions to pester the court sculptor who had not finished his commission. In Milan, Leonardo did not have to work hard to earn his keep by doing the things that he knew how to do – above all, by painting. In one way this is a pity for us: we would have more great paintings, and fewer sketches, if Leonardo had had to deliver his work for cash during the years in Milan, when his gifts flowed most easily. But in another way we can be grateful that Leonardo in those years of his middle life did not have to do the things he could do so well, which somehow were becoming distasteful to him. Leonardo in Milan grew impatient with his own gifts; he did not care to paint, he disliked the likenesses that he could catch so swiftly, the tricks of light and shade, the surface appearances. His interest was more and more in the structure of things, and as a result his notebooks are now full of sketches which are always, as it were, taking nature to pieces. He did not want to copy: he wanted to understand.

An indication of how his mind was working during these years may be seen in the beautiful portrait of a mistress of Lodovico Sforza, painted soon after Leonardo arrived in Milan. The sitter, who could have been no more than a girl when he painted her, was probably Cecilia Gallerani. The ermine which she holds in her arms was an emblem of Lodovico, and is probably also a pun on the girl's name. And in a sense the whole picture is a pun, for Leonardo has matched the ermine in the girl. In the skull under the long brow, in the lucid eyes, in the stately, beautiful, stupid head of the girl, he has redis-covered the animal nature; and done so without malice, almost as a matter of fact. The very carriage of the girl and the ermine, the gesture of the hand and the claw, explore the character with the anatomy. The painting is as much a research into man and animal, and a creation of unity, as is Darwin's *Origin of Species*.

The notebooks of Leonardo are as unexpected, and as personal, as everything about him. There are about five thousand pages of them which have been preserved. Each page is a wonderful jumble of drawings and notes, in which a piece of geometry, a horse's head, an astronomical conjecture, and a flower stand side by side. A photo-graph shows all this with Leonardo's transparent clarity, but it does not show the delicate scale on which Leonardo worked. Many of the pages in the notebooks, crowded with detail, are no bigger than a man's hand. This is perhaps another expression of Leonardo's with-drawn and indrawn character, and so, no doubt, is the mirror writing which Leonardo used, writing with his left hand. The shading in his drawings is left-handed also, but it is not certain that he painted with his left hand. It is possible that he had damaged his right hand in Florence, and that thereafter he still used it, but only for the most delicate parts of his pictures. The pocket notebooks, the left-handed shading, the mirror writing, express something else, too, in Leonardo's character: a determination to do everything for himself, in his own way, down to the smallest detail. Witness, for example, his anatomical drawings showing the hollows and blood vessels in the head – drawings so exact that they have been compared point by point with photographs made by X-ray or by radioactive tracers. It is not only the enormous scope of his researches that is impressive, it is the absorption, the meticulousness, and the intensity with which he looked for the mechanism behind what he saw. Leonardo was not merely an original man, in the sense that he had two or three profound and new ideas. He had a passion for looking afresh at everything that came into his life, no matter how trivial the occasion. In this sense, he was not merely an original but a perverse man; and perhaps all the oddities of his life reach back into the childhood of the lonely boy.

'Intellectual passion drives out sensuality,' Leonardo wrote on a page of his notebooks. But perhaps his tragic and unfulfilled life proves that when the intellect becomes the subject of such a passion, it ends by being a kind of perversion.

Leonardo's notebooks from this time are full of the penetrating observation of nature, particularly in the anatomical drawings; and

Anatomical study of a woman
by Leonardo da Vinci
Royal Collection, Windsor Castle

are full, too, of a springing invention which was fired by his observation. He had long been absorbed by the flight of birds, and now it led him to invent a parachute and a form of helicopter. The fact that the latter did not work may be blamed on the age in which he lived, which did not understand, and could not have commanded, the mechanical energy necessary for flight. He observed, one hundred years before Galileo, that the pendulum might be used to make a clockwork keep equal time. He saw that red light penetrates through mist and that blue light does not, and so devised practical rules for giving depth to the painting of landscapes. There are mechanisms on his pages here and there which he noted from others, but the bulk of what he outlined was original, and it included various types of bridges, a mechanical excavator, machines for grinding needles and mirrors, a rolling mill, an automatic file cutter, an instrument for measuring wind speeds, and a self-centering chuck. Here is a characteristic invention, which characteristically goes into every essential detail:

A Way of Saving Oneself in a Tempest or Shipwreck at Sea

It is necessary to have a coat made of leather with a double hem over the breast of the width of a finger, and double also from the girdle to the knee, and let the leather of which it is made be quite air-tight. And when you are obliged to jump into the sea, blow out the lappets of the coat through the hems of the breast, and then jump into the sea. And let yourself be carried by the waves, if there is no shore near at hand and you do not know the sea. And always keep in your mouth the end of the tube through which the air passes into the garment; and if once or twice it should become necessary for you to take a breath when the foam prevents you, draw it through the mouth of the tube from the air within the coat.

There is no wonder that, as Leonardo grew more absorbed in the mechanism of nature, the work which he had come to Milan to do was put off further and further. At last, in 1493, it could be put off no longer. Lodovico Sforza was arranging to marry his niece to the Emperor Maximilian. Leonardo made a full-sized model of the statue of Francesco Sforza on horseback in clay. The bronze to cast the statue was gathered, too, but that had to be sent off next year to make cannon for Lodovico's allies. Lodovico was now deep in intrigue, trying to marshal one group of the city-states of Italy against another. Finally he invited the French to come into Italy on his side, and they, as treacherous as Lodovico, entered Milan in 1499. Lodovico fled, but a year later they took him prisoner.

Leonardo also fled from Milan in that year, a defeated man now nearing fifty, who had given the richest years of his life to a second-rate tyrant with a passion for power. The French archers had used the clay horse and its rider as a target, and there remained in Milan little to show for Leonardo's spent years except a painting of the Last Supper which began to moulder on its damp convent wall even before the artist died. The prior had complained that Leonardo had been dilatory in finishing even that, and Leonardo in revenge had said that he would paint the prior for eternity into the figure of Judas. Yet, characteristically, when it came to the point, Leonardo had done something more profound with the figure of Judas: he had moved Judas out of the place that the Middle Ages had assigned to him and had put him on the same side of the table with Jesus.

Leonardo lived for twenty years after the fall of Milan, wandering irresolutely from one city to another, and from one commission to another, without ever again settling down to any one. In 1502 he served briefly in the train of Cesare Borgia as military engineer. This was the same treacherous campaign on which Niccolò Machiavelli was present – the one which provided the Florentine diplomat with a portrait of undeviating ambition for *The Prince*.

Soon after, Florence commissioned two patriotic pictures of battle scenes, one from Leonardo and one from Michelangelo. Leonardo's drafts of the picture survive, but the painting itself deteriorated almost immediately. During this time Leonardo painted a portrait of the third wife of a local merchant named Giocondo. This is the *Mona Lisa*, which in its day was admired for the warmth of its flesh tones, and which time and varnish have now turned to the faint green of ice in a landscape of rocks.

Leonardo went back to Milan from time to time to make sketches, now, for another horse and rider. This time the rider was to be Gian Giacomo Trivulzio, that Italian condottiere who had fought on the side of the French in the battle for Milan and had overthrown his one-time master and Leonardo's patron, Lodovico. Once again, nothing came of this monument. Then, in 1513, the son of Lorenzo de' Medici became Pope Leo X, and Leonardo went to Rome, where Raphael and Michelangelo had been working for some years, and there received several papal commissions. The story goes that Leonardo began, upon his arrival, to make the varnish for one picture before he started to paint it, and that Leo X observed, sadly and wisely, 'This man will never do anything, for he begins to think of the end before the beginning.'

The King of France at last offered Leonardo a retreat without obligation near Amboise, and there he spent the remainder of his life, from 1516 until 1519. His self-portrait, drawn a few years earlier, shows him as a man looking much older than his sixty years, full-bearded and patriarchal, his eyes veiled against emotion and his mouth set bitterly, and the distress of an old age full of regrets for the wonderful things that he had planned and never finished now fills his notebooks. Once he had been so sure of his own gifts that there had seemed to be an infinity of time in which to fulfil them. In those confident young days he had written:

I wish to work miracles; – I may have less than other men who are more tranquil, or than those who aim at growing rich in a day.

Now he was conscious every day of the merciless erosion of time, which leaves nothing of the living vigour and beauty of a man if the man has not perpetuated them in his own creations. Leonardo is looking into his own face when he thinks of Helen of Troy and, borrowing from Ovid, writes:

O Time, thou that consumest all things! O envious age, thou destroyest all things and devourest all things with the hard teeth of the years, little by little, in slow death! Helen, when she looked in her mirror and saw the withered wrinkles which old age had made in her face, wept, and wondered to herself why ever she had twice been carried away. O Time, thou consumest all things! O envious age, whereby all things are consumed!

The works of art that Leonardo left behind are indeed sadly few – not a whole statue, about a dozen finished paintings, some fine anatomical and mechanical drawings, and otherwise only the thousands of sketches. For some artists with one small gift, this might be enough; but when we consider the prodigious talent of Leonardo, the instant eye, the exact hand, and the penetrating mind, we understand why he scribbled desperately on page after page of his later notebooks: 'Tell me if anything at all was done . . . Tell me if anything at all was done . . .'

And no doubt Leonardo was right to think that he had wasted his life; but he was wrong to think that he had wasted his gifts. At bottom, his true gifts were not those of a painter, for his painting, original as it was, was not out of the reach of his contemporaries. As a painter Leonardo was in the stream of the Renaissance tradition which Botticelli, Raphael, Michelangelo, and others were also helping to form. Leonardo's most profound gifts were of another kind, and make him seem modern to us today, five hundred years after he lived.

The first of the gifts which made Leonardo a pioneer was his absorbed interest in the structure and mechanism of nature. The science of his day has hardly a hint of this, because it was still dominated by a magical view of man. The alchemists of Leonardo's time believed that they would command nature only by breaking the natural order of things, by casting a spell over nature which made her function in a way contrary to her own laws. They wanted to bewitch the world, and to gain power by forcing it to obey them instead of the laws of nature. Leonardo realized, as his contemporaries did not, that we command nature only when we understand her, when we enter into her processes and give them scope to work naturally. He was full of contempt for those who wanted to force nature to do the impossible: 'O speculators about perpetual motion, how many vain chimeras have you created in the like quest? Go and take your place with the seekers after gold.'

Leonardo's second pioneering gift was to see that the structure of nature also reveals her processes, which are perpetually in movement and in development. The way a skeleton is hinged, the way a muscle is anchored, the way a leaf is veined – all such knowledge tells something about the functioning of the organism and therefore, in the end, about the whole cycle of its growth. Leonardo dismissed the easy appeals to vital forces and the spirits that inhabit living things with which his age fobbed off all questions; he looked for the strict mechanism by which living things move and act; and he saw that mechanism as something dynamic. This dynamic quality is present even in his simplest sketch of a machine, and in his old age it expressed itself in a growing preoccupation with the forms of plants and of flowing water. Leonardo did not think that a scientific analysis of the processes of nature deprived them of life; on the contrary, he wanted the analysis to express their changing and living movement.

Third, and most important, Leonardo understood that science is not a grand parade of a few cosmic theories, of the kind that Aristotle and St Thomas Aquinas had propounded. Until Leonardo's time a theory was expected to give a general explanation of some large phenomenon, such as the motion of the moon, and no one then asked whether the theory could also be made to match the precise times at which the moon rises and sets. The detail was not thought important, and any discrepancy between theory and fact was shrugged off as a point of detail. Leonardo for the first time elevated the detail so that it became once and for all the crucial test of a scientific theory. He was seldom misled by what the classical medicine of Galen said in general about the functioning of the heart or the way that the eye sees; he drew what his dissection showed him, and then asked how it could be squared with the vague medical beliefs which were then accepted.

Here we are at the centre of Leonardo's pioneering mind. Because he had an exact eye, because he was a painter for whom nature lived not in generalities but in the very shape of a flower or a waterfall, he was at the opposite pole from the theorizing scientists of his own age. Leonardo did not therefore lose interest in science: he transformed it. Only a painter could have forced science to change its outlook, and to become as dedicated as his art was to the discovery of the natural order in the minute detail of its structure. Leonardo *was* that painter, who is the true pioneer of science as we practise it.

His interest in what was new made him unwilling to look back; his gaze was outwards and forwards into nature. His passion for the exact turned him towards mathematics, his passion for the actual urged him to experiment, and it is significant that these two dominant themes – logic and experimentation – have remained, ever since Leonardo's time, at the base of scientific method.

It was natural that, with these gifts, Leonardo should have quarrelled with the classical and literary Renaissance in which he was brought up and should have turned to a more popular and naturalistic Renaissance. It was natural that he should give up pictures for machines, and that his machines should have that subtle quality of human intelligence, of one operation controlling another, which to-day we call automation. It was natural that these interests should take him from the rich merchant culture of Florence to the brutal thrust for power of the Sforza and the Borgia. And it was natural and inevitable that a life spent at the courts of such men should have about it the modern ring of our own age, the pointless planning of pageants and machines of war, the aimless postponement of every constructive scheme, and the final despair of a great mind that from childhood has been baffled by an alien world. At the end of his life Leonardo wrote constantly of his visions of the cruelty of man to man, and what he foresaw links his gangster age to ours:

Of the Cruelty of Man

Creatures shall be seen upon the earth who will always be fighting one with another with very great losses and frequent deaths on either side. These shall set no bounds to their malice; by their fierce limbs a great number of the trees in the immense forests of the world shall be laid level with the ground; and when they have crammed themselves with food it shall gratify their desire to deal out death, affliction, labours, terrors, and banishment to every living thing. And by reason of their boundless pride they shall wish to rise towards heaven, but the excessive weight of their limbs shall hold them down. There shall be nothing remaining on the earth or under the earth or in the waters that shall not be pursued and molested and destroyed, and that which is in one country taken away to another; and their own bodies shall be made the tomb and the means of transit of all the living bodies which they have slain. O Earth! what delays thee to open and hurl them headlong into the deep fissures of thy huge abysses and caverns, and no longer to display in the sight of heaven so savage and ruthless a monster?

ROME: SPLENDOUR AND THE PAPACY

ROME was a city caught, like an old man, in memories, delusions, and dreams. Even when fighting (and not too successfully at that) the little town of Tivoli, medals were struck bearing the proud title, *Roma caput mundi*: Rome, the world's ruler. By 1400, however, even the great days of the Middle Ages seemed remote to realistic men, and gone forever. For most of the fourteenth century the popes had lived at Avignon in France, in the great and luxurious Palais des Papes that looms above the Rhône, where the broken Roman bridge became a symbol of the Church's break with its own past. To Avignon went the clerics, lawyers, and merchants who harvested and spent the wealth which a pious Europe poured into the papal lap. It was to Avignon that Francesco Datini, the famous merchant of Prato, went to make his fortune as a small but ambitious boy of fifteen. And make it he did, in his determined, hardheaded, Tuscan way, selling silks, jewels, works of art, damasks, swords, silverware, cloth, even salt – anything that would make the money grow, although the profits on his insurance and his banking interests nagged at his conscience. Through men like Datini, Avignon prospered and Rome lost; and, of course, the artists too went where the money was, and Sienese artists painted the frescoes that adorned the Palace's walls.

True, in Rome a few cardinals still flaunted their courtesans, and a few saintly men continued to dedicate themselves to the liturgical worship of God and the relief of the poor. Even the Curia functioned, although ever more slowly. But the absence of the Papacy was killing Rome as inexorably as a cancer. The vast ruinous buildings, combined with constant plague, stifled hope, depressed the spirit, bred despair. In this dark world the great, furious Roman tribes – the Orsini, the Colonna, the Frangipani – made their sport, and what a sport it was! They tossed each other into the Tiber, and when a pope ventured to enter Rome, they chased him into the fortress of Sant' Angelo or frightened him – like the aged Gregory XII – into the remoter corners of the Patrimony. They terrorized the citizens, raped the nuns, robbed the monks, pillaged the churches. To compound confusion, from 1378 to 1429 there was an antipope as well as a pope, and in 1409 even three authentic successors of St Peter – a glorious opportunity for rebellion, riot, and plunder. King Ladislas of Naples prowled about the broken-down streets of Rome, extorting what he could and decapitating whom he dared. Popes and kings hired the toughest, most brutal condottieri – including Braccio, who, according to a chronicler, enjoyed the sufferings of others, and for his pleasure would throw a few men from the highest towers in Rome or drop a prisoner into a boiling cauldron. After years of anarchy the Romans were willing to believe anything and nothing. When John XXIII, afterwards struck from the list of the popes and accused of a huge catalogue of crimes, the least important of which were incest, sodomy, and murder, swore that he would defend them to the death, they replied that they would rather eat their children than surrender to his enemies. During the same night John XXIII flew under the cover of darkness, taking all the portable wealth he could lay his hands on, and the Romans opened their gates the next morning, their children undevoured. Such a kaleidoscope of brutality, such a cascade of violence, broke the government of the city in pieces and reduced it to a poverty and a misery it had not known since the barbarian invasions.

No one in 1425 could have foreseen that Rome was about to be reborn (not spiritually – the Renaissance popes were not to prove men of the spirit – but physically, artistically, and politically). St Peter's, the Vatican, the churches, the tombs, the squares, the great

Castel Sant'Angelo, 1491
Drawing from the Codex Escorialensis, *Biblioteca del Escorial*

palaces and gardens of Rome which now entrance the eye and delight
the heart, were brought into being and gave an impetus to the pursuit of beauty that the stern moralities of the Counter-reformation
could not stop. For two hundred years the beauty of Rome became
the pride of the Papacy. The downward plunge into anarchy and
destitution and poverty was checked by Martin v, himself a Colonna
and a Roman. During his pontificate (1417–31) the dreadful split in
the Church was cured, if not quite healed. Furthermore, he proved
a good administrator and such a fearsome personality that he secured
peace for the city. He checked the robberies, violence, and murder,
and stimulated the city's trade. With the papal court back in Rome,
back came the pilgrims and supplicants, back came the merchants,
and back came the life-blood – the papal tax harvest that was reaped
from Europe's peasantry. And so the Roman soil was fertilized again,
for without wealth no Renaissance was possible. The next pope,
Eugenius IV, had to flee down the Tiber in a rowboat, disguised as a
monk, and eluded capture only by a hair's breadth. For years he kept
his court at Florence, where he patronized the humanists and bided
his time, while he left Rome to be pacified by a ferocious bishop,

191

Vitelleschi, who razed cities, hanged and decapitated barons, slaughtered right, left, and centre, and probably met his own end by poison (possibly with Eugenius' connivance). By such murderous methods were the popes re-established. The calculated savageries of Cesare Borgia, that were to astound a later generation, were unusual only in the beauty and dexterity of their timing.

To be secure in Rome, the Papacy needed to control the States of the Church which stretched in a broad diagonal across the long leg of Italy. During its residence at Avignon and the Great Schism (1378 to 1417), men and cities had naturally usurped papal rights and privileges, and what they had won by force they would not yield by persuasion. Excommunication, interdict or anathema left them unmoved. These had been flung about so wantonly by rival popes at each other that they had lost much of their force. Indeed, it seemed to the popes that the Church could only get back its own by acting like any other power in Italy. By alliance, by diplomacy, by war, the Church might wrest its possessions from alien hands. Its wealth permitted it to hire the ablest condottieri, including the great Francesco Sforza as well as Federigo da Montefeltro. Having been a plaything of the great powers, the leaders of the Church wished to secure independence by giving the Church great temporal and political strength. That being so, they looked for a leader not among the saints nor usually among the scholars (Nicholas v and Pius ii were exceptions) but among the administrators and natural politicians. They looked for worldly men, men of powerful personalities, tough fibre, and quick decision. And again, as the power of the Papacy steadily grew through temporal measures such as war and diplomacy, so did the need for such qualities in a pope seem ever more necessary. This is the explanation of what so many now find difficult to understand – of popes such as Alexander vi or Julius ii. Alexander vi, whose lusts repelled even the tolerant age in which he lived, was a very hardheaded diplomat and excellent administrator, whose policy undeviatingly pursued what was thought to be a necessity for the

Five Renaissance Popes
1. NICHOLAS V, 1447–55
2. CALIXTUS III, 1455–8
3. PIUS II, 1458–64
4. ALEXANDER VI, 1492–1503
5. PAUL III, 1534–49
Bibliothèque Nationale, Paris,
and Appartamento Borgia, Vatican

Church – temporal power, expressed in the overlordship of central Italy. Julius II, even as pope, loved war, loved to get on his horse, to feel the weight of his armour and hear the blood-call of battle.

So, by and large, the Renaissance popes were worldly men, pragmatic, tough, concerned with power. And like many hardheaded, ambitious men they did not wish to be outshone by their rivals in the symbolic display of wealth and greatness. They were determined to build vast churches, huge palaces, magnificent fountains; to employ the finest painters, sculptors, craftsmen; to collect the loveliest antiquities, the most resplendent jewels, the most remarkable books, the most exquisite manuscripts. These things, like their armies, were necessities of state, and the cost irrelevant. So hand in hand with the resurgent power of the Papacy went the artistic Renaissance in Rome; and because the popes controlled more wealth, the result was more splendid than anywhere else.

Rome was full of priests, monks, nuns, churches, monasteries,

The seven pilgrimage churches of Rome
Print by Antoine Lafréry, Gabinetto Nazionale delle Stampe

convents, holy relics, miraculous shrines, healing images. Every year thousands of pilgrims from all corners of the Western world made their way to it in penitence and in hope. Most were simple people to whom the sight of a piece of the True Cross or a saint's leg justified the dangers and tribulations of their journey. They cared nothing for the whispered rumours of the Pope's children, of his poisonings, murders, or even the alarming sensualities of the Borgia. Twenty thousand of them reverenced Alexander VI, in the great Jubilee year of 1500 – unmindful of his lusts. For them the mounting grandeur of Rome was a wondrous thing, a visible proof of the glory of their Church. Humanist criticism of the Church's venality, corruption, immorality, and obscurantism fell on deaf ears. A Savonarola or a Bernardino of Siena might momentarily stir this multitude with a sense of the world's unrighteousness, but the vast mass of the Western world was locked in an accepting piety, and the luminous sins of the popes and cardinals were a matter for gossip but not for radical rage. Throughout the Renaissance, with its political and personal immorality and its intellectual scepticism, Rome remained the centre of the Western world's religion. From this atmosphere of worship no pope could escape, and it became subtly interwoven in the Renaissance in Rome.

There is no need to follow the twists and turns by which the Papacy gradually re-established its dominion over the Patrimony or to describe how from time to time this was endangered by popes trying to create hereditary dominions for their children (Cesare Borgia, for example), a tendency which scores of Orsini and Colonna died bloody deaths to prevent. The treaties, battles, and plots have faded to near-oblivion; there remain, however, in all their greatness, the treasures of the Vatican, its library, its antiquities, its sculptures, its paintings. And the Vatican is but a fragment of Renaissance Rome; the *Laocoön* and the *Apollo Belvedere* belong to it as much as St Peter's or Via Giulia, for a reverence for her own past grew with her new delight in beauty.

The revival of Rome began, like the Renaissance itself, with litera-ture. The Italian Papacy, at the time of the Schism, had many Tuscans in its service, among them Poggio, one of the luckiest of the human-ists. After Petrarch's discovery of lost letters of Cicero the search for ancient manuscripts intensified, and Poggio's instinct seemed to lead him unerringly to his target like a pig to truffles. Perhaps he was more thorough, more remorseless than the rest; whatever the cause, his haul was prodigious. In the Swiss monastery of St Gall he unearthed the entire works of Quintilian; other highlights of his discoveries were the poems of Lucretius, discourses by Cicero, treatises on architec-ture by Vitruvius and on agriculture by Columella. The rich patrons of Italy rushed to buy them or to have them exquisitely copied and illuminated, for the competition to possess first-rate classical manu-scripts splendidly illuminated was as keen as that for French impres-sionists among present-day millionaires. Tommaso Parentucelli, the son of a surgeon, who became Nicholas v, was as addicted to books as the Borgia family was to women. 'What was unknown to Parentu-celli,' said Pius ii, 'lay outside the sphere of human learning.' He encouraged his secretaries to ransack old monastic libraries, and he employed an army of copyists. Terrified by the fall of Constan-tinople, he sent his emissaries scurrying to Greece and collected a few Greek codices at vast expense. He paid extravagant prices for the work of translation as well as for the books themselves: indeed, he offered ten thousand gold pieces for a fine translation of Homer. He employed the best of all classical scholars, Lorenzo Valla, who had proved some of the most hallowed documents in the papal Curia to be forgeries. As well as being a destructive scholar of genius, Valla was a satirist with the bite of acid, and his favourite targets were priests, monks, and cardinals. In fact, during the pontificate of Eugenius iv, Rome had been too hot for him. Nicholas v welcomed him and employed him. And, of course, the Pope created a fitting setting for his great library: the books were housed in the Vatican and exquisitely bound in red velvet with silver clasps. Philosophers, rhetoricians, poets, historians, philologists, grammarians, and teachers of Latin and Greek all were welcome in the new palace of the Vatican that Nicholas was creating, whether their work fortified or undermined the authority of the Papacy. Only a few setbacks marred the triumphant development which Nicholas had started. As with so many aspects of the Renaissance, Sixtus IV was also involved in the extension and adornment of the Vatican library. Even Alexander VI added to it, although his interest in learning, and it was a genuine one, expressed itself in the patronage of the University of Rome. Between them Nicholas and Sixtus laid the foundations, and secured some of the rarest treasures, of the greatest library in the Western world.

Although the reverence of most popes for the literature of antiquity was profound, their attitude towards the visible remains of ancient Rome was more haphazard. The collection of coins, of bronzes, and of statuary had been the cult of a few cardinals even as early as 1400; and naturally, as the fashion for antiquity spread, so did the desire to acquire genuine works of art of classical Rome and Greece. But the vast ruins of Rome were a different matter. The huge Palatine Hill, upon which had stood the immense palaces of the emperors, had become an incoherent mass of rubble – broken arches, paths, and masonry covered in sage and thyme and rosemary, crowned with olive trees, and grazed by sheep. It was a desolate, rural place – a paradise only for the meditative humanist brooding on the mortality of greatness. The Arch of Constantine was buried in ruins and covered by houses; the Colosseum was a mound of tumbled marble; everywhere there were broken columns, remains of theatres, circuses, stadiums; and medieval houses spread like weeds in and out over this ruined city. These crapulous vestiges of a glorious past were harder to cherish, and although an occasional pope paid lip service to the need for their preservation and issued Bulls for it, the majority plundered them for building materials or razed them to the ground for their new projects. Nicholas V removed 2,300 wagon-loads of marble from the Colosseum in a single year, as well as quarrying from the Circus Maximus, the Forum, the Arch of Titus, and the Temple of Venus. Even that great patron and connoisseur Sixtus IV took stones from ancient buildings and built a bridge across the Tiber from the masonry of the Colosseum. A few dedicated men, like the great architect Brunelleschi, dug and measured and drew the ancient buildings; but most men were drawn to them, like the robbers of the pyramids, by the hope of a lucky find, for the search for antiquities had revealed masterpiece after masterpiece of ancient art, culminating in 1490 in the discovery of the *Apollo Belvedere* in a Roman villa. Even if the great plundered the ruins or ignored them, there were humble scholars whom they fascinated, and the best of these was Ciriaco de' Pizzicolli, who wandered throughout the classical world, measuring, sketching, describing the visible remains of antiquity. Antiquarian studies, however, were largely confined to medals, coins, inscriptions, marbles, and bronzes, things which could be collected and displayed: there were, of course, not enough, and forgeries soon abounded, to the confusion and despair of posterity.

Although the popes had little wish to preserve, as in aspic, the ruins of Rome, they dearly desired to restore its architectural supremacy. The popes recovered a ruined city shrunk to a tiny area of Imperial Rome, and fields and orchards and wild, overgrown places abounded. Nicholas V, fortunately, possessed a touch of megalomania; fortunately, because size and space are vital principles of architectural splendour. He not only dreamed, but also planned, a vast new Rome, dominated by a new St Peter's, a new papal palace, and protected by an invincible Castel Sant' Angelo. The medieval popes had lived in the indefensible and oft-burned Palace of St John Lateran, but on their return from Avignon it was so ruinous that they had taken up residence in the Vatican Palace, which had been the guest palace for emperors and kings. Nicholas V sent for the great Florentine architects Rossellino and Alberti, men totally hostile to the Gothic, and as addicted as the Pope to classical antiquity. All the gold and silver of the West would scarcely have been sufficient for the multitude of churches, convents, monasteries, palaces, theatres, gardens, piazzas, towers, walls, and fortifications which they planned. The cost did not daunt the Pope. He tore down the ancient Roman temples near St Peter's and began slowly to lay the foundations of his new basilica. At his death the whole of what is now the Vatican City was scarred with trenches for the huge walls of his dreams. They were never fulfilled, but Sixtus IV, Alexander VI, Julius II, and Leo X completed the destruction of medieval Rome and created the new city of the Renaissance that was to prove worthy of him.

Sixtus IV, born in poverty, ruthlessly pursued greatness. Sensual, self-indulgent, decisive, an excellent administrator and generous patron, he is in many ways the most typical of Renaissance popes. He showered gold on his nephews (one of whom was to become pope as Julius II) and stopped short of no means to get his political ends. He helped to promote the Pazzi conspiracy and, in fury at its failure, placed Florence under the Interdict. His personal immorality gave rise to the wildest rumours; but the lack of restraint in the satisfaction of his appetites provoked an extravagance that was entirely beneficent for posterity. Not since the days of the emperors had Rome witnessed such junketings. Here is a description of the food at the banquet given by Sixtus when a bastard daughter of the King of Naples arrived in Rome to meet her future husband:

Before them were carried wild boars, roasted whole in their entire hides, bucks, goats, hares, rabbits, fish silvered over, peacocks with their feathers, pheasants, storks, cranes and stags; a bear in its skin, holding in its mouth a stick; countless were the tarts, jellies, candied fruits and sweetmeats. An artificial mountain was carried into the room, out of which stepped a livery-man with gestures of surprise at finding himself in the midst of such a gorgeous banquet; he repeated some verses and then vanished. Mythological figures served as covers to the viands placed on the table. The history of Atlas, of Perseus and Andromeda, the labours of Hercules were depicted

life size on silver dishes. Castles made of sweetmeats and filled with eatables
were sacked and then thrown from the loggia of the hall to the applauding
crowd. Sailing vessels discharged their cargoes of sugared almonds . . .

By such means, perhaps, Sixtus obliterated the memories of his
hungry youth, but many of his indulgences were less transitory. His
taste in building was as simple and as austere as his delight in food was
riotous and fantastic. He widened streets, constructed bridges, built
hospitals, erected churches, gave land to all who would build houses
and palaces. He encouraged his cardinals to foster the splendour of
Rome: the market was expelled from the Piazza Navona and the
building of its churches and palaces begun. There was scarcely a ward
of the city that Sixtus did not improve or adorn, but his greatest
glory is the chapel in the Vatican that bears his name. Utterly simple
in design, it served merely as a frame for its adornment, and for this
purpose Sixtus brought the best artists in Italy to Rome – Signorelli,
Botticelli, Perugino, Pinturicchio, Ghirlandaio, Rosselli. Later, in the
pontificate of Julius ii, who wished to complete his uncle's work,
these frescoes were dwarfed by the superb ceiling by Michelangelo,
for which the Sistine Chapel is so famous. Such, however, was the
galaxy of painters in Rome in the 1470s that they founded their own
guild, that of St Luke, which afterwards developed into the famous
academy. Although painters and sculptors and architects had been
patronized by the popes long before Nicholas v and Sixtus iv (Giotto
had created mosaics and painted frescoes for the old St Peter's, and
Fra Angelico had adorned many churches), yet with their pontifi-
cates papal patronage moved into a new dimension. It touched all
aspects of art and learning. Possessing great wealth and sublime
authority, many of the popes rose to the enormous visions of
Nicholas v. The Basilica of St Peter's – the work not of one but of a
plethora of geniuses: Alberti, Bramante, Raphael, Michelangelo,
Bernini – is the most impressive Christian monument in the world,
yet it is essentially a product of the Renaissance. The treasures of the

Vatican Palace – paintings, sculpture, antiquities, ancient manuscripts, and rare books – are incomparable, yet in 1420 the Papacy possessed no more perhaps than three hundred books, and scarcely any antiquities or pictures or statues of merit. To the sensual, warlike popes who ruled from 1471 to 1521 Rome owes a great deal of its present beauty.

What a strange gallery these popes make, yet essentially they are as much creatures of the Renaissance as Michelangelo's *Adam* or Donatello's *David*. The strangest of all is doubtless Alexander VI, whose name has become a byword for lust and cruelty. Certainly he was a man of strong, animal passions, driven remorselessly by his instincts. His attachment to his mistress, Vannozza, who bore him the terrible Borgia brood, was profound and life-lasting, no matter what other temporary indulgence he permitted himself. He loved his children to desperation, with a fierce physical passion. When one son was stabbed and thrown into the Tiber, probably by another son, Cesare Borgia, his grief astounded the cardinals whom he called to a consistory in order to bewail the loss of his child. So deep was his grief that, in tears, he swore not only to reform his own life, but also the Church's. His animal spirits, however, soon reasserted themselves, and his slavish devotion to his son Cesare became the bane of Italy when he resolved to create for him a great Italian kingdom. After spectacular victories in which, with French aid, Cesare overcame the great, seemingly impregnable fortresses of the Romagna, as well as Urbino, he seemed to Machiavelli to be the destined ruler of Italy. Machiavelli admired the way Cesare welcomed his enemies as friends and then neatly strangled them. By such stratagems were the Orsini obliterated. The speed, the decision, the timing of Cesare had an almost physical perfection. Yet, as in some Greek tragedy, the fates kept a bitter end in store. Before Cesare could consolidate his power, his father died; at the time he himself was prostrated with a loathsome and debilitating sickness. Stripped of power, he became a pawn of popes, kept on sufferance, banished to prison in Spain, and

Pope Julius II *carried by his Swiss Guards*
Cartoon by Raphael, Louvre

finally was killed in a brawl in Navarre. The life of Alexander's daughter, Lucrezia, was marked by a similar irony of fate. The Pope loved her with an almost incestuous passion. He heaped wealth on her; no delight was too sumptuous or too lascivious to be denied her. No husband was worthy of her charms: one was declared impotent by Papal Bull; one was assassinated. But Lucrezia lived on long after her father's death, her life threaded with tragedy and stultified by a wearisome piety that mocked her past. The depth and ferocity of the Pope's passion for his children have made him an ogre of history, making men forget his astonishing dignity, his overwhelming physical charm, and the immense presence as well as that animal vitality which made him as unwearying at work as at pleasure, and the bull his proper emblem. His irresponsible virility was scarcely in keeping with the tiara, but his pontificate was far from disastrous for the Papacy. He brought its temporal possessions more firmly under its control, and even though his intention to transfer these temporalities to his own family would, if realized, have ruined the Church, yet the possibility that this could be achieved was so remote that the success of Cesare merely redounded to the advantage of the Papacy.

That advantage was brilliantly exploited by Julius ii. Sixty years old when he was elected pope, he possessed the strength and decision of a man half his years. He loved action, hated the French, loathed the great Roman families, not one member of which he elevated to the purple, and detested the tyrants of Perugia and Bologna who usurped the temporal power of his Church. Defeat merely increased his energy, and in all his dealings this tough, thick-set priest was bold, decisive, and single-minded. His aim was the absolute independence of the Papacy from emperors, kings, or Romans, for without that temporal independence its claims to universality in a world of national states, he realized, would be meaningless. As in politics, so in art, Julius never vacillated. Nor did he play safe. Hearing of the abilities of the young Raphael, he sent for him from Florence, ordered him to obliterate paintings by Piero della Francesca, Signorelli, Perugino,

Sodoma, and the rest and to cover the walls of the rooms now known as the Stanze of Raphael with subjects of his own choice. The result is one of the great glories of Renaissance Rome. In architecture Julius showed the same sweeping vision, the same decisive action. He patronized Bramante, a man whose dreams were as grandiose as Julius could wish, accepted his colossal plans with alacrity, and taxed the faithful. Nor was it in any way surprising that Julius, who always stared life directly in the eye, should contemplate death with the same robust realism. Michelangelo's designs for his tomb entranced him; after all, it was the largest and most ornate mausoleum conceived in Europe since Theodoric's, but he could not bridle his impatience with the sculptor's slow progress, his creative doubts and endless reconsiderations, which drove the Pope to such furious quarrels that Michelangelo left Rome in anger and the project came to a standstill. Nor did reconciliation speed it forward – long after his death, a part of Julius' tomb went up in the little church of San Pietro in Vincoli; his bones lie in an undistinguished grave in the Vatican. Julius' furious spirit did not always meet such adamantine opposition.

The triumph of the Renaissance Papacy received its most splendid illustration in the coronation of Julius' successor – the young Giovanni de' Medici, son of Lorenzo, who became pope in 1513. at the age of thirty-seven. Bull-necked, pop-eyed, red-faced, he totally lacked the presence and ferocity of an Alexander VI or a Julius II. The cardinals in conclave had decided to avoid aggressive, virile temperaments. They had had enough of them. Leo x belied his name. Subtle, intuitive, sophisticated, he charmed with his generosity, affability, and sweetness of manner. Discretion veiled his private life, and his character and his education gave him a range of intellectual interests and sympathies not matched by a pope since Nicholas v. Bred in riches and nurtured in luxury, he had no compunction in using the wealth of the Church in splendiferous pageantry. Since the days of the emperors the Romans had never witnessed a procession comparable to his, as it made its way from the Vatican to St John

The Piazza del Campidoglio, Rome, designed by Michelangelo in 1538. Photo: Dmitri Kessel

Lateran. Cardinals and bankers vied with each other in the display of artistic treasures or the construction of ceremonial arches. Agostino Chigi erected an eight-column arch and festooned it with his best pictures and sculpture. Apollos, Ganymedes, Bacchuses, Minervas, Venuses, nymphs and dryads, emperors and princes, the best antiquities that Rome had to offer lined the Via Triumphalis, sharing it with the newly painted apostles and prophets of Christendom. The procession itself equalled its setting. Two hundred and fifty abbots, bishops, patriarchs, and cardinals were matched by the representatives of Italy's great families. The Gonzaga, Este, Sforza, Bentivoglio, Colonna, Orsini, Baglioni, nobles of Florence, patricians from Venice, knights from the Romagna, the Duke of Urbino in black velvet, Lucrezia Borgia's husband released from excommunication for the occasion, and the rebel Cardinal, Alfonso Petrucci, whom Leo, four years later, was to have executed, were set like jewels amidst chamberlains, standard-bearers, guards, and acolytes. On that day passions were buried, no stones were hurled, no angry shouts drowned the plainsong, no daggers flashed in the cruel sun. All paid homage to the fat, perspiring, red-faced Pope, clad in white, sitting side-saddle on his white palfrey. Eighty years earlier no pope could have risked his life and throne in such a spectacle.

Although Rome steadily increased in splendour, and the Pope's authority waxed majestic, violence, turmoil, and chicanery still threaded the papal annals with the scarlet of battle and murder. Enemies of papal power abounded: the French, the Spaniards, and the Milanese had found no resolution to their dynastic ambitions, and the Venetians had not given up their belief that security could only be achieved by raping the Church of its north-eastern temporalities. What was more, the wealth of the Church proved insufficient for its needs. Taxes grew grievous, the sale of indulgences more blatant. Across the Alps criticism of clerical worldliness, of monkish foolishness, of papal avarice, of Roman decadence, had often been sharp and prolonged. Under the stimulus of national needs, criticism developed a political and social purpose. And Luther, who might easily have met his end at the stake like another Savonarola, became the founder of a reformed Christianity that came to see the Pope as Antichrist and Rome as the whore of Babylon. The tribulations of the Reformation dimmed the lustre of the Papacy; yet the heretic Germans were remote and their future uncertain, and it was a more immediate tragedy that jolted the Romans and the Church out of the gilded sweetness of Medicean rule into a sterner, harsher world. In 1527 the soldiers of the great Habsburg ruler Charles V, whose dominions embraced the Spanish as well as the German Empire, sacked Rome efficiently, brutally, completely. After the death of Clement VII, another Medici who succeeded Leo X, the growing rift with Protestantism and the shock left by the devastation of Rome bred a sterner spirit in the Church and Papacy. The more flamboyant aspects of the Renaissance were suppressed: speculation went out of fashion; dogma was more sharply defined at the great Council of Trent; the Holy Office and the Index maintained its purity; the new order of Jesuits soon dominated the school and the confessional, and men of ruthless will and unbending morality sat on the throne of Saint Peter, marshalling and leading the resurgent forces of Catholicism. They deplored paganism; repressed the licentiousness of the Romans, religious and secular; insisted on sacred subjects in art and clapped fig leaves on the statues of antiquity. So great, however, was the impetus of the Renaissance that they could not stop it. For centuries Rome continued to grow in beauty, and became, as no other city, the embodiment of the arts, if not the spirit, of the Renaissance.

COMENTARIORVM
MAXIMI PRAEF

perio comminuitur · Qu
nominis gloriam querim
dulcedinem aliquam ha

POPE PIUS II

by Iris Origo

THE ROAD that winds up from the eleventh century *pieve* of Corsignano – roughhewn in the golden stone of the region and containing the font in which Aeneas Silvius Piccolomini was christened – to the perfect little Renaissance city of Pienza – named after Pope Pius II – is a short one. But the ascent it symbolizes was one unusually swift and high even in a period in which able men quickly made their mark – the ascent which led a clever country boy from a humble secretary's desk to Peter's throne. A shrewd statesman, an elegant humanist, an inquiring traveller – keenly addicted to the learning of the past, but equally alive to any new ideas or discoveries of his own time – witty and urbane, sceptical and adaptable, he might be considered an entirely typical figure of the Renaissance, had he not, at the very summit of his career, devoted his last years to a vast and impracticable idea which was more closely in harmony with the spirit of an earlier age: the last Crusade. To carry out this plan, he cast aside every obstacle suggested by expediency or prudence and certainly hastened, though well knowing that his scheme had failed, his own death.

Aeneas Silvius Piccolomini, the son of an impoverished country nobleman who had been a soldier of fortune, was born in 1405 in the little Tuscan village of Corsignano, on the bare, dust-coloured hills of the Val d'Orcia. A clever boy, he was sent by his father at the age of eighteen to Siena, the city which he called 'sacred to Venus'. There, while certainly not neglecting the charms of the beautiful Sienese women, he ardently pursued his legal studies with the celebrated jurist Sozzini, and later on continued his classical studies in

Florence with Filelfo. Too poor to buy all the books he needed, he would sit up at night copying out long passages from the volumes lent to him by his friends – once even setting his nightcap on fire, as he nodded over his work. Cicero, Virgil, Livy, these were his first models, and among the moderns, when first he began to write verse, Petrarch. His first glimpse of the efficacy of eloquence, when he saw the whole congregation of Siena swept off their feet by the sermons of the famous popular preacher St Bernardino, excited him so much that he pursued him to Rome, to ask whether he, too, should not follow the same path. But St Bernardino firmly dissuaded him, telling the future Pope to return to the worldly pursuits for which he was apparently more fitted.

It was thus not as a priest but merely as a young scholar with some legal training that Aeneas' career began. Cardinal Capranica, passing through Siena on his way to Basle to claim redress from the Ecumenical Council in his quarrel with Pope Eugenius IV, took him with him as his secretary – and in Basle the young man at once found ample scope for his talents. The Council – which had recently reaffirmed its supremacy even over the Pope, and which had the support of both the King of France and the Emperor Sigismund – was confronting two vast tasks, the destruction of heresy and the reformation of the Church. There Aeneas made the acquaintance of most of the great European prelates and observed their intrigues and counter-intrigues; he fostered the cynical detachment already inherent in his Tuscan blood; and he acquired the adaptability, the breadth of vision, and the persuasive eloquence which were to lead him to success. In his *Commentaries* he related, with disarming vanity, that he once held his audience so riveted by his words that for two hours no one even spat!

For twenty years he led a wandering life between Switzerland, Germany, and Austria. He was sent on missions all over Europe: to James I of Scotland – probably for the purpose of inciting fresh border-raids against England – to the Hussite heretics of Bohemia, and to the hermit-duke Amedeus of Savoy, whom he described as leading, in his luxurious hermitage on the Lake of Geneva, 'a life of pleasure rather than of penitence'. He became known in Germany as 'the apostle of humanism'. He accepted a post in the chancery of Frederick III, negotiated the marriage of the young Emperor to Eleonora of Portugal, and later went to meet the young bride and to escort her and her bridegroom to Rome. Ambition, he quite frankly admitted, was to his mind the chief spur to every human activity. But he also found time to make love to many pretty women (declaring chastity to be a philosopher's virtue, not a poet's, and sending home one of his bastards to be brought up by his father at Corsignano, 'so that another little Aeneas may climb on your and my mother's knees') and to write some scurrilous tales and a little satirical treatise on the miseries of life at court, as well as the poems which caused him to be crowned as poet by the Emperor. To all this he added a formidable list of more serious works, which included treatises on education, on rhetoric, on the Holy Roman Empire, and even on horses; histories of Bohemia, of the Goths, of the Council of Basle, of the Diet of Ratisbon, and of the Emperor Frederick III; and some *Lives of Illustrious Men* – and finally, after becoming Pope, the famous *Commentaries*.

It was not until the age of forty that he returned to Rome, obtained the forgiveness of Pope Eugenius IV, and conducted the negotiations which led to the reconciliation of the Papacy with the Empire – and it was only two years later, in 1447, that he at last took orders. After this, the speed of his preferment was remarkable. Within a year he became Bishop of Trieste and resumed his travels between Italy, Austria, and Bohemia; in 1449 he was made Bishop of Siena; in 1456 Calixtus III nominated him Cardinal of St Sabina; and two years later, in 1458, he was elected Pope.

Success comes most swiftly and completely not to the greatest or perhaps even to the ablest men, but to those whose gifts are most completely in harmony with the taste of their times. The Renaissance man admired versatility, scholarship, eloquence, diplomacy, and an inquiring and balanced mind; above all, he valued style, both in life and letters. All these were qualities possessed by the new Pope to a very high degree. '*Aeneam rejicite, Pium suscipite*' (Reject Aeneas and accept Pius), he wrote, with a harking-back to the Virgilian phrase which had also determined the choice of his new name – and it is certainly true that he abstained for good, after his ordination, from the loose living and scurrilous writings of his early years, and lived a life of great industry, sobriety, and benevolence. 'I do not deny my past,' he wrote to his friend John Freund, 'but we are old, nearer to death . . . I have been a great wanderer from what is right, but I know it, and I hope the knowledge has not come too late.'

He was not exempt from one fault of many other pontiffs: nepotism. Three members of his household (including his nephew Francesco) were given the cardinal's hat at the same consistory, another nephew, Antonio Piccolomini, was made commander of Castel Sant' Angelo, and his sisters were richly endowed with both money and palaces.

The fullest picture of his daily activities is to be found in the book which was the mirror of his times and of himself: his *Commentaries*. This is not only one of the most readable autobiographies ever written, but also a historical record of many of the important events of Pius' time, seen with a sharp eye and a ripe judgment, and enlivened by brilliant sketches of men and places, and by perceptive reflections on human nature. '*Nil habuit ficti, nil simulati*' – nothing was there in him of deceit or pretence, wrote one of his earliest biographers – and indeed this book carried these qualities so far that when it was first published in 1584 (during the Counter-reformation), it was thought necessary not only to prune it severely, but even to ascribe its authorship to its copyist, Gobellinus of Bonn, so that 'matters which the heretics gladly seize upon' should not come from a pope's pen. Now that the full text is again available, however, we are afforded an unvarnished picture of the Pope's contemporaries. It is not always flattering. He described the Florentines as 'traders, a sordid populace who can be persuaded to nothing noble'. When once Pius asked the Bishop of Orta what he thought of Florence and he replied that it was a pity that so beautiful a woman had not a husband, the Pope replied, 'She lacks a husband, but not a lover.' As though to say she had no king, but a tyrant, meaning Cosimo. Of the Bolognese he wrote: 'They are cruel rather than brave at home, while abroad they are known to be cowards,' and many pages were filled with attacks on the Venetians, who drew back from their promises of alliance against the Turks, while he said, 'They favoured the war against the Turks with their lips but condemned it in their hearts.' 'Glorious deeds,' the Pope said, 'are not embraced by democracies, least of all by merchants, who, being by their nature intent on profit, loathe those splendid things that cannot be achieved without expense.'

The tyrants of the Italian states were described with an equally sharp pen. Cosimo de' Medici, indeed, was admitted to be 'more lettered than merchants are wont to be', but Borso d'Este was depicted as 'listening to himself when speaking, as though he pleased himself better than he did others', and as a man 'whose mouth was full of flattery mixed with lies'. And Sigismondo Malatesta, for all his brilliance of mind, artistic sensibility, and military skill, was described as 'a man essentially pagan' and 'so avaricious that he never shrank not only from looting but from theft, so ruled by his passions that he raped his daughters and his sons-in-law. He surpassed all barbarians in cruelty'. The Pope publicly declared that, just as some holy men are canonized, so Sigismondo should be 'enrolled as a citizen of Hell'. On the steps of St Peter's his effigy was burned, bearing the inscription: 'Sigismondo Malatesta, son of Pandolfo, king of traitors, hated by God and man, condemned to the flames by the vote of the Holy Senate.'

It is when he is writing of the members of his own Curia, however, that Pius II's indictments are most startling. Shortly before his death he addressed a secret consistory of his cardinals: 'Like businessmen who have failed to pay their creditors, we have no credit left. The priesthood is an object of scorn. They say we live for pleasure, hoard up money, serve ambition, sit on mules or pedigree horses, spread out the fringes of our cloaks and go about the city with fat cheeks under our red hats and ample hoods, that we breed dogs for hunting, spend freely upon players and parasites, but nothing in defence of the Faith. Nor is it all a lie!'

Yet when Pius met true saintliness or valour, he was swift to recognize it. It was he who canonized St Catherine of Siena and who, in describing the entry into Vienna of the humble Franciscan friar Giovanni da Capistrano – 'with so tiny a body, so advanced in years, so dried up, exhausted, all skin and nerves and yet always serene' – at once recognized in him the attributes of a saint. He also gave a singularly detached and impartial account of the story of Joan of Arc, 'that astonishing and marvellous maid', ending with the comment, 'Whether her career was the work of God or a human invention we would not like to say.'

But where his regard was not awakened, no figure was so eminent as to escape his darts. He described James I of Scotland as 'smallish, hot-tempered, and greedy for vengeance', and said of his former master, the antipope Felix v, that when he appeared without his beard, he looked like 'an unsightly monkey'. Before the assembled Curia he referred to the Cardinal of San Marco as 'the buffoon of your Order', and to the brilliant, unscrupulous French Cardinal d'Estouteville of Rouen as 'a slippery fellow who would sell his own soul'. And here is his account of another prelate, Jouffroy, Cardinal of Arras – a man 'made mad by too much learning' – 'He wanted to seem devout and would say Mass, sometimes in the Basilica of St Peter's, and sometimes elsewhere. By face and gesture he would show how much he was carried away, drawing sighs from the bottom of his chest, weeping and, as it were, conversing with God. But before he had taken off his sacred vestments and left the altar he had cuffed one or another of his servants who had made some slight mistake in his ministration . . .'

His description, too, of the conclave by which he himself was elected Pope is as cynical as it is convincing. 'The men having most power in the College . . . summoned the others and demanded the Apostolate for themselves or for their friends. They implored, promised, threatened; some, even, without a blush and forgetting all modesty, spoke in praise of themselves . . .' Aeneas' chief rival was the Cardinal of Rouen, and many were the intrigues which took place in the latrines of the Vatican ('as being a private hiding place'). The French Cardinal openly distributed promises of honours and posts to those whose support he thought he could obtain, but the next morning Aeneas called in turn upon *his* friends – appealing to the loyalty of one prelate and the vanity or self-interest of another. In the end nine votes for him and six for the Cardinal of Rouen were dropped into the golden chalice. But still the required majority had not been obtained. For a while no man dared to commit himself. 'All sat in their places, silent, pale, as though they had been struck sense-less. No one spoke for some time, no one opened his mouth, no one moved any part of his body, except the eyes, which turned this way or that. The silence was astonishing, astonishing, too, the appearance of those men, as though you had found yourself among their statues . . . Then the Vice-Chancellor Rodrigo [the future Pope Alexander VI] rose and said, "I accede to the Cardinal of Siena!" And his words were like a sword through Rouen's heart . . .' Another followed him, but still one vote was lacking, that of the old, fat Cardinal Prospero Colonna. As he rose he was seized by each arm by the cardinals of Nicaea and Rouen, who tried to hustle him out of the room. But before they could do so, he shouted, 'I, too, accede to Siena, and I make him Pope!'

Pius II's *Commentaries*, however, will not now be read chiefly for their account of the intrigues of the Curia or of the politics of the

Italian states. What gives them their peculiar flavour is their revelation of the point of view of a Renaissance man. 'My spirit is an inquiring one,' Aeneas wrote of himself in his youth, and in this he never changed. As an antiquarian, his curiosity embraced Christian and pagan monuments alike. In England he admired the stained-glass windows of York Cathedral and the shrine of Saint Thomas à Becket in Canterbury, 'at which it is a crime to offer any metal less than silver', but he was no less interested in the translation of Thucydides in St Paul's Cathedral, and in being told that Newcastle was founded by Julius Caesar. In Hadrian's Villa he tried to reconstruct the origins of the ruins. On his visit to Federigo da Montefeltro, the Pope and condottiere discussed not the politics of the day, but the arms used in the Trojan War. On his way to the Congress of Mantua he turned aside to search for the labyrinth of Clusium described by Pliny, and visited the house called Virgil's Villa. Even in his last years, crippled with gout, he was carried in his litter to Tusculum, Tibur, and Falerii; he examined 'with great pleasure' the Roman ship recently dug up in the Lake of Nemi, and rowed down the Tiber to Ostia, speculating about the Latin name of the fine sturgeons he was given, and the site of one of the Roman palaces. At Albano he visited the old monastery of San Paolo, which its new owner, the Cardinal of Aquileia, had transformed into a fine villa surrounded by gardens, and the deserted church belonging to the Cardinal de Foix, which was 'without roof, altar, or doors' and served only as a stable for cattle and goats. 'These,' he dryly commented, 'are the Canons appointed by the Cardinal of Albano to perform God's service day and night.' With regard to the preservation of ancient monuments, however, his own conduct was somewhat inconsistent. When, on the Appian way, he found a man digging up some stones of the Roman pavement, he sharply rebuked him, bidding Prince Colonna never again to allow the public road to be touched, and he even issued a Bull forbidding the use of ancient columns and statues for making mortar. But he himself used, to build the Loggia della Bene-

dizione and the marble steps leading up to St Peter's, many fragments
from the Colosseum, the Forum, or the Baths of Caracalla, and he
constructed most of the great new fortress at Tivoli with material
from the amphitheatre of that city.

He was in some ways singularly free from the superstitious beliefs
of his time, rebuking Borso d'Este for 'heeding the pagan folly' of
his astrologers, and refusing, even after being racked with fever for
seventy-five days, to summon a magician who was 'said to have
cured of fever two thousand men in the camp of Niccolò Piccinino'.
But he told a Saxon student who asked him whether he knew of a
Mount of Venus in Italy, in which the magic arts were taught, that
'in Umbria . . . near the town of Nursia [Norcia], there is a cave
beneath a sharp rock, in which water flows. There, as I remember to
have heard, are witches, demons, and dark shades, and the man who
is brave enough can see and speak to the ghosts and learn the magic
arts.'

In his travels he always investigated eagerly, if sceptically, any
local legend or tradition. In Scotland he was fascinated by the legend
of the Barnacle Geese, which told 'of a tree growing on a river bank,
whose fruit rotted if it fell to the ground, but if it fell into water, it
came to life and turned into birds; but when he [Piccolomini] went
thither and made inquiries, eager for a miracle, he found that it was
a lie . . .' When he visited the slopes of Monte Amiata, he looked for
the herb called Carolina because, according to tradition, 'it was once
revealed by God to Charlemagne as a cure for the plague' and he
succeeded in finding it – 'a herb with prickly leaves which cling to
the ground and are set around a flower similar to that of a thistle'. He
added, however, 'Pius considered it a fable invented by Charlemagne's admirers.'

He had an observant eye, too, for the different sorts of men and
manners that he met upon his travels. In Scotland – where he spent
one night in a rough farmhouse, with the goats picking the straw out
of his pallet – he observed with interest that the white bread and wine

that he had with him were such rarities that 'pregnant women and their husbands drew near to the table, fingering the bread, sniffing the wine, and asking for a taste'. He noticed, too, that 'nothing gives the Scots more pleasure than to hear the English abused'. In Basle he was impressed by the well-built stone houses and well-kept gardens, with fountains 'as numerous as those of Viterbo', and in Vienna – according to his *Life of Frederick III* – by the comfortable dining-halls with stoves and glass windows, where songbirds were kept, as well as by the fine churches and spacious cellars. He even described a convent for the redemption of penitent prostitutes, 'who sing hymns in the Teutonic language day and night. . . . But if one of them is caught sinning again, she is cast into the Danube'. But he also complained of the rough German table manners, of a court in which any falconer or stable-boy was more welcome than a scholar, and above all, of the gross drunkenness. He described how Heinrich, Count of Gorizia, would wake up his two little boys by a virtuous Hungarian lady in the middle of the night to pour wine down their throats. When the sleepy children spat it out, he turned upon his wife, shouting, 'Strumpet, these brats are none of mine!'

Perhaps the most delightful passages in the *Commentaries*, as in Pius' letters, are those which reflect his passion for natural beauty. He might, indeed, be considered, with Petrarch, the first of the Romantic travellers. At Viterbo he went out almost every day at dawn 'to enjoy the sweet air before it grows hot and to gaze at the blossoming sky-blue flax'. At Bolsena he insisted on being rowed out to the islands in the lake, and whenever possible, he preferred to hold his consistories out of doors, especially in the great beech woods of Monte Amiata, 'beneath this tree or that, and also by the sweetly running stream . . . Sometimes it happened that as the Pope was signing documents the dogs flung themselves upon some huge stag hiding nearby, which would drive them back with its horns or its hoofs and make off with all speed for the mountains'. Often, too, he picnicked with his Curia in a meadow or poplar grove – though whether his cardinals, mostly elderly and urban gentlemen, enjoyed this habit is not related. One evening, as the Pope was returning home through some meadows, a cowherd, 'seeing the golden litter carried by its porters and surrounded by horsemen . . . milked a cow that was near him and, full of joy, offered to the Pope the bowl which he used for eating and drinking, filled to the brim with milk . . . Pope Pius . . . was not too proud to put his lips to the black and greasy bowl.'

One of Pius' most endearing traits was his simple enjoyment of homely pleasures: the cheese of Monte Oliveto, 'which Tuscans consider the best in the world', the fresh trout which he saw caught on the Monte Amiata, and the engaging antics of his sister's baby. He even devoted a whole page to the misadventures of his poor little puppy, Musetta, who first fell into a cistern full of water and, when rescued at the last gasp, 'was taken to the Pope, to whom she continued to whimper for a long time as if she wanted to tell him about her danger and stir his pity', but then was bitten by a large monkey, and finally, having climbed up on a high window sill, was seized by a violent gust of wind and dashed upon the rocks. The Pope sadly commented that, like some men, she was plainly fore-destined to a violent end.

He described with relish the horse and foot races in Pienza, where a small and beardless grown-up slave inserted himself among the boys and defeated a little boy from Pienza, 'with fair hair and a beautiful body, though all bedaubed with mud, who . . . bewailed his fortune and cursed himself for not having run faster. His mother was there, a handsome woman, comforting her child with gentle words and wiping off his sweat with a towel.' 'The Pope and cardinals' – so ends this chapter – 'watched from a high window with no small merriment, though in the intervals they were busy with affairs of state.'

The occasion of these events was the inauguration of the cathedral and palace which the famous Florentine architect Bernardo Rossellino had built at Corsignano – now renamed Pienza – as a summer residence for the papal court. The little city is still as perfectly harmonious a work of art as the early Renaissance has produced – the cathedral being flanked on one side of a little paved square by the papal palace, and on the others by the episcopal palace and town hall. Some smaller palaces were built nearby for the cardinals and their courts. The cost, however, was so much higher than the original estimate that everyone expected the architect to be cast into prison. But the Pope, after inspecting the buildings, sent for him and said: 'You did well, Bernardo, to lie to us about what this undertaking would cost us. Had you spoken the truth, you had never persuaded us to spend so much money, and this fair palace and this church, the loveliest in all Italy, would never have existed. . . .We thank you, and we consider you deserving of special honour.' And he issued a Bull forbidding the defacing of any of the church's walls or pillars, the building of any other chapels or altars, or any other change that might mar the church's perfect symmetry. 'If any do otherwise, may he be anathema and absolvable only by the authority of the Bishop of Rome, except in the hour of death.'

This happy return to his native city was perhaps the last carefree incident of the Pope's life. His remaining years were obsessed by a single idea: the coercion of the reluctant princes of Christendom to fight against the Turks.

It is not difficult – even without attributing to Pius II the religious fervour of an Urban II or a Saint Catherine – to understand his motives. He was well aware of how closely Hungary and Austria, and beyond them Italy herself, were threatened by the rising ambition of that astute and designing sultan, Mohammed II. His historical imagination was intensely conscious of the ancient traditions of the Holy Roman Empire, and of the Papacy as the saviour of Christendom. And as he himself would have been the first to admit, his sense of drama was fired by the image of himself as the central figure in the most significant of all wars, once again leading princes and peoples against the Crescent in the name of the Cross.

Long before his accession, Aeneas had tried to awaken the European princes to the Turkish menace. At the coronation of Frederick III he had pointed out that Hungary had become the last bulwark of Christianity, and when Constantinople fell he was among the first to realize that henceforth the doors of Europe would always remain open to the Turk. 'I see faith and learning,' he wrote, 'destroyed together.' Aeneas implored both the Emperor and the Pope, Nicholas V, to convoke a European congress at which the princes would agree to a truce with each other, 'and turn their arms instead against the enemies of the Cross'. A Diet was actually held at Ratisbon, at which the few delegates who came voted for the Crusade, but only a few months later, when another congress was held in Frankfurt, most of them had already changed their minds. 'They would not listen to the names of Emperor or Pope, but said they were deceivers and greedy men, who wanted to make not war but money.' Aeneas was still struggling to persuade them to confirm their promises, when the sudden death of the Pope 'rent the web that had been so long in weaving'.

Immediately after his accession Pius returned to the charge. He summoned another congress at Mantua and, though crippled by gout and suffering from stone and bronchitis, decided to attend it himself. 'It is all-important,' he had written, 'that a war should begin well, for the end of a war is often implicit in its beginnings.' Certainly the beginning of this one foreshadowed its failure. The Pope set forth for Mantua with most of his cardinals, but when he arrived there, he found himself almost alone. His court implored him to go home again. Had they been brought here, they asked, to discuss a Crusade with the Mantuan frogs? Messengers from Thomas Palaeologus of the Morea (the southern part of the Peloponnesus) brought desperate appeals for help, but there were few to listen to them. The Duke of Burgundy now said that he was too old to come. The King of France, exasperated by the Pope's recent support of the accession to the Kingdom of Naples of Ferrante of Aragon, sent word that he could join no Crusade so long as he was still at war with England. England – torn by the Wars of the Roses – sent a similar message. Frederick III was engaged in invading the Kingdom of Hungary, while the envoys of that country - which alone, in the recent past, had defended Europe against the Turks – bitterly complained of this new menace. No single voice was raised to echo the old Crusading cry: '*Deus lo vult* – it is God's will!' Of the Italian rulers, Borso d'Este declared that his astrologers forbade him to attend; Malatesta suggested the employment of Italian mercenaries, but only to get their pay for himself. The Florentines and Venetians both feared the loss of their eastern trade, but Venice promised to furnish sixty galleys, if every expense was paid from the general treasury and she was given the supreme command of the naval forces and awarded the spoils of the war. 'To a Venetian,' the Pope commented, 'everything is just that is good for the State; everything pious that increases the Empire.'

Yet when at last he was in the presence of those envoys who did come, the Pope showed much of his old fire. He had learned to conceal his physical pain so well that it was only revealed by his yellow colour and drawn features and by an occasional compression of his lips. The French, in return for their participation, demanded the reestablishment of the Angevin rule in Naples, and believed that the Pope's illness would at once cause him to yield. But he declared; 'Though I should die in the middle of the assembly, yet shall I reply to that proud-stomached delegation!' Speaking with as much eloquence and energy as in his youth, his cough ceased, and the colour returned to his old cheeks. Even his most bitter opponents admitted that he had 'spoken like a Pope'. Moreover, in an attempt to shame the princes into following his example, he declared that he himself would lead the Crusade. 'We can be borne in Our litter to the camp.' On 14 January 1460 the Holy War was formally declared, and, discouraged but not defeated, the Pope started on his long journey home.

Before actually embarking on the Crusade, however, Pius II made one last curious effort to come to terms with the infidel – one which, if successful, might well have changed the course of European history. In a long and eloquent letter he attempted to convert the Sultan Mohammed II to Christianity. If he accepted baptism, the Pope wrote, a second Roman Empire might arise in the East, with Mohammed at its head. Pius reminded the Sultan that Clovis had brought Christianity to the Franks, and Constantine to the Romans; he depicted a Europe once more united and, for the first time in centuries, at peace. The epistle – which now reads more like a fine literary exercise than a political document – was widely circulated in Europe, but whether it ever even reached the Sultan is not known. Certainly no reply was ever received in Rome.

It was now plain that the Turks could be conquered only by arms. In a last attempt to arouse the Roman people the Pope decided to display to them – in what Gregorovius calls 'one of the most curious scenes of the Roman Renaissance' – a singularly precious relic: the skull of the Apostle Andrew, which the exiled Despot of the Morea, Thomas Palaeologus, had brought to him – 'the symbol of the Empire of Constantine and Justinian, and of the Church of Origen and Photius'. Three cardinals, who had gone to fetch the head at Narni, were met at the Ponte Molle by the Pope and the other cardinals, and after a solemn *Te Deum* they accompanied it in procession to St Peter's. 'It was a splendid spectacle,' Pius wrote, 'to see those old men walk on foot through the mud holding palms in their hands and wearing mitres on their white heads . . . Some who till then had lived delicately and could hardly move a hundred paces except on horseback, on that day . . . walked two miles through mud and water with ease.' All along the route, windows were hung with tapestries and lit up with torches and oil lamps; altars were set up at street corners, branches of fragrant shrubs were set alight. 'Any man who possessed paintings or a fine and lifelike statue displayed them in the portico before his door.' Little stages were set up, on which children, dressed as angels, sang or played musical instruments.

Finally, on reaching St Peter's, the Pope stood at the top of the marble stair before the church and displayed the head to the assembled crowd, renewing his own vow to the Apostle 'to recover thy sheep and thy dwelling-place on earth', and calling upon God to deliver Christendom from the Turks. 'Then there arose a great sound, like the murmur of many waters.'

In the following spring, since the Turkish army was engaged in Bosnia, the Venetians, who had concluded an alliance with Hungary, decided that the moment was propitious to send off their own fleet to the Peloponnesus. ' *We* are already at war,' they declared. Pius had no illusions about the Venetian motives, but, as he pointed out to the Florentine envoys, even though the Venetians were 'seeking the Peloponnesus and not Jesus . . . if Venice is victorious, the Church will be victorious. . . . This war is our common war.' Moreover, at just this moment, a most fortunate event had come to strengthen the Pope's hand. In the wooded hills of Tolfa, which were within the Patrimony, some mines of alum, the precious dye until then imported from Turkey, were discovered. This Pius declared to be a miracle, and at once set aside all its profits for the Crusade. On 22 October 1463 he issued the Bull *Ezechielis*, repeating his determination to lead the troops of Christendom himself. 'In our spirit, old as it is, and in our sick body there is a determination to make war upon the Turks.'

Already, however, he realized that many of his allies had failed him – in particular Francesco Sforza of Milan, Louis XI of France, and his vassal the Duke of Burgundy. The Venetian troops in the Peloponnesus had been swiftly defeated by the Turks and their commander killed. The only troops to reach Ancona were a handful of unscrupulous adventurers, greedy for gain and loot. The Archbishop of Crete was appointed to weed them out, rejecting all those who had neither arms nor money.

Nevertheless, on 14 June 1464, in a solemn ceremony at St Peter's, the Pope took the Cross, and four days later, so ill that he had to be carried on to his barge, he set forth. Turning back at the Ponte Molle for a last glimpse of Rome, he bade his city farewell, declaring, 'You will never see me alive again.' In all the history of the Crusades there are few episodes more pathetic than this journey of the dying Pope up the Tiber and across the Apennines – well aware that his enterprise was doomed. Often, as they drew near the coast, his attendants would draw the curtains of his litter, so that he might not see the bands of deserters who, scenting the prospect of defeat, were fleeing home before they had even begun to fight.

When the Pope reached Ancona, no Venetian ship was to be seen, and day after day, from the windows of the bishop's palace at the summit of the town, Pius scanned the Adriatic in vain for the galleys of St Mark. The city was now short of food and water and a pestilence had broken out, and the Pope himself was wasting away with dysentery.

When at last, on 12 August, the Doge Cristoforo Moro sailed in with twelve ships, Pius was too ill to receive him. 'Until now,' he said, 'it was a fleet that was lacking. Now the fleet has come, but I shall not be there.' Two days later, feeling his end to be near, he summoned to his bedside the prelates who had come to Ancona with him, gave them his blessing, and told them that he was leaving them to finish what he had begun. Then, left alone with his nephew, his secretary, and his old friend Cardinal Ammanati, he once again exhorted the latter not to draw back. 'Urge my brothers to go on with the Crusade . . . Woe befall you if you draw back from God's work.' Asking for his friend's prayers, he lay back and died before the dawn.

On the next day his body was carried to the cathedral, where the Doge pronounced a long and insincere oration over it and then at once set sail for Venice, while the cardinals hurried back to Rome to elect a new pope. The last Crusade was over, with the death of the only man who had believed in it.

VENICE: THE GOLDEN YEARS

O N Ascension day, 997, Doge Pietro Orseolo stayed his galleon in the great sea-gateway that joins the Venetian lagoon with the Adriatic, poured a libation on the sea, and received the blessing of his Patriarch before he sallied forth to annihilate the Dalmatians. For eight hundred years that ceremony was repeated, growing in complexity and splendour as Venice herself grew rich and powerful, until it became one of the great ritual pageants of the Western world. The huge state barge of the doges, the *Bucentaur*, ablaze with crimson and cloth of gold, drew away from the Piazzetta to the chants of massed choirs. The Council of Ten, the Signory, the patricians and ambassadors, followed in their gilded gondolas. At the Porto di Lido the Doge, standing on the poop of the *Bucentaur*, cast a golden ring into the waters, declaring 'O sea, we wed thee in sign of our true and ever-lasting dominion.' The mixture of paganism, Christianity, and Orien-tal splendour was as symbolic of Venice as the marriage to the sea.

The sea linked Venice with Byzantium, the market for her goods, the protector of her liberties, the model of her state, the teacher of her crafts, the fountain of her arts. Under Byzantium's protecting wing Venice had grown to greatness, great enough to rend and despoil the Empire in the Fourth Crusade, yet not great enough to save the imperial city in its days of crisis when, in 1453, the surge of the Turkish hordes overwhelmed it. The loss proved grievous, but not disastrous, for by that time the sources of Venetian power were scattered throughout the seas of the Western world.

Venice lived by her ships. Thanks to them, the desolate mud flats had flowered in stone. To this strange water-borne city they brought riches, power, and security. Only twice in its history did enemy vessels sail into the waters of the Venetian lagoon, and both times the enemy was annihilated. To the landward its defences proved equally inviolate. The Venetians made their ships in the great Arsenal that was the wonder of Europe in the Middle Ages. Its two miles of forbidding fortifications enclosed the most formidable armoury in the Renaissance world. Thousands of workmen toiled there, and a new galley was produced every hundred days. These ships could be commissioned with amazing alacrity. From the Arsenal to the lagoon the ships moved as on a conveyer-belt – masts, sails, oars, stores, and weapons were quickly loaded as the vessel slowly passed each storehouse. Most fittings on each galley were standardized, so that replacements could be stored in all Venetian warehouses, whether they might be in Southampton or Tyre; any crew could be moved to any ship without further training, or a fresh crew could be made up from survivors in battle. And every galley, whether used in commerce or in war, belonged to the state: no patrician, no matter what his wealth might be, could possess a Venetian galley. Such precise regimentation, such absolute control, gave Venice its pre-eminence over its rivals and enabled it to ship a crusading army to the Holy Land without overstretching its resources. The other maritime powers of Italy hated the supremacy of Venice. Genoa ruined herself in a long and desperate war, which ranged from the Bosporus to the lagoon itself, in an attempt to crush Venice and despoil her of the riches which her great fleet carried for her merchants. By 1400 Venice had proved herself invincible; indeed, she had become the centre of a sea-borne empire. Zara, Ragusa, Crete, and many Aegean Islands belonged to her absolutely: trading communities, enjoying extraterritorial privileges, had been established in Constantinople, Acre, Tyre, Sidon, Alexandria. Venetian merchants were as familiar with the Black Sea as the Adriatic; her ambassadors were to be found in Isfahan and in

Cairo; her travellers, stimulated by the stories of Marco Polo, reached Sumatra and Ceylon long before Vasco da Gama rounded the Cape. And even though the Venetians never ventured to such far-flung places as the Genoese at the height of their greatness, their contacts with the East were more stable, more secure, and made up in volume for what they might lack in diversity.

By 1450 Venice was the only power in Italy, save for the Papacy, that was truly cosmopolitan, one whose interests required not only a great fleet but also a complex intelligence system. Venice needed to know the intentions of the Shah of Persia, the Count of Flanders, the Sultan of Cairo, the King of France, or the Duke of Ferrara. And every merchant, every priest was expected to spy for his country's good. The Signory knew at once the deepest secrets of the most carefully guarded conclaves of the Papacy, for the patriarchs of Venice put loyalty to the state higher than the command of the Church. The carefully, beautifully written, well-informed, judicious reports of the Venetian residents in London, Paris, or Bruges now form some of the most reliable sources not only for the history of Venice, but also for the

Reception of a Venetian Ambassador in Cairo,
by a follower of Gentile Bellini, Louvre

Fourteenth-century trader's arithmetic book
Coll. Thomas Marston, New Haven

history of England, France, and the Netherlands. In the great building of the Archivio Centrale, next to the Frari church, is the greatest collection of archives ever accumulated by a single city. Altogether this contains approximately a quarter of a million books, documents, and parchments. For the fourteenth and fifteenth centuries there is a multitude of papers, a plethora of facts, a pyramid of accounts, still awaiting the toil of the historian. The reason for it all lies in the attitude and methods of the famous, or infamous, Council of Ten who, throughout the Renaissance, were the absolute rulers of the most highly organized state west of Byzantium.

The Council of Ten believed in knowledge, in facts: nothing was too trivial, too remote. They were as interested in the words and actions of a shopkeeper in the Campo di Santa Maria Formosa as in the gossip of the harem at Samarkand. So voracious was their desire to pry that, throughout Venice, they set up the famous Lions' Mouths by which Venetians could inform the Council anonymously of their suspicions of their neighbours. On this knowledge the Council acted swiftly and silently, for no public trials enlivened the Venetian scene, and there were no appeals. Once found guilty, the prisoner was sometimes quickly and efficiently strangled in the dungeons; or thrown into a part of the lagoon reserved for the purpose, where no fishing was allowed; or hanged by one leg from the pillars of the Doge's Palace; or quartered and distributed about the city; or buried upside down in the Piazzetta; legs protruding; or beheaded – as a public spectacle – between the great pillars on which stand St Theodore with his crocodile and the winged lion of St Mark. That was how the great condottiere Carmagnola met his end, when the Council discovered that he was prepared to sell Venice to her enemies. But most traitors went silently in the night, their broken bodies sending a shiver of horror through the waking city as dawn gilded the palaces and churches.

This formidable engine of government ruled with equal efficiency all departments of the state – finance, diplomacy, the navy, the army, the welfare of the city – and it would tolerate no real rivals. In the last resort the safety of the state, for which the Ten were responsible, overrode all other considerations. The powers of the Doge had been so ruthlessly suppressed (he could not even display his own armorial bearings) that he had become a mere ceremonial idol – a figure for pageants and formal acts of state. The Church, too, bowed to the state. No bishop, no parish priest, could officiate in Venice unless Venetian born. When placed under the Interdict by Pope Sixtus IV, the Patriarch fell discreetly ill, and the Council told the clergy that they would treat as a traitor any priest who refused to celebrate the offices of the Church. The clergy ignored the Interdict. During the most savage years of the Counter-reformation, the Council protected the historian Sarpi, whom good Catholics regarded as little better than a Lutheran. In Venice there were no divided powers. Its immense wealth and its colossal maritime power were ruled with the iron will of a modern dictatorship. Unbridled capitalism might flourish on the Rialto, but the Doge's Palace was close cousin to the Kremlin.

The Council of Ten did not consist of permanent rulers. Its powers, if not its final authority, were partly shared by the Collegio or Cabinet; and beyond these there was a more numerous body still – the Senate or Signory from which the councils were appointed. No one, however, by a decree of 1297, could sit on these bodies unless his ancestor had been a member of the Great Council between 1172 and 1297. In 1319, in order to make certain that the purity of this oligarchy should be maintained, the heraldic officers of the republic drew up the famous Golden Book, the *Libro d'Oro*, as a perpetual studbook of Venice's aristocracy. This revolution, for it was nothing less, deprived the mass of Venetians of all the political rights they had possessed. The murmurs and rebellions against it were quickly and ruthlessly suppressed, and, by the Renaissance, the patrician families of Venice were as secure in their political and social power as the English aristocracy of the eighteenth century. A patrician's life was not, however, one of gilded leisure. The aristocrats were expected to officer the fleets; trade was not regarded as ignoble; and the far-flung Venetian possessions required patricians for their government. Like the guardians of Plato's republic or the proconsuls of British India, these men were expected to lead lives dedicated to the state. Power and prestige might be theirs, but undeviating loyalty, exemplary courage, and unflagging generosity were the price they paid. If they aspired to the Doge's throne, they were aware of the risks, the dungeons, and the strangler's silent visit; if they sought glory in battle, their spirit was steeled by the grim epics of Venice's history – Admiral Dandolo, who bashed out his brains against the timbers of his galley the night the Genoese defeated him, or the neatly folded skin of Admiral Bragadino, flayed from his living body by a sportive pasha. Such is the dulcet beauty of Venice, with its time-eroded buildings swathed in the opalescent light of the lagoon, that it is all too easy to forget the stern, unyielding, harsh, and dedicated spirit that inspired its rulers in their days of greatness.

Venice, however, was Janus-faced. Her commerce might be regimented, her aristocracy disciplined and controlled, her people subjected, yet she was cosmopolitan as no other city in Europe was. The crowded wharves of the Rialto and the Riva degli Schiavoni saw Gentile and Jew, Moslem and Greek, haggling over rich cargoes from the Orient. The Germans possessed a vast warehouse – decorated with frescoes by Giorgione – on the Grand Canal; the Turks, another, which had been the palace of the Pesaro family. Venice possessed the earliest ghetto in Europe, and the Armenians followed their religion for centuries without fear of the Inquisition. All the nations of Europe mingled with the races of the Near East. They were brought together by the simple fact that Venice was the greatest market of the Western world. Anything could be bought and sold in Venice, but the principal commerce was in luxuries – in spices, slaves, gold, silver, glass, silks, damasks, jewels – cargoes that were small in bulk but huge in worth. Throughout the barbarian times, when Venice grew to greatness, Europe lacked the sophisticated skills and crafts that were commonplace in the Eastern Empire, or in Syria and Egypt; and in return for products from these places, Venice could offer the cheap raw materials that a primitive Europe produced – hides and tin from England, fine cloth from Flanders, raw silver from Bohemia, copper and steel from Germany. And there were the pilgrims. Decade after decade, century after century, in peace or in war, rich and devout Christians won their way to heaven via the Holy Places, to the great profit of the Venetians. For centuries the Crusaders warred in the eastern lands, and the Crusaders paid; paid for themselves, their armies, their horses, their necessities – and Venetians did not believe in bargains. In spite of their great wars – against the Genoese, the Greeks, the Turks – Venice waxed rich: rich on man's craving for luxury, for ostentation, for self-indulgence, on the pride of life and the lust of the eye. All the skills that she encouraged were luxury crafts rather than industries. The glass manufacture of Murano, based on secrets learned in the East, was guarded by the Council of Ten: for any workman with the knowledge of its manufacture to leave Venice was an act of treason. The Council hunted him down and killed him. Along with the monopoly in glass went another – the making of mosaic: this art, derived from Byzantium, was practised only in Venice. Venetian jewellers had no rivals in the late Middle Ages, and emperors and kings sent there for their crosses and sceptres. Few Italian cities could rival Venice in the splendour of its silks, and none in the beauty of its lace. In Venice everything was for sale – love along with the rest. She boasted more courtesans than Rome. Their charges were carefully catalogued, and they were incomparable in skill as in price. They, too, had their rivals; the competition from homosexuals was so severe that the harlots complained loudly to the Council of Ten. As the wealth and prosperity of Europe lifted, so the riches of Venice soared.

On the threshold of the Renaissance, Venice possessed an unrivalled trade, and a stable and immensely powerful government firmly in the hands of its patricians. It was a city of hatchet-faced merchants. Jacopo Loredan entered in his great ledger: 'The Doge Foscari: my debtor for the death of my father and uncle.' After Foscari had been

Glass bowl
Toledo Museum of Art

harried to death and his son killed, Loredan wrote on the opposite page, 'Paid.' In 1450 that was the spirit of Venice. By 1550 a gentler, softer, more self-indulgent atmosphere had turned Venice to a city of carnival: still strong, still rich, still capable of sacrifice, but essentially an empire in defence, wishing for a secure isolation in which to enjoy her immoderate riches. And this change was brought about partly through a change in strategy – itself the result of the growth of the Renaissance state – and partly through the spirit of the Renaissance itself.

Safe in the security of the lagoon, the strategic problems of Venice had been largely distant and maritime. Her diplomacy had been directed solely to the pursuit of trade, and the acquisition of territory had been subordinate to these ends. Throughout the High Middle Ages the Venetians had excluded themselves from Italy (sometimes they hinted that they owed allegiance not to the West but to the Greek Emperor at Byzantium), but when it suited their purpose they forgot the East and made a token gesture to the Emperor of the West. So successful had this policy been that many influential doges and patricians regarded it as the foundation of Venice's glory. They felt that any deviation would ruin the state, and the deviation that they most feared was that the government would succumb to those who demanded that Venice should extend her frontiers on the mainland and take her place as a great power in Lombardy. The problem was one that all expanding commercial empires were to face: Did the needs of commerce require the political control of its channels? So long as the plain of Lombardy was divided up between a multitude of petty powers, Venice had little to fear, but in the fourteenth century the dominant powers in northern Italy became fewer and fewer, and the danger of their enmity was brought home to the Venetians when Carrara, the despot of Padua, joined with the Genoese in the war that Venice saved on the very threshold of defeat by winning the great battle of Chioggia in the lagoon itself. The safety of the lagoon, let alone Venetian trade, depended upon the control of the great rivers –

the Brenta and the Piave – that had cost the republic huge sums to canalize and divert from the lagoon. Beyond the rivers were the easy Alpine passes, particularly the Brenner, through which Venetian trade flowed to Northern Europe. And there were subtler motives at work – everywhere in Italy small city-states were going down like ninepins through the onslaught of Milan, Florence, Rome, Naples, and if the Venetians wished to be heard in the councils of Italy, they needed to acquire far more Italian territory than a few muddy islands and river mouths in a shallow lagoon. Finally, after the defeat of Genoa and before the collapse of Constantinople, Venice had plenty of money and plenty of young aristocrats ready for a venture.

Although the debate, particularly at the time of Doge Foscari, seemed bitter and prolonged, Venice was drawn inevitably into the vortex of Italian politics and war. Once embroiled, strategic needs forced her to push her frontiers ever westward and southward against Milan and Rome. Her vicissitudes were many, but her successes built up like a coral reef which, no matter how frequently it is submerged, continues to grow. There were years of danger, particularly when Venice struggled single-handed to keep the Turks confined to the eastern Mediterranean; there were even darker days when all the princes of Italy combined with her enemies in the League of Cambrai to ruin her. But Venice triumphed. Her frontiers stretched from Lake Como in the west to Trieste in the east, from the high Alpine valleys in the north to Ferrara in the south. And these rich territories were ruled with wisdom and restraint. No local customs were violated, no local law abrogated, no families uprooted. About all that the republic did there was a hardheaded, bourgeois realism. The possession of Verona, Vicenza, Padua, Bergamo, Brescia, Treviso, and the rest added enormously to Venetian wealth in spite of the cost of the wars their capture entailed.

The patricians found they could tap the riches of the *terraferma*, as they called the Lombard plain, far more easily than they could the Oriental trade, rich as it was. The Turks were in Constantinople, and the frequent, costly, and bloody struggles that resulted made eastern trade more difficult and more uncertain than it had been in the time of the Greek emperors. That trade had always entailed risks, from pirates, shipwreck, or the hazards of the sea, but money in farms on the rich alluvial plains of the mainland brought in a high, steady return. In addition, there were choice opportunities in the captured towns – real estate, banking, insurance, partnerships in trade and industry – yet it was the land that attracted the Venetians. For centuries their rich families had built their villas and landscaped their gardens on the Giudecca and Murano. There, in the summer evenings, they had escaped from the heat and stink of Venice for their *fêtes champêtres;* for the music and dalliance that are so brilliantly portrayed by Giorgione and Titian. But tenements and warehouses crept along the Giudecca; Murano was eaten up by the ever-expanding glass works, so the lovely sweeping curves and gentle slopes of the valley of the Brenta or the wilder hills of Cadore drew the Venetian aristocracy to the rustic but sophisticated life of the countryside. There Palladio built the most exquisite villas in the Western world, villas that were to inspire the architects not only of eighteenth-century England, but also the planters of Virginia. Their walls were painted by Veronese and by Tiepolo; their owners' portraits by Titian or Tintoretto. Here they created an indulgent Arcadian life that stood in harsh contrast to the battle-scarred days of Venice's heroic growth. As ever, the strength of merchants was sapped by the delight in being landed gentlemen.

The same spirit was at work in Venice itself; the city had become stuffed and bloated with possessions. Although it proved tenacious still, in clinging to what it had, it grew ever more indifferent to adventure. No Venetian galleys probed the secrets of the New World; no hard-headed merchants sought gold in tropical Africa. Perhaps it is not surprising that the early, exploratory, heroic phase of the Renaissance passed Venice by. Only, as it were, when the market in Renaissance goods was established did Venice enter it, but then she did so with a *panache* and a brilliance all her own. And furthermore, her proud independence and her utter indifference to the ideological strife of the sixteenth century enabled the spirit of the Renaissance to flourish long after it had been strangled elsewhere in Italy. Venetians, by the very nature of their experience in life, were quick to adopt technical improvements or to exploit the commercial possibilities of artistic development. The Flemish discovery in oil paintings was quickly adopted by Venetian artists; the market for bronzes after the antique was flooded by Venetian craftsmen; family portraiture was a commonplace in Venice while it was unusual elsewhere. Whenever the calculating eye of the Venetian entrepreneur saw a main chance, he seized it. Printing, scoffed at in Rome and patronized in Milan, rapidly became a luxury industry with a growing mass market in the capable hands of Aldus Manutius and his family. The famous Aldine Classics were the first comprehensive, standardized sets of books produced. They lacked the beauty and rich ornamentation of the earlier books that attempted to ape the illuminated manuscripts, but about the Aldine Classics there is a spare and efficient functionalism. Elegant, not ornate, moderate in price, and easy to read, they were all that a book should be. Yet this was but one of over two hundred presses in Venice in 1500. Here the new printing trade, carefully nurtured and protected by the state, flourished as nowhere else.

Venice exploited with exceptional skill the bourgeois delights from which a growing public of increasing affluence derived intense satisfaction. Indeed, as her political and military power gently, almost imperceptibly, ebbed, she became the symbol of self-indulgence and sensuous living – a city of extravagance, urbanity, and sophistication, an aristocratic Bohemia in which the future was forgotten in the day's delights. In the end, bereft of all but the pageantry of power, the Venetians, as hardheaded as ever, plucked their profits from the gaping provincial nobility of Western and Northern Europe. But between 1450 and 1570, the great years of the Renaissance in Venice, there was still vigour enough in Venetian commerce, achievement enough in

A palace designed by Jacopo Bellini
Louvre

Venetian arms, to create legitimate pride. The lords of Venice could still live in an aura of greatness without any sense of falsity. Yet the weakening, the softening, was spreading everywhere as decade followed decade, like the growth of self-indulgent fat on an old warrior. This atmosphere of transition was exceptionally fertile for Venetian art, even though it sapped its power.

The Signory had always believed in the value of art as propaganda. They were willing to pay high prices for huge frescoes in the Doge's Palace that celebrated the heroic deeds of the republic or the noble acts of its great men. Indeed, after the doges died, they might be willing to immortalize them in a splendid portrait. And when it came to a pageant, their hard fists opened willingly. They delighted in parading the might and splendour of the republic. Saints' days, the acquisition of a new relic, the anniversaries of notable victories, the solemnization of treaties, the visits of monarchs and princes, the presentation and dismissal of ambassadors – all provided opportunities for glorious display, a kaleidoscope of colour in which the costumes of the senators were as glorious as those of the ecclesiastics. As they wound their way through the Piazza, or in and out of the Doge's Palace, the powerless populace became visually aware of the greatness of their masters. It was a lesson, the Signory thought, that could not be learned too often – and they commanded Venice's outstanding artists to immortalize their pageants in paint and to embellish the walls of the Doge's Palace with the glories of the republic. Powerful guilds and rich patricians, with that quick eye for an opportunity, followed suit – and the life stories of Venice's favoured saints in a peculiarly Venetian setting covered the charity schools and hospitals, the churches and monasteries of the city. Skilled craftsmen and painters had always been in demand in Venice, and the great personalities of Venetian art – the Bellini family, Giorgione, Titian, Carpaccio, Tintoretto, and Paolo Veronese – were surrounded by traditions that went back to the early Middle Ages. In Venice, because demand had been so heavy and the commissions so large, painting had to be a family affair, a workshop, almost a factory. The properties used for backgrounds were handed down generation after generation, some of Giovanni Bellini's reappearing in canvases a hundred years later. Every great Venetian painter was something more than an individual artist at work; he was the director and inspiring genius of a studio of painters in which brothers, wives, sons, daughters, journeymen, and apprentices all worked together. Naturally, this increased output, and it enabled a painter like Tintoretto to cover acres of wall and roods of canvas in his long and active life; so, too, was it easy for the Bellini and Titian to produce hundreds of portraits and scores of pictures of pageants and religious mythology. Venetian art exists in abundance; indeed, in Venice the feast is almost surfeiting – every church, every monastery swarms with masterpieces. This abundance, this astonishing fertility, reflects the three strands in Venetian life, its vigour, its wealth, and its sensuous delight. Of all painting of Renaissance Italy, the Venetian is most alive to colour, to the warm sensuous delight in flesh and clothes and landscape played upon by light and shade. The Venetian master could move with consummate ease from painting a vast wall glorifying the state to the representation of the intimate enjoyment of physical love, yet whatever he might be painting there was warmth, and the reality that the Venetian knew. The huge *Paradise* of Tintoretto, the largest painting of its age, was peopled with Venetians. In Gentile Bellini's

Cardinal Bembo, by Titian
National Gallery of Art, Washington

Miracle of the Cross, the canals, the gondolas, the roof tops and chimneys of Venice are all there. In Carpaccio's *Saint Ursula*, a Venetian girl sleeps in her bedroom; under the thin guise of a Christian story the rich, sensuous life pulsates, reflecting the splendour of the city.

Although the life of Venice was glorified in this way, individual men were not. An occasional doge, when dead, a patriarch or two, a brilliant condottiere, might be immortalized in a superb portrait or a statue – but the majority of portraits by Bellini or Titian have lost the names of their sitters, for they adorned the walls of those ordinary patricians who had no place in history – only the luck to be born in Venice at a time of artistic greatness. Yet how evocative are these portraits, how infinite their variety, and how sharp the sense of the transience of living and loving men that broods over them. Nostalgia emanates from things Venetian like miasma from the lagoon; the streets of Venice echo with a sense of loss. The poetry of existence, the sadness that veils a sensual life, informs not only the best Venetian painting but also the writing of its one outstanding literary genius – Aretino. In him were mirrored the conflicting images of man – the cosmic and the noble, the moral and the obscene – that were to hypnotize the creative writers of Europe for generations.

Venice at the crossroads of her destiny created a society of exceptional complexity. It was still the city of hard-headed merchants, still the city of enterprise and ingenuity, still the city of the all-pervading, all-powerful state, of the swift and terrible justice. Its claim to dominion over the sea did not ring hollow: the hieratic splendour of the Doge had not been reduced to a quaint old-fashioned pageant. Yet the Renaissance settled on Venice like a golden haze, sweetening life, softening the edges. Venice had lost the future; from the city of commerce she was becoming the city of carnival. And this feeling of the future lost was already pervading much of the attitude to life of Venetian men and women, drawing them to the luxurious life which they could so easily afford, to the new delights in painting, music, architecture, and letters that the Renaissance produced in such abundance. Rome itself could scarcely vie with Venice in the splendour of its new buildings both public and private. The splendid façades of Sansovino had given the Piazzetta its permanent face, and scattered about the canals and islands of the lagoon were the churches and monasteries of Palladio. Its artistic luxuries were incomparable (so many craftsmen possessing such an ancient tradition were bound to throw up genius after genius in the visual arts), and its gold and silver, armour, jewellery, bronzes, glass, lace, printing, and bookbinding – indeed all the arts and crafts that adorn the life of man – were practised not only with the highest skill but also in a profusion that made Venice both in its lagoon and on the mainland, the most affluent state of Italy. The splendour of its new palaces of white marble, porphyry, and serpentine overwhelmed generations of foreigners, while the profusion of its merchandise bewildered them. Philippe de Comines, nobleman of France, ambassador of its King, rich, sophisticated, much travelled, was as entranced by the Grand Canal – '*la plus belle rue que ie croy qui soit en tout le monde, et la mieulx maisonnée*' – as the merry, uncouth joker Thomas Coryate of Somerset, who walked all the way there and gaped, open-mouthed with amazement, believing himself in paradise. Other cities might possess nobler paintings, statues, buildings; the spirit of the Renaissance maintained in Florence a more heroic aspect, in Rome its expression was more grandiose. But nowhere did it permeate more thoroughly the daily life of a city and its people than in Venice.

The Doge Francesco Foscari, by Lazzari Bastiani
Museo Correr, Venice

DOGE FRANCESCO FOSCARI

by H. R. Trevor-Roper

I N 1423 the old Doge of Venice, Tommaso Mocenigo, lay dying. The prosperity of the city was now at its height; this indeed was the golden age of the republic. But for a generation grave problems had clouded the city's future, threatening not only its security and its carefully nurtured wealth, but its very survival. Now it seemed at the parting of the ways: should it concentrate on its empire abroad or on its base at home? For both were threatened.

The empire abroad was centred in the Aegean Sea, although it extended to the factories in Constantinople and on the routes to the Middle and Far East. Here the threat came from the Ottoman Turks, now settled in Europe, with their capital at Adrianople, and pushing into the Balkans. All·the efforts of Venice were needed to keep them out of the Aegean, and for years that had been the prime object of Venetian diplomacy.

The threat to the home base came from closer quarters: from new powers which were rising ominously in and around Italy. Hitherto, Venice had been able to build up its empire abroad because its neighbours at home had given little trouble. Bishoprics, communes, petty princes – they could not be ignored, but equally they offered no temptations compared with the huge profits of the Levant. So the republic had practised a policy of the balance of power, involving the minimum of direct intervention. But now these petty neighbours were becoming part or projections of greater powers, and these greater powers were threatening the very life of Venice. The rulers of Hungary and Naples were closing in on its Adriatic lifeline. Above all, a menacing new state was pressing down the valley of the Po. For this was the time when the free republics of Italy were gradually being converted into despotic princely states; and the greatest of these states was the new duchy of Milan, under the Visconti family. Having crushed the liberties of Milan, the Visconti were creating around it an even larger hinterland or *retroterra*. In the south they had absorbed the great mercantile republic of Genoa, which, being confined between the Ligurian Alps and the sea, lacked such a *retroterra* in which to fight. In the east the Visconti were pushing towards another great mercantile republic, which was squeezed between the lagoons and the sea – Venice.

How could the republic ensure its survival? The answer, according to some Venetians, was to enlarge its own *retroterra*, the Venetian *terraferma* – a process which had already begun, with the annexation of Padua, Vicenza, and Verona. But there were others who distrusted this policy. Land wars, they said, were costly; they distracted the city from its real task, in the East; they created a new class of landed nobility and made the city dependent on condottieri; and was it not precisely out of the landed nobility and condottieri that the powerful new group of princes, which threatened the liberties of all Italian cities, was rising?

The Doge Mocenigo was one who argued thus. As he lay dying he summoned to his bed the ducal councillors and there delivered a famous speech. The war for the *terraferma*, he said, had shattered the finances of the republic. It could not be continued. The wealth of Venice lay in manufacture, trade, and shipping: only by keeping to these pursuits, and to peace, would the city master the wealth of Christendom. Therefore they must be careful to appoint a sound successor to himself. Then he went down the list of the possible candidates. Bembo, Loredan, Mocenigo, Contarini – the political members of the great mercantile families who formed the closed aristocracy of Venice – there was something to be said for them all. But at the end he warned them explicitly against one man: Francesco Foscari, he said, was proud, ambitious, unscrupulous. If he were Doge, it would mean war, war, war . . .

To us there may seem something unbalanced in such a warning. Already by that time the republic had achieved its perfect aristocratic form – a form which was to be final (in all essentials) for centuries. Gone were the days when the people had power of election; since 1297 the Greater Council, the legislature and electorate of the republic, had been 'closed' – that is, confined to the nobility, who in turn kept careful control over their own membership. Gone, too, were the days when the Doge, however elected, had exercised personal power. By now successive 'ducal promises' – the conditions which the nobility, after observing the faults of each Doge, imposed upon his successor – had reduced the Doge to a mere figurehead. If offered the dogeship, a Venetian nobleman was unable by law to refuse it. Once elected, his power was narrowly circumscribed. He was unable to travel outside Venice. Neither he nor his sons could marry foreigners without permission. Neither his sons nor his personal officers could hold public positions under him (except as ambassadors or naval commanders, in which jobs they could not make trouble at home), and his official councillors, without whom he could do nothing, not even open a formal letter, could not be chosen by him. His income was fixed and his expenses limited, lest he should raise a party by bribery. His authority over the citizens was reduced, lest he should raise a mob in his support. He was not even allowed to give himself social airs. He could not set up his escutcheons in public places, nor answer to honorific titles. To foreigners, as representative of the greatest, richest republic in Italy, he might be *Serenissimo Principe;* at home, in that republic, he was only *Messer lo Doge.* And finally, he could not even lay down his office at will: except with the consent of his six councillors, ratified by the approval of the Greater Council, he could not even abdicate. Why then should an ambitious man want to be doge, and what could an ambitious man do, even if he were doge?

Nevertheless, Mocenigo's warning cannot have been entirely groundless. The Venetian constitution may have been completely aristocratic, and its aristocratic character may have been jealously preserved by a perpetual subdivision of authority, indirect elections, and a complex tissue of checks and balances. But even the most perfect constitution is operated by men with human passions, and the more complex a constitution is, the more certainly it falls into the hands of skilful politicians; and skilled politicians, even with the old rules, may play a new game. In the fifteenth century a new game was being played in all the republics of Italy. Faced by new problems, their old constitutions were crumbling, and new men – sometimes patricians rising out of their midst, sometimes condottieri in their service – were building up despotic rule. This had already happened in Milan, with the Visconti; it would happen again, with the Sforza. Soon it would happen in Florence, too. Cosimo de' Medici might begin as *pater patriae*, 'the first citizen' of the republic. He would end by founding a dynasty that would last for centuries. Remembering this, no one can assume that even the Venetian constitution was proof against overthrow from above by an ambitious doge who, as a war leader, might build up a new form of patronage and power. Such at least may have been the fear which inspired the Doge Mocenigo to warn his fellow noblemen against electing, as his successor, Francesco Foscari.

Who was the man who aroused these fears? The great Venetian aristocrats are always somewhat impersonal figures. The very system, with its intense jealousy of individual power, tended to depersonalize them. For it was the essential character of the Venetian republic that all personality was ruthlessly subordinated to the state. Instead of the cut-throat private enterprise of Genoa, or the brilliant individualism of Florence, here we see only an impersonal state capitalism, an implacable reason of state, an official state culture entirely hostile to 'the cult of personality'. So the official records of Venice do not bring to life even a controversial personality like Foscari. And yet he certainly was a controversial character. His whole reign shows it – a fact which is demonstrated, first of all, by the battle over his election.

Foscari, it is clear, was determined to be doge. Moreover, from the point of view of Mocenigo and his friends, he was an outsider. That was why they so feared him. He was also young (at fifty he was the youngest of the candidates); he was regarded as poor by the great 'nabob' families, although he had enriched himself by marriage; he was experienced (after sharing his father's exile in Egypt, he had held most of the great elective offices of the state); and above all – and this was what Venice particularly distrusted – he was ambitious and the head of a party. Moreover, this party was particularly suspicious to the great mercantile aristocracy, like the Mocenigo, that customarily ruled Venice, for it was a party of 'the poor nobles', the lesser noblemen, the radicals, the 'Westerners' who favoured war by land – as distinct from the 'Easterners' with their Levantine interests. We are told that, as Procurator of St Mark's, Foscari had used the large cash balances in his hands to create his following; he had relieved the wants of poor noblemen, given portions to their daughters, and made himself dangerous by their support. No doubt he had won other support by his merits, too. And finally, as was soon to be shown, he was a consummate election manager.

When the forty-one electors met, Foscari was not the favourite. He was too impulsive, too controversial, too committed to a policy. The favourite was Pietro Loredan, the admiral of the republic, who was also determined on office. But Loredan made the mistake of speaking confidently on his own behalf, which lost him votes. Foscari was much more prudent. Although his rivals did not know it, he had already nine ballots safely in his pocket. These voters acted as a bloc, but they did not reveal themselves until they had quietly contributed to the defeat of all the other candidates. Instead, they allowed it to appear that they, too, were opposed to Foscari. Then, suddenly, at the tenth ballot, they all plumped for the outsider and carried him into the ducal chair.

Thus began the longest ducal reign in the long history of the Venetian republic. Foscari, who always liked *panache*, hastened to celebrate his victory. For a whole year he dazzled the city with feasts and pageants. The new Sála del Maggior Consiglio – the Hall of the Great Council – was opened with splendid ceremony. He fetched his wife, the Dogaressa, in triumph to the Palace in the ducal galley, the *Bucentaur*, attended by the noblewomen of Venice. These spectacles, incidentally, were something of a sop to the non-noble citizens of Venice who in that year lost their last vestigial rights in the government of the republic; but it is doubtful if their personal emphasis pleased the aristocracy. Then the Doge settled down to the business of government.

The character of Foscari's reign can be described in three words – pageantry, war, and dissension. There were feasts and spectacles of unexampled magnificence. There was also – as Mocenigo had prophesied – constant war for the *terraferma*. And thirdly, there was the undying jealousy and hatred of those whom Foscari had defeated – particularly of the Loredan family, whom he had pipped to the post. The pageantry gave his reign its outward splendour; the war its real content; and the hatred of the Loredan brought it to a tragic end.

The outward splendour was shown in many ways. New palaces, public and private, rose by the Grand Canal and the lagoon. The Rialto bridge was rebuilt. Paolo Uccello worked on mosaics in St Mark's, Antonio Vivarini in San Pantaleon. Famous visitors were received with ever greater pomp and show. In 1428 it was the Prince of Portugal whom the *Bucentaur*, escorted by a fleet of boats, fetched in to a banquet attended by two hundred and fifty ladies dressed in cloth of gold and silk and jewels. In 1438 the Emperor of Byzantium himself, in his great time of trial with the Turks, condescended to come in person to Italy, with his brother the Despot of the Morea and the Patriarch of Constantinople, ready to accept the supremacy of the Roman Church in return for Western aid. When the *Bucentaur*, covered with red silk and golden emblems, carried the imperial party from the Lido, the whole lagoon was full of boats, flying banners and playing music, with oarsmen clad in cloth of gold. In 1452 even this event was eclipsed when the Holy Roman Emperor followed the Emperor of the East to Venice, and was drawn in triumph by the *Bucentaur* and the gaily coloured boats up to the Grand Canal. By the next year the last Emperor of the East had perished in the sack of his capital, and the Doge Foscari would receive in Venice the fugitive scholars and salvaged treasures of Byzantium.

In Byzantine eyes, the fall of Byzantium was due to Venetian indifference. All through the reign of Foscari, it was said, the military resources of Venice had been turned too exclusively to the West. But this was hardly a fair judgment. The threat from the West was a real

The Healing of the Demoniac, detail, by Carpaccio
Gallerie dell' Accademia, Venice

threat, as the fate of Genoa showed. And besides, in the first year of Foscari's reign there had been a great success in the East. In that year the Greek governor of Salonika, the emporium of Thessalian grain (Venice lived on imported grain) and the northern watchtower of the Aegean, gave or sold his city to Venice rather than lose it to the Turks. So the East, it seemed, was safe. Meanwhile, the republic had obtained an invaluable ally for war in the West. It happened that at this time the greatest condottiere in Italy, the man who had himself re-created the power of the Visconti in Milan, now, on some slight, deserted his master and offered his services to Venice. This was Francesco Bussone, known as Carmagnola. The Venetians could hardly resist such an opportunity. It was against a background of this double security provided by Salonika in the East and Carmagnola in the West that the republic, in 1425, made a league with Florence and declared war on the revived, aggressive power of the Visconti.

Thus, within three years of his accession, Foscari was carrying out the policy that had always been associated with him. There can be no doubt that it was his policy: there exists the speech with which he persuaded the republic to make war. Of course, given the Venetian constitution, one can be sure it was not his policy alone, for he had only influence, not authority. Nevertheless, it seems that it was his influence, combined with circumstances, which weighted and held the scales. Even twelve years later, in 1437, that personal prestige was extraordinarily powerful. In that year the Doge sat, day after day, at the bedside of his son Domenico, who was dying of the plague. Foscari's supporters feared that he, too, would catch the infection, and then what would they do? The lives of many, they said, depended on his: if he were to fail, the fortune and the forward policy of the state would be in peril. Clearly, if men could say this, the Doge was no mere chairman. The forward policy of the state depended particularly on him in 1437, when those initial advantages which had made the western war popular a dozen years earlier had disappeared.

In fact neither Salonika nor Carmagnola lived up to their promise.

Salonika was the first to go. In 1430 the Turks captured and sacked it; the slaughter was terrible, the loss final. From now on the Aegean Sea lay open to the Turks, with the wealth of Venice in it, scattered among subject islands whose Greek inhabitants preferred (or thought they preferred) Turkish conquest to Venetian exploitation. In the same year an attempt was made to assassinate the Doge. And as for Carmagnola, like so many condottieri, he proved thoroughly unsatisfactory. At the head of one of the greatest armies that had been seen in Italy, he somehow failed to be as victorious in Venetian as he had been in Milanese service, and he remained suspiciously familiar with his former employer and present enemy, the Duke of Milan. The Venetians offered to make him lord of Milan if he would only conquer it, but still he consumed time and money in mere parades or took cures at the baths of Abano. Finally the Venetians lost patience. With their usual circumspection, they did nothing rashly or openly, but invited Carmagnola to Venice to meet the Doge and discuss future strategy. He never saw the Doge. Instead, he was whisked from the palace to prison, tortured, tried, and condemned. When his sentence was discussed, the Doge voted for mercy, but was overruled, and Carmagnola was sentenced to death and beheaded. That was in 1432. After that the republic employed other, less dangerous condottieri.

So by 1432 Foscari's policy was faced with difficulties on all fronts. He sensed the obstacles, and next year asked to resign his office. It is said that he asked again in 1442 and again in 1446, and this suggests that he was an impulsive man, impatient of obstruction, easily discouraged by defeat. But the Venetian aristocracy, or perhaps his supporters in it, would not allow him to give up his office. On each occasion they reminded him that, by the constitution, he could not resign except with the assent of the six councillors and the Greater Council. It was an answer which he was later to remember and to use against his enemies.

Meanwhile the forward policy continued. The war for the *terraferma* went on. It was very long, lasting, with brief interludes, for thirty years. It was also very costly; the first ten years alone cost seven million ducats. It had its dramatic incidents – among them the bringing of Venetian ships over the mountains from the river Adige to Lake Garda; it had its disappointments, too – the most bitter being the gradual slide of the Florentines, out of commercial rivalry, towards the side of Milan. But in the end the war was successful. It carried the westward frontier of the *terraferma* to its furthest and final limit, to incorporate the provinces of Brescia and Bergamo, and the Doge solemnly received them as imperial fiefs. He also obtained Ravenna as a papal fief. And before his death he inspired and signed a new treaty – a league with Florence and Milan, Rome and Naples, which was to preserve the liberty of Italy. It would have been a great triumph had it lasted: all we can say is that at least it outlasted Foscari.

So the pageants and the war went on. But meanwhile what of the third feature of Foscari's reign, the enmity of his rivals? This, too, was very long – long and bitter, as Venetian enmities always were. For if Venice, with its exaltation of state service, was free from the strife of parties which ruined every other Italian republic, it was enlivened, even more than the others, by fierce personal and family feuds. In particular, the Doge Foscari never escaped the bitter hatred of the Loredan family. He had defeated them in 1423. They remembered their defeat, and in after years, with their allies the Donà and the Barbarigo, mercilessly persecuted him at his weakest point – his family.

At the time of his election, one objection to Foscari had been his large family, whose members, it was suggested, would feed on the resources of the state. This danger did not materialize, for of his five sons, four died young of the plague. The last survivor, who alone had heirs, and to whom the Doge was devoted, was Jacopo, a young man of cultivated tastes – a Greek scholar and collector of manuscripts – but indiscreet ways. In 1441 his marriage to Lucrezia Contarini had been one of the most magnificent of the many spectacles which the Doge gave to the city. There had been boat races, feasts, and illuminations, with the city adorned in scarlet and cloth of gold, a great tour-

nament before thirty thousand people in the Piazza San Marco, and
two hundred and fifty horsemen had ridden in cavalcade over the
Grand Canal on a specially built bridge of barges. But in 1445 Jacopo
Foscari was secretly denounced for receiving gifts from Filippo Maria
Visconti, the Duke of Milan. At that time Francesco Loredan, the
nephew of the defeated candidate, was one of the three chiefs of the
Council of Ten, the secret political police of the republic. His ally
Ermolao Donà was another, and the Ten decided to act at once. They
ordered the arrest of Jacopo and excluded the Doge and his kinsmen
from all their deliberations on the matter. Then sentence was pronounced: Jacopo was exiled to Nauplia in Greece, and all his goods
were confiscated. In vain the Dogaressa begged to see her son; the
orders were given, and the name of the Doge himself was placed, with
ruthless, impersonal irony, at their head. Before they could be executed there was a hitch, and then, on grounds of health, the place of
exile was changed to Treviso, which was both nearer and more comfortable; but the humiliation to the Doge was no less. It was after this
bitter defeat that Foscari made his third attempt to resign; but he was
forced to remain in office and drink the dregs of the cup.

Before long, however, the Doge was able to score a point. In 1447
he made a moving appeal to the Ten, and the Ten consented, not on
grounds of humanity but (a typically Venetian reason) 'because it is
necessary at this time to have a prince whose mind is free and serene,
able to serve the republic', to remit the exile of Jacopo, now sick in
body and mind. But the reunion of the Jacob and the Benjamin of the
house of Foscari did not last long. In 1450 the Loredan family found
another pretext, and resumed their attack.

That year one of Jacopo Foscari's judges, Ermolao Donà, was murdered, and Jacopo was at once suspected. Again the Doge's son was
arrested; he was even tortured; and although nothing was proved and
he was probably innocent (it is said that another man afterwards confessed to the crime), the Ten, having gone so far, were afraid to go
back. They sentenced him, without proof, to exile, and this time there

A RESOLUTION CALLING FOR THE DOGE'S ABDICATION, VOTED BY THE COUNCIL OF TEN, THE PRIVY COUNCIL AND THE GIUNTA, A BODY OF TWENTY-FIVE NOBLEMEN.

There is no one who does not thoroughly comprehend how useful and altogether how essential to our State and to our affairs is the presence of a Prince, without which, as becomes manifest from the results, the greatest inconvenience and detriment are apt to arise to our State which, since it has by infinite clemency of our Creator been bequeathed to us by our forefathers hereditary and fair to look upon, we are bound to preserve with all our power and to hold dearer to us than our very life. And although this our city is furnished with holy laws and ordinances, it is of little avail if they be not executed, if the observance of the same be relaxed. The presence of the Prince besides in the councils, at audiences, in the transaction of affairs of state – how desirable it is, how glorious it is, it would be superfluous to point out. All are aware that our most illustrious Prince has vacated his dignity for a great length of time; and from his advanced age it is not at all to be expected that he will be able to return to the exercise of the functions appertaining thereto. How pernicious his absence and incompetence are is more easily understood than explained. Wherefore: it is proposed that by the authority of this most excellent Council and the Giunta the resolution be agreed to that the Privy councillors and the chiefs of the council shall repair to the presence of the most illustrious Prince and declare to him our opinion, that the government of our city and State; (which as his Highness knows very well is excessively arduous) cannot be carried on without the constant presence and cooperation of a Prince; also considering how long his Excellency has for personal reasons renounced all share in this government, and that there is no hope that he will be able at any time hereafter to discharge his duties according to the exigencies of this state; and [considering] that his absence is threatening to involve consequences such as we are assured from his affectionate patriotism, he can never desire to witness; – on these grounds which his Excellency in his supreme wisdom will readily appreciate, we with the aforesaid council of Ten and the Giunta have decided upon exhorting and requesting his Serenity, for the evident and necessary welfare of our State – his native land – freely and spontaneously to abdicate, which on many accounts he ought to do as a good Prince and a true father of his country, and especially as we provide that he shall have for his support and proper maintenance from our Office of Salt 1,500 gold ducats a year for life as well as the residue of his salary due to the present day. Also that if it happen that the same most illustrious Prince, on this declaration being made known to him, shall demand time to consider, he may be told that we are content to wait for such answer till tomorrow at the hour of tierce.

were no second thoughts; he was carried off to Crete. Even in Crete his movements were watched, his indiscretions observed; and in 1456 it was reported to the Ten that he was planning, or at least discussing, revenge with foreign help. The Ten (of whom Jacopo Loredan was now one of the chiefs) immediately decided that the matter was 'of the greatest importance'; and once again the Doge's son was fetched back for a trial.

Now began the final tragedy of the Doge's reign, the tragedy which Byron converted into his drama *The Two Foscari*. Before this third trial it was admitted that Jacopo's projects were entirely academic, and that being in Crete, he could do little or nothing to harm the republic; but that made no difference. He was tortured and judged guilty, and the remorseless Jacopo Loredan urged that he be publicly beheaded as a traitor between the columns of the Piazza. Even the Ten drew the line at this, and the prisoner was sentenced to renewed exile in Crete, this time in prison. Before returning to Crete, he was allowed to see his father, now eighty-four years old. He begged the Doge to intercede for him. 'Jacopo,' replied the old man, 'go and obey your country's commands, and seek no more.' But when his son had gone, he threw himself upon a chair, weeping and crying, 'O pietà grande!' Within a few months he was shattered by the news that his last son was dead in Crete.

The Doge's distress was his enemies' opportunity, and they now decided to complete their victory. The Doge, they said, was too old; he was distracted by grief – the grief they had caused him; he could no longer attend to business. Therefore must he go. The Council of Ten met and decided to demand his abdication (*see opposite*). Their message was brought to the Doge by Jacopo Loredan. But now the old man had his revenge. He turned on them the argument they had used against him in the past; by the law, he said, he could not abdicate unless the councillors proposed and the Greater Council agreed. Here, too, he obeyed his country's laws. Baffled, the Ten consulted again, reinterpreted the law to suit their convenience, and told the Doge of their reinterpretation; but still he kept to the old interpretation and would not move. Finally they sent him an order: he was to resign and clear out of the ducal palace within eight days. If he did so, he would receive an adequate salary and a doge's burial; if not, he would be driven out and all his goods confiscated.

It was a completely illegal demand, but the Doge was powerless. He gave in. The ducal ring was taken from his finger and broken, the ducal cap from his head. He promised to leave the palace. Then, seeing pity in the eye of one of his visitors, he called to him and, taking his hand, said, 'Whose son are you?' 'I am the son of Messer Marin Memmo,' was the reply. The Doge said, 'He is my old friend. Ask him to come and visit me so that we may go in a boat for solace; we will visit the monasteries.' The next day he left the palace. Wearing his old scarlet robe of state, he stepped forth, bent but unaided except by his staff. As he went to the stone steps leading down to the water his brother Marco urged him to go to his gondola by the covered stair. 'No,' replied the Doge, 'I will do down by the same stair by which I came up to my dukedom.' A week later he died – of rage, it was said, on hearing the bells announcing the election of his successor.

The people of Venice were indignant at the indecent deposition of the Doge who had reigned so long, who had enjoyed all the honours and prestige of government, whose figure and personality were so striking, whom the emperors of East and West had visited, and who had given them such splendid shows. There was much murmuring against the usurpation of the Ten, and even the Doge's enemies were now a little ashamed that they had not waited another week for a natural death. When Foscari was dead they gave him a splendid funeral, in spite of the protests of the former Dogaressa at this solemn humbug. He was buried in the church of the Frari, and a majestic Gothic-Renaissance monument commemorated his achievement – conquest of the *terraferma*. Meanwhile the Ten withdrew from the invidious limelight, until the furore over their indecent treatment of the old Doge had abated somewhat. But there was no denying that they had won a notable victory. From now on the constitution was not only clearly oligarchical; it was also clear where the centre of oligarchical power lay. It lay with that inner ring of self-elected councillors who could mobilize, even against the Doge, the Council of Ten.

Thus ended the long reign of Francesco Foscari. It ended, as it had begun, in bitter personal controversy, and even today historians dispute its significance. It has been said that it was Foscari who diverted the attention of Venice from East to West, sacrificing Salonika and Constantinople to Bergamo and Brescia. This diversion, it is added, led to disastrous consequences fifty years later, when the powers of Europe united against 'the insatiable cupidity of the Venetians and their lust for power'. And yet, one may answer, could any other doge really have acted differently? Before Foscari's time the dilemma had been there: if the land powers of Europe would not unite against the Turks, a sea power could not defeat them alone; and could Venice ignore the western threat, or the ominous example of Genoa? Other historians have dwelt on the fear of princely despotism; they have represented the Loredan as incorruptible republicans, Catos inexorable in the cause of the constitution. But is there in fact any evidence that Foscari ever entertained thoughts of altering the constitution? Perhaps in his early years he did (though we can only judge from the suspicion he inspired); but how seriously could an old man of eighty have threatened the established power of the oligarchy? In the end it was not he but his enemies who broke the constitution. He submitted to its most humiliating rules, malevolently applied; his foes broke through its last restraints in order to humble him.

Nevertheless it must be admitted that Foscari's reign was crucial in Venetian history. Whatever his personal aims, they were in the end subordinated and absorbed by the impersonal Venetian system. During his term of office the last Milanese republic was converted into the duchy of the Sforza, the great Florentine republic into the domain of the Medici, but the jealous republicans of Venice, whatever their

259

motives, and whether they were right or wrong in their personal suspicions, positively strengthened their republic. They accepted the policy, and then crushed the personality, of the one man who might conceivably have recreated the old ducal power, so long undermined. And their victory over him was final. After 1457 the republic no longer feared the Doge. Before that date seven doges had been assassinated, nine had been blinded and exiled, twelve had abdicated, one had been sentenced to death and beheaded, two had been deposed. But after that date all is peace inside the republic. The Venetian constitution survived intact through the era of the native princes. It kept its independence when the other Italian states fell under foreign rule; it resisted the Papacy during the Counter-reformation; and it was to be praised, in the seventeenth century, as the most perfect model of government for any mercantile state which aspired to be free, effective, and independent.

Engraving of the fire of 1577
Museo Correr, Venice

THE IMAGES OF MAN

Venice, Rome, Milan, and Florence were, physically speaking, new cities – cities in construction littered with scaffolding, scarred with half-realized plans. The villas, the taverns, the lounging places in the piazzas and gardens were filled with earnest argument about the new cathedrals and palaces. The statues that adorn the Piazza della Signoria at Florence gleamed with an almost raw whiteness. The Piazza San Marco at Venice shook itself free from the clutter of stalls, bakers' shops, and latrines to acquire the beauty that we see. In Milan the new citadel of the Sforza drew a wondering crowd of enthusiasts. In Mantua, Parma, Naples, Perugia, Viterbo, Genoa, indeed in all the towns of Italy, it was the same story – a new physical world was being built that buried or obscured the old barbarisms. In the churches and monasteries scarcely a year passed without a new masterpiece being painted on the walls. Today the blackened surface and faded pigments baffle the imagination and make it difficult to recapture the sharp impact that these pictures had on the eyes that first saw them, and the same is true of statues and bronzes staled by centuries of reproduction and plagiarism. Impossible, too, to recapture the novelty of books, the miracle that it must have seemed to scholars to possess their own Virgil, their own Cicero, or to see their own poems and plays and familiar letters stacked by the hundreds in printers' shops. To this fresh, lavish, and splendid world were being added new horizons, and old certainties were dissolving as rapidly as the old scenes. Stories from Portugal and Spain, tales from Genoese sea captains, the gossip of the Venetian Cabots, told of a wondrous world of continents before undreamed of.

Soon speculation became certainty, and the fables of Marco Polo and Mandeville gave way to the sober statements of mariners. The discoveries of Columbus, of the Cabots, of a whole generation of Portuguese in the Eastern Seas – 'such great adventures as Fate had to no former age allowed' – confirmed the belief, already held by many men and women, that the age to which they belonged was original and new, and that the immediate past was dead. Undoubtedly such convictions bred a sense of liberation and encouraged a belief in the unique quality of personal destiny. Men began to create new images of themselves – a habit as old as man himself, but always fresh and entrancing.

'Men,' wrote Alberti, 'are themselves the source of their own fortune and misfortune.' 'O supreme generosity of God the Father,' apostrophized Pico della Mirandola, 'O highest and marvellous felicity of man. To him it is granted to have whatever he chooses, to be whatever he wills.' Man was heroic, destined by his own nature to greatness or to failure, but eternally alone, eternally himself. If born wise, then

Self-portrait, Leon Battista Alberti
National Gallery of Art, Washington

he might of course benefit by the wisdom of the past; if sensitive, he would gain from philosophy and religion; if apt, he could acquire the education of a gentleman. In the last resort, however, all rested on himself – on his nature and on his luck, that curious personal destiny, controlled of course by God, but a mystery that could never be unlocked except by time. Portents and the conjunction or combustion of the stars might, as in a riddle, hint an answer, but essentially man was alone with fate. This attitude was deeply bound up with the growing capitalism of society, in which the merchant sought a profit by gambling on his own ingenuity, but there lay between these ideas a barrier of unawareness, like that which lies between the unconscious drives of a man's personality and his rational self. To the men who lived in the fifteenth century, this view of man – his individuality, his lonely destiny, his isolation – had nothing whatsoever to do with the active world or its expanding horizons. For them it was a new truth, self-evident, eternal, inescapable. As this attitude to man gathered momentum, it spread to places and communities that were unripe for its reception. Also it became entangled in the strong, clinging, wayward tendrils of the past. Men were still priests, monks, scholars, soldiers, aristocrats, and merchants, and each profession, each community, each class possessed rules, regulations, beliefs, and attitudes already centuries old. On these the new conception of man worked, but, in working, suffered its own sea change.

Yet the concept of man, untrammelled, as a creature of destiny, but with his destiny provoked by his own self, enthralled most of the sensitive spirits of the Renaissance. Its fascination is beautifully illustrated in the growth and development of drama and the theatre. Plays there had been in medieval Europe, but they were a looking glass of morality, not a mirror of man. They had concerned themselves, often in an intensely human way, with God, Christ, the Virgin, with the Creation or the Flood, or with personified moralities – vices like Lust and Sloth, virtues like Chastity and Humility. The humanists and their circle found these plays barbarous. They took delight in Plautus

COLISEVS SI VE THEATRVM

Setting for a farcical comedy of Terence, Venice, 1497

and in Terence, in the obscenities and the jokes, the brave declamations and fateful tragedies of individual men and women, crude as they were, two-dimensional as they might now seem; to us they are caricatures rather than living men, yet the change from the immediate past was very great. So, too, in history, the humanists looked for heroes, not men, looked for the individual life lived on a scale of intensity and drama beyond the range and experience of common mortals. And this spirit spread through literature like a dye. All aspects of a personal life – birth, love, marriage, ambition, defeat, senility – were blown up, endowed with an excess that in the hands of a genius, a Tasso or an Ariosto, acquired a heroic and universal significance. If

265

the dramatists, poets, rhetoricians, and novelists were often second-rate, if their creations now seem bombastic and ridiculous, they entranced their contemporaries. Nothing was more fashionable at any court than plays, masques, the declamation of set speeches, the recitation of poetry, or even the reading of familiar letters between humanists. Of course, these fashionable literary banquets were concerned with more than the heroic nature of man. They provided settings for the display of ancient learning, for the parade of the esoteric, for the language of concealment that all literary coteries delight in cultivating. And they also gave an opportunity for display – a physical setting was required, and all Renaissance man's delight in ostentation and sumptuous adornment was given full rein. The masques, poetic entertainments, and dances were produced regardless of cost; the drama itself created its own special theatre with scenery as spectacular and as realistic as the world was ever to know. Yet overlaid as the setting might be with a distracting luxury, time and time again the theme of poem or play or philosophic oration harked back to the lonely plight of man, to his capacity for heroism and for tragedy. Sometimes this was threaded with comic realism, with the sense of man's absurdity; at other times a portrayal of his vigorous instinctive life flashed over both the comedy and the tragedy. But always the writers were drawn back, as indeed were the painters and sculptors, to man – enlarged, ennobled, romanticized.

This attitude toward man did not remain merely a theme for the arts; it spread into society, modifying customs, penetrating politics and changing them. The belief – often unconsciously adopted – that man's instincts and abilities must find their own destiny, be it what it may, influenced sexual practices more profoundly than any other social conventions. In the Middle Ages there had been sinners galore, priests, cardinals, popes who could not resist the itch of concupiscence; novices had been thrust into monasteries at too hectic a period of their adolescence; nuns found that the time of waiting for their heavenly groom lay heavily on their hands. And the laity, as ever, found the desires of the flesh pushing them through the barriers of accepted morality. But in the Middle Ages these things were wicked, a matter for penance and sorrow; matters to be suppressed and eradicated. A wandering scholar might glorify the sins of his flesh in a lyric, but medieval society condemned them. Not so in the Renaissance. Sex was *par excellence* the expression of the individual man. Nor were the humanists confined by Christian or Hebraic morality: they had read their Plato; they knew of the lives and loves of the gods. Jove had his Ganymede, why could not they? So Aeneas Silvius sends his bastard to his mother and father so they will have something of him to love. Pietro Aretino asks the Duke of Mantua to send him a boy that struck his fancy. Lorenzo Valla spends the leisure from his exacting scholarship in the Vatican library writing some of the most brilliant, and certainly the most obscene, familiar letters, a literary activity which Machiavelli, too, enjoyed with relish. The follies of Alexander VI provided no more gossip for Rome than did the follies of Aretino in his old age for Venice. Not since the days of Petronius had public men indulged themselves in such unmeasured erotic fantasy.

Untrammelled by convention, dominated by instinct, swept along by his nature, fulfilling his fate with the agility of an acrobat, yet true to his inner essence, his mysterious *virtù* – this was the compulsive image which Renaissance man created for himself. Instead of the stage being the mirror of life, it seemed rather as if the characters of melodrama had usurped the true characters of men. In no other man of this age is the image more sharply mirrored than in Pietro Aretino – the first Bohemian.

'I am a free man,' Aretino wrote, 'I do not need to copy Petrarch or Boccaccio. My own genius is enough. Let others worry themselves about style and so cease to be themselves. Without a master, without a model, without a guide, without artifice, I go to work and earn my living, my well-being, and my fame. What do I need more? With a goose quill and a few sheets of paper I mock the universe.' And he did, riotously, splendidly, until in his vigorous sixties he roared too vehemently at a bawdy joke, had apoplexy, and died. But what a life he had lived – shameless, selfish, magnificently free from humbug and splendidly creative.

Born the legitimate son of a poor shoemaker of Arezzo, Aretino passed himself off as the bastard of a gentleman until a fellow citizen, in a moment of rage, blew the *gaffe*; then Aretino boasted the truth as vehemently as he had paraded the lie. He received no serious education. He turned up for a time, in his late adolescence, at Perugia, probably living as a painter's apprentice. Already he had started to scribble sonnets. He next appears in the household of the great Roman banker Agostino Chigi (as a domestic servant, his enemies said, who was quickly dismissed for pinching the silver). Aretino claimed Chigi, however, as patron, not master. Whatever his situation, Chigi's household gave him a lifelong taste for luxury, feasting, and pomp. Rome also offered him a golden opportunity for his natural literary genius.

At the corner of the Piazza Navona, a worn antique statue had become a curious sort of notice-board. Learned lampoons of the Pope's government and the leading personalities of Rome were stuck to it. It was called Pasquino after a bitter-tongued schoolmaster. Later another statue in the Campus Martius was used in a similar way, and then the two statues took to having dialogues. These were known as pasquinades. Most of them were dull and pedantic, but risky in a mild way because of the freedom of their criticism. Aretino changed all that – his opportunity came on the death of Pope Leo x. To press the claims of his candidate, Cardinal Medici, afterward Clement VII, Aretino launched a series of unbridled lampoons against the cardinals. Every vice they may have practised (and Aretino's imagination was rich), every dishonourable event in their own lives or their families', was widely and mercilessly pilloried. To make it worse, these verses were printed and sold as handbills. Rome rocked with laughter; princes asked their ambassadors for copies. No one believed that such impudence could go unpunished, but it did. Aretino demonstrated the power of the pen; he became the 'scourge of princes'. However, when an old Dutchman was elected Pope, Aretino thought he would cool his heels in Mantua. There the Gonzaga enjoyed his talents and boasted of his presence at their court, but with the election of Cardinal Medici as Clement VII, Aretino was summoned back to Rome to regale the papal court with his wit and license. At Rome he began to write his superb comedy *La Cortigiana;* of course in Italian, and with complete disregard for the models of Terence and Plautus that were thought sacrosanct. His reputation for wit and daring soared to new heights. His fancy, however, became powerfully stimulated by sixteen remarkably obscene drawings by Giulio Romano that an enterprising publisher was about to have engraved. For each, Aretino provided a sonnet as explicit and as indecent as the picture. This did not endear him to his patron the Pope, who lacked the temperament and interests of the Borgia. At the same time Aretino was cuckolding as many husbands as he could. After a bad brawl in which he was nearly killed by an irate husband, the Pope's protection abruptly ceased. So off went Aretino to join the famous condottiere Giovanni delle Bande Nere. In that great captain, Aretino saw a mirror image – a man compelled like himself to follow his star, to fulfil his own life on his own terms, outside society, beyond custom, a man of destiny. With Giovanni he rejoiced in the freedom of military life, whose sweetness and pain were heightened by the dark presence of death. For a man of Aretino's powerful imagination and strong instincts, the grandeurs and miseries of war proved deeply enriching. The death of Giovanni acted as a traumatic experience which Aretino described in one of the most remarkable letters that he ever wrote. In it he depicted in language that was simple, grave, and noble, the last hours of a heroic man, triumphing over pain, accepting death, making his own terms with God as he had done with man. After Giovanni's death, Aretino felt more keenly his isolation from society; in his bitterness he poured his acid scorn on popes and princes. However, he had to live, and with his usual journalistic flair he brought out an almanac in which he flayed men and affairs by predicting the year's events. Its vast success enabled Aretino to settle in Venice – free, secure, rich from his pen: princes tumbled over themselves either to obtain a few flattering lines of prose from him or to avoid mention altogether; even the Pope forgave and pampered him; everything he wrote sold handsomely. He lived like a prince on the Grand Canal, his *palazzo* full of women and boys – the Aretines, he called them. There he offered profuse hospitality, gargantuan banquets and feasts of love, orgies of literary gossip. Titian was drawn to him like a moth to a candle. He painted him over and over again, and in return Aretino pushed Titian's paintings on his patrons. They drank together, rioted together, lived the Bohemian life of the writer and artist that became one of the most seductive and compelling images of man, at once creative and destructive, and one that still had the power to hypnotize long after they were dead. Aretino's life gave great impetus to the idea that the artist was beyond morality, outside society, a spirit dedicated only to the compulsive needs of his art. At the same time he invested this image with a nobility, a certain grandeur, and the possibility of tragedy. The end of a free man could be brutal, harsh, and black with pain; in the midst of a riotous life those shadows were with him. Titian saw them in his face, and painted them.

Of course there were men who were alarmed by Aretino, shocked by his life, disgusted by his writings, who condemned him roundly. Christian morality and the precepts of the Church were to the majority of men not shackles on the instinctive life but principles by which it should be lived. Yet in spite of themselves many were drawn to the image that Aretino or men like him presented. And some were honest enough to admit it. True, they tended, like Machiavelli, to discover man as a free agent more in princes and in captains of war, in the life of decision and action, than in writers and the writer's life. In war and politics, if anywhere, man was solitary, alone, without friends, and of necessity, they believed, without principle. To survive, to succeed, to kill before being killed, such were their destined lives. And this image artists evoked in painting as Machiavelli did in prose; the profiles, the faces of the Renaissance princes, have a terrible majesty, an aloofness, a dedication beyond the reality of common men.

So complex a society, of course, created many images that expressed its needs and hopes and aspirations, and not all mirrored egotism and the pursuit of fame. To some, Aretino or Cellini with his 'Men like Benvenuto . . . stand above the Law' were tedious. Men yearn to belong, to be secure, to be accepted. At a time when the courtly graces were being practised in London, Paris, Dijon, or Avignon, the rocky fortresses of Urbino, Rimini, or Orvieto were full of raw robber barons, uncouth, scarcely literate. Few despots could boast a long ancestry: within a mere three generations the Sforza rose from peasants to princes; even the Medici had modest origins. Rich Italy might become, but many of its prosperous men felt insecure in the luxury they could afford. Yet there existed, for them, antique patterns of behaviour. The knights of the late Middle Ages had developed chivalry into a code of manners, a complex dance of love as intricate as a tarantula's; Greece and Rome offered guides to gentility and sophistication. Above all there was Plato to teach them the efficacy of education; human nature, they hopefully believed, could be moulded to what men might desire it to be.

This attitude was formulated most effectively by two men – Vittorino da Feltre, who ran an academy for boys and girls at Mantua, and Baldassare Castiglione, who became the arbiter of taste for the western world. Education, they both maintained, was more than learning: it was breeding, which might give what the heritage of blood had conferred on the nobles of the Middle Ages. Those knights had been required to learn the manners as well as the skills of the warrior's trade, to be 'a verray parfit gentil knight', but the training did not confer gentility. That they inherited or, more rarely, won on the field of battle. The men of the Renaissance were concerned, however, to turn sow's ears into silk purses, peasants into princes.

The rough soldier of fortune and the uncouth merchant from the counting-house wished to appear as men of breeding, as connoisseurs of taste, as representatives of antique virtue. Even though they spurned the fortune of birth, cared not a rap for legitimacy, they could not bear to be considered barbarous. Barbarity was shown in a man's deportment, in his attitude to women, in his pleasures, and, of course, in his possessions. Some things were easier to eradicate than others. Giovanni della Casa thought no perfect gentleman would thrust stinking fish under the noses of his friends, or closely examine the contents of his handkerchief, or sit so that the more intimate parts of his person were revealed, or pick his nose, or spit, or break wind. The fact that della Casa found it necessary to expatiate on such things in his handbook of gentlemanly behaviour indicates the rudeness, the roughness, and the untutored nature of much of Renaissance society. But della Casa wanted more than behaviour free from physical offence. He also stressed that no man could be a gentleman without modesty, without being 'very desirous of beautiful things, well-proportioned and comely,' and squeamish of all that was not. To achieve this, Vittorino da Feltre and his imitators thought that all activities of the child should be directed to that end. Gentility, they maintained, was not an attribute of correct conversation or well-chosen clothes, on the contrary, it was the whole being of man; indeed, the highest perfection a man could achieve was to be immediately recognized as a gentleman.

The qualities of soul, the aspects of refinement and sensibility, which marked off the perfect gentleman were, of course, subject to endless debate, in which the classics were ransacked for precepts. Vittorino established a certain canon of requirements: the body as well as the soul needed to be brought to perfection. Exercise, quickness of eye, control of the muscles, and grace of movement were linked to moral qualities which the proper use of the body promoted – courage, hardiness, stamina, indifference to pain and discomfort. Intellectual exercises, like physical ones, were aimed at building character, developing moral qualities, and for this purpose classical antiquities and mathematical knowledge had special merits: the former

was full of the most excellent precepts, the latter revealed the harmonies of man and nature. Although many of the qualities which Vittorino sought in his pupils had been qualities of knightly perfection in
earlier times, his attitude to boys and girls and to their educational
needs was nearer far to Plato than to Aristotle. Above all, he believed
that a gentleman should be literate and his aesthetic senses refined by
teaching. Nor did he believe gentility to be conferred by birth; he
educated the poor with the rich.

With the growing leisure and the growing secularization of life in
the Renaissance, social pleasures became a pursuit in themselves. As
ever with an emerging class, opulent but insecure, many yearned for
the aristocratic distinctions of a previous age – long genealogies, em-
blazoned arms, the somewhat archaic extravagance of the joust and
tourney. Some humanists, however, would have none of this hanker-
ing after the trappings of feudal nobility. 'The longer the line of bold
miscreants,' wrote Poggio, 'from which a man traces his descent, the
further he is removed from true nobility.' For him nobility lay in the
individual heart and cultivated mind, in a man's nature and education
– not in his birth. There was endless debate – snobbery, a desire for
exclusiveness, drawing one way; a pride in the freshness and strength
of their own world and times pulling another. In drawing rooms of
courts, in the lounging places of piazzas, in tents on the battlefield, in
the country houses of bankers, men discussed over and over again the
nature of men and the way of perfection. Or they argued on how they
should act in love or in war, or what attributes they should cultivate,
or which passions they should despise and suppress. Naturally men
arose who became by common consent arbiters of such matters, and
the greatest of these was certainly Baldassare Castiglione, who was,
as might be expected, the son of an ancient, noble, but very poor
family, a man whose birth drew him towards the old, but who lacked
any future except with the new and emerging world of his own time.

His, long, grave, handsome face with its expression of almost careless elegance became the image of what an aristocrat and a gentleman

Portrait of a young man, possibly Guidbaldo II, Duke of Urbino, 1514–74,
by Bronzino
Metropolitan Museum of Art, New York

should look like. Everyone – kings as well as commoners – immediately recognized his quality. His presence at court was eagerly sought, and he conferred immortality on Urbino by writing of the conversations about the nature of a gentleman in which he had participated under the aegis of its blue-stocking Duchess. And in his *Book of the Courtier* there is portrayed another image of Renaissance man, distinct from Aretino's man of destiny; for Castiglione's man was a social being.

Belonging though he did to the knightly class, Castiglione was open-minded about birth. It was better to be born noble, easier to become a true gentleman if one were, but it was not, he reluctantly conceded, essential. Knightly virtues were, however, a necessity, for fighting, the pursuit of arms, the cult of honour, were the life of action to which a gentleman must dedicate himself. So courage and strength were prime virtues, and the exercise of the body a necessity. Horsemanship, fencing, wrestling, swimming, tennis – all things which gave the body suppleness and grace and power were proper pursuits for a gentleman. Naturally he must excel, but should avoid seeming to do so; above all he must cultivate grace of movement, and this Castiglione thought could only be achieved by the practice of *sperzzatura*, nonchalance, 'so as to conceal all art and make whatever is done and said appear to be without effort and without almost any thought about it.' Polish was as necessary as prowess, in exercises of the mind as well as the body. The gentleman was, of course, literate, knowledgeable about the classics, and eloquent. Learning must be lightly, negligently worn. Of course he should be quick in conversation but never thrusting, amusing but never mocking, humorous but never coarse, learned but never pedantic. And he must avoid being precious: eschew archaisms, never fear to use accepted colloquial speech, nor even bits of French and Spanish if they were in use in the society he frequented.

After the mind and the body came sensibility, connoisseurship. According to Castiglione, a gentleman might even be taught to paint

– as, indeed, the Greek and Roman aristocrats had been. Music and its appreciation were necessities: music composed the mind, directed thought to gentle pleasures, inculcated a love of harmony. Music was essentially *right*. The lighter expressions of art as well as the weightier were proper pastimes – dances, masques, the parade of rhetoric, and, naturally, the pursuit of love (love, however, not lust). The conquest of the heart, the possession of the mind, were a courtier's targets: the consolations of lesser delights were not altogether to be despised, even though they were improper subjects for conversation. A certain hypocrisy made for social ease.

About all activities, from the discussion of philosophy to the tilt of a hat, there must be ease, grace, and nonchalance; nobility must shine through. The princes of Italy might be murderers, adulterers, traitors, violators of boys and girls, but Castiglione depicted them as they desired themselves to be, just as Titian painted them as they wished to look – distinguished, set apart by their *virtù* and destiny from other men, yet full of ease, grace, nobility, and charm. The image created by Castiglione and his imitators, for his book enjoyed a vast success, increased the civility of Italians, made their courts a byword for sophisticated living. The cleanliness of their homes, the decorum at their tables, the beauty of their clothes and furnishings, the elegance of their manners, became models for the rude provincial gentry of the northern countries. Indeed for many generations Italy became an obsession for the less sophisticated nations of Europe, for it provided Europe not only with images of men, but also with a mirage of aristocratic and courtly life. Of course between image and reality there was frequently enough of a chasm. Most men could not live like Castiglione. Crude manners, vulgar habits, coarse pleasures, the instinctive life of which Aretino sang, lurked even in the courtier. The importance of Castiglione lies in the fact that men thought they *ought* to be like his Courtier, and valued men who seemed to achieve it.

In the High Renaissance, aristocratic attitudes triumphed over the rough bourgeois spirit of its earlier days. Certainly in so doing the

Knight in a Landscape, by Carpaccio
Thyssen Collection, Lugano

idea of what an aristocrat should be suffered a profound change. The armed knight, chivalry itself, became, as in *Don Quixote*, a pathetic joke. Much of the world in which the new aristocracy moved with such elegance grew, after all, out of the activity of merchants, bankers, and seafarers, not out of feudalism. But the code of manners which evolved was not a merchant's code; it had little to do with the traditional attitudes of the middle class. By 1530 much that Alberti had written about the family in the fifteenth century wore an old-fashioned air, and lives devoted to the pursuit of gain were regarded as vulgar. Castiglione and others like him had helped to define the terms by which men were included in or excluded from gentility. It was essentially a private world with its own scale of values, but one that twinkled with recognition symbols. Style in the turn of a phrase or the cut of a cloak; fields of knowledge, of taste, even of sport, that a gentleman might know or practice; attitudes to love, to religion, to the prince – all these things marked off the gentleman from the man. The rich could achieve this exclusive world only by leaving the counting-house behind and getting away from the rattle of the loom.

This, as we shall see, had profound consequences, and still has, for Western society. But the importance of the dominating image of man created by the Renaissance lies in this: it arose after the heroic age of Italy's commercial and industrial expansion was past. It belonged to the gilded twilight world of a luxurious but defeated society – defeated not only by the discoveries of the outer world which had given Western Europe the future, but also by the exceptional resilience of its traditional class structure which triumphed over the pragmatism, the disorder, the violent economic and political changes, of Renaissance Italy.

It was against this world of Castiglione – a society at once charming, elegant, inbred, and effete – that Aretino and his followers had to rebel, and so present the image of a genius for which conventions are but naught. Castiglione taught men how to belong, Aretino how to live.

FEDERIGO DA MONTEFELTRO

by Denis Mack Smith

For a brief fifty years, a little hill town in the northern Marches was one of the great cultural centres of Europe. Urbino was the birthplace of Raphael and Bramante. Sculptors were drawn there from Milan and Florence, architects from Siena and Dalmatia, painters from Spain and tapestry workers from Flanders. Paolo Uccello worked inside its hospitable walls; so did Piero della Francesca and Melozzo da Forli. Baldassare Castiglione emigrated from Mantua in order to live there, and was sent as the special envoy of Urbino to England, taking with him a painting commissioned from Raphael as a present for the English King. And as a result of Castiglione's much-translated *Book of the Courtier*, people all over the Western world heard of this remote mountain town, and learned from the standard of Urbino a code of manners, a way of courtesy and refinement, which became the norm of polite behaviour.

The duchy of Urbino and its standards of taste in art and manners were created by Federigo da Montefeltro, whose unforgettable broken-nosed profile portrait by Piero della Francesca has helped to make him one of the best known of Renaissance personalities. Earlier Montefeltro princes had won no special reputation either in politics or culture. For three centuries they had governed no more than a few dozen square miles in the Apennines, sometimes as feudatories of the Holy Roman Emperor, but usually owing nominal allegiance to the Pope. The soil and climate were indifferent, but the precipitous hill villages were easily defensible, and their hardy mountaineers fought well, with the result that the rulers of Urbino remained independent, even though they never owned a port on the Adriatic and never penetrated far down the alluvial valleys into the fertile coastal plain of Ancona. Federigo, who ruled from 1444 to 1482, was the greatest of the Montefeltro dynasty. He consolidated several scattered mountain fiefs and extended them into a state three times larger than his original inheritance. His duchy, which reached from the environs of San Marino in the north to beyond Gubbio in the south, was about sixty miles each way at its longest and broadest, and included perhaps four hundred villages and 150,000 inhabitants. Its independence was maintained by playing off one potential enemy against another – Rome against Venice or Florence against Rome – and luckily two of the strongest Italian states, Naples and Milan, were sufficiently remote from Urbino and sufficiently threatened by Rome or Venice to be generally friendly.

Like many prominent contemporaries, Federigo was born illegitimate. As a boy he spent a year as a hostage in Venice and then went to Mantua, where he was taught by Vittorino da Feltre, the greatest educator of Renaissance Italy. Vittorino ran a boarding-school where princes mixed with poor scholars and were given a severe classical education based on Latin and mathematics. The aim was to form character as well as mind and body. Federigo was taught frugal living, self-discipline, and a high sense of social obligation. He was made a connoisseur of literature and the arts, and also had to practise the manly sports, riding, dancing, and swordsmanship – all the accomplishments, in fact, which Castiglione later prescribed for the perfect courtier. Religion and scholarship were equally cultivated, but with a practical application: philosophy was made a guide to the art of living, and gracefulness and self-possession were inculcated as training for public life. As Federigo himself said later, Vittorino had instructed him 'in all human excellence'.

Few details are known about Federigo's early life. In 1432, at the age of ten, he was knighted by the Emperor, and five years later, after returning from Mantua to Urbino, he was married, after an engagement which dated from his early childhood. A few months later he set out for Lombardy with a company of eight hundred men to learn the art of war under a professional condottiere who was fighting against Gattamelata. Fighting was the occupation to which most contemporary princes were dedicated, and especially so in Urbino, where the Montefeltro family compensated for the poverty of the land and their remoteness from any significant trade routes by selling their services and their army to one side or other in most Italian wars. This was to be Federigo's chosen career. While his half brother Oddantonio succeeded their father as ruler of Urbino in 1443, Federigo himself seemed doomed to the traditionally subordinate life of the poor, illegitimate relation. But in 1444 the young Oddantonio, because of violent indignation against his debaucheries, was assassinated and his body torn to bits by the town mob. At first Federigo seems to have been refused entry to Urbino, but eventually he was chosen to succeed 'by the voice of the people' after promising not to revenge the murder.

Probably the chronicler who called this an election by popular acclaim was not romancing, for contemporaries unanimously praised the young Federigo, and later generations looked back to his reign as a golden age. Any patron as generous as he could no doubt buy adulation from that narrow but important group of writers which handed down what was likely to become the verdict of history, but with Federigo there were no dissentient voices even among commentators who did not benefit from his generosity. Unlike many Renaissance rulers, he avoided the accusation of cruelty and extravagant self-indulgence. He was magnanimous to his foes, and was rewarded handsomely when they preferred to surrender to him rather than run the risk of sack. He was also exceptional for his time in never deserting his allies for gain, and never was he known to break his word, not even when urged to do so by a papal legate. This honesty and trustworthiness were unusual in such a treacherous and brutal age. Federigo's great enemy, Sigismondo Malatesta, was in this respect more typical. Sigismondo was no less picturesque, no less refined and tasteful a patron, and equally fierce a fighter, but his atrocious cruelties were legendary; his dishonourable treatment of allies and his brutality towards subjects were common knowledge, and so was his failure to withstand such a prince as Federigo, who possessed the trust of ordinary people.

The biographers of Federigo (Raphael's father was the first of them) were concerned mainly with military exploits, and consequently there is little information about other aspects of his reign. We know, however, that he had to grant a charter of liberties at his accession. Taxes were to be reduced, some kind of public educational and medical service was promised, and the populace was to have some say in electing magistrates. Probably we should have heard further about this charter if he had governed harshly. According to one chronicler, 'revisers' were sent round the country to investigate grievances and relieve poverty, and grain from Apulia was stored away so that prices could be kept steady when the harvest failed. Certainly Federigo was more generally accessible than most Renaissance rulers. Vespasiano da Bisticci described how at mealtimes the doors would be opened so that anyone might address him between courses. Furthermore, 'When he rode out he met none who did not salute him and ask how he did. He went about with few attendants; none of them armed . . . He would often go afoot through his lands, entering now one shop and now another, and asking the workmen what their calling was, and whether they were in need of aught. So kind was he, that they all loved him as children love their parents. The country he ruled was a wondrous sight.' This affability and accessibility were remarkable at a time when assassination was a common form of political behaviour. The benevolence of Federigo's despotism was famous throughout Italy. Where his brother was said to have burnt a page alive for some minor lapse, Federigo was merciful to all offences save blasphemy. The few recorded instances indicate a man who was just and humane, who prudently considered the welfare of his subjects. A ruler who was so often away on campaign could not afford serious discontent at home.

An important reason for this unusual domestic tranquillity was the profits of successful war, which kept taxes low. Federigo's salary, together with the wages of his army, and perhaps not least the booty they captured, were the means by which a poor country for a while became rich, civilized, and content. His employers included two kings of Naples, two dukes of Milan, and three popes, and even in winter, when not fighting, he insisted on a substantial retainer fee from them. He commanded a good price particularly because of his tried loyalty, for Federigo never kept up relations with both sides simultaneously and never surrendered an allegiance until the end of his stipulated *condotta*. His income also reflected the fact that for many years no other general possessed quite his prestige. Less brilliant than many previous condottieri, he was nevertheless more successful than any in avoiding defeat, and both Castiglione and Vespasiano proudly, if not quite accurately, boasted that he lost not a single battle even when heavily outnumbered.

Federigo was known for keeping exceptionally good discipline among troops. When he met the enemy, his usual technique was to be prudent in the early stages of a battle and impetuous and daring the moment he observed some weakness in his foe's deployment. As a young man he had lost an eye in a tournament, but otherwise he was fit and tough. People admired his swift unexpectedness, the mastery and modernity of his complicated siege works, his skill in carrying heavy guns through difficult mountain country, and his tested ability to endure fatigue, hunger, and wounds. Others admired his charity and the pains he took 'to mitigate the horrors and miseries of war'. Machiavelli derided the safety-first tactics of professional condottieri, and incorrectly asserted that not a single man was killed when Federigo fought the great Colleoni at Molinella in 1467. The two captains certainly met after this battle to exchange civilities, for chivalry was not extinct, but Machiavelli wrongly assumed that wars were necessarily going to be more decisive and more justifiable in the sixteenth century, when they became less humane and more destructive. Federigo had to satisfy his employers, or he would have been without a job. Wars of independence and imperialism were as real in the fifteenth century as later, even if they were smaller and less lethal.

Federigo's first regular patron was the powerful Sforza family, for whom in 1445 he helped to win Pesaro at the same time that Fossombrone was acquired for Urbino. This earned him an excommunication because it was at odds with papal ambitions, and it also increased the enmity of the Malatesta. Sigismondo Malatesta controlled a large stretch of coast above Ancona. His state and Federigo's were too close to avoid friction, and they shared an insecurity and lack of natural frontiers which led to quarrelsomeness and aggression. In between his struggles with Sigismondo, Federigo in 1448 raised an army for the Florentines. Several years later he contracted to serve the Aragonese dynasty in Naples, and this arrangement lasted almost all his life. The throne of Naples was at this point contested by the French Angevins, who found considerable support among the Neapolitan baronage, but Federigo in 1460 helped the Aragonese to resist the invaders, and in the following year he captured the important town of Aquila.

While Federigo was preoccupied in southern Italy, a Malatesta army invaded Urbino and papal territory. The ferocious Sigismondo was therefore 'canonized to hell' by the Pope and burnt in effigy before St Peter's, while his excommunication for heresy, uxoricide, incest, and other crimes was pronounced by Cardinal Nicholas of Cusa. Federigo, as captain-general of the Church's forces, seized this opportunity to destroy his rival's power for good. Sigismondo's heir was taken prisoner when Fano fell after a difficult and damaging siege, but Federigo released him without ransom despite the fact that contemporary practice made such hostages a legitimate and profitable asset. In addition to Fano, Senigallia was captured, and all that remained to the Malatesta was Rimini. Sigismondo, on his knees, publicly recanted his atheistical beliefs. Most of the Malatesta empire was claimed by the Pope and the papal nephews. Federigo, however, was allowed some fifty townships, which made him more powerful than any other ruler throughout the Marches and the Romagna. Although still a pigmy among the giant states of Milan, Venice, and Naples, he sometimes held the balance of power in Italy.

At this time the Papacy was trying to enforce its suzerainty and taxation rights over the seignorial families who ruled in central Italy. Pius 11 had exploited the rivalry between Montefeltro and Malatesta, employing one to subdue the other, and in 1465, his successor Paul 11, appointed Federigo *gonfaloniere*, or captain, of the Church's forces, in order to extend papal power still further. The condottiere from Urbino was now a famous man in Italy. In 1467 he was made commander of a league of states alarmed at the aggressive imperialism of Venice. The Venetians, retreating before the Turks on the far shore of the Adriatic, were attempting to compensate for these losses by pushing their empire westward and southward in Italy, to the consternation of their neighbours and the Pope. Federigo's own state was among those upon which both Rome and Venice might have ambitions, and this dual threat increased in direct proportion to his general political success.

In 1468 Sigismondo Malatesta died, and the Pope tried to annex Rimini. At this point Federigo, who had hitherto been more frightened of Venice, recognized the danger of further papal aggrandizement. He was a devout and loyal son of the Church, but not without qualification, for he could see that Venice and Rome between them were gradually swallowing up the Romagna. Even more alarming, the popes were trying to conquer principalities for their sons and nephews before another family succeeded them in their sacred office. Against this danger Montefeltro and Malatesta made common cause out of self-preservation, and instead of renewing his lapsed *condotta* with the Pope, Federigo supported the claims of Roberto Malatesta to Rimini. The ruler of Urbino, as captain of a league which included Naples and Milan, as well as other Romagnol *signori*, routed the papal army at Mulazzano.

Federigo's first wife, Gentile Brancaleoni, had died in 1457 leaving no children. He then married Battista, daughter of Allessandro Sforza of Pesaro. Battista's face is almost as well known to us from Piero's portrait as her husband's. Married at thirteen, she died at twenty-five, leaving one son, many daughters, and the reputation of being a formidable blue-stocking who had governed the state in her husband's absence and could extemporize publicly in Latin. Federigo's half-sisters had married into the neighbouring dynasties of Sforza, Gonzaga, and Malatesta; two of his daughters were bestowed upon papal families, the Colonna and della Rovere, and a third upon Roberto Malatesta, the illegitmate son of his old enemy. The circle of appropriate families being limited, there was an inevitable tendency to inbreed.

In 1472, the year Battista died, Federigo was asked by Lorenzo de' Medici to raise an army against Volterra in Tuscany. (Lorenzo was defending the mining interests of Florentine citizens against nationalization in Volterra.) The military task was easy, but after the town had surrendered, Federigo could not restrain his soldiers from a terrible sack. Discipline in mercenary armies was always a problem, especially since the prospect of loot was an inducement for enlisting recruits, but this was a solitary lapse on Federigo's part. For himself he seized only a polyglot Bible of great rarity and beauty, and he was then escorted in triumph to a civic banquet in Florence and given a helmet adorned by Pollaiuolo. Another distinction received soon afterwards was the Order of the Garter from England, and this emblem became a common motif in the decoration of his palace. Such was his reputation outside Italy that special embassies arrived not only from England and Hungary but from Persia and Trebizond. A further triumph came in 1474, when Sixtus IV, solemnly receiving him in St Peter's, changed his traditional title of Count to Duke. This acknowledged that Urbino had now reached a special position of independence and strength that distinguished it from other small city-states. It also acknowledged the Pope's need for military support for his nephews, and the formal concession of the title was designed to seal the alliance.

Federigo served Sixtus well. He tamed the insubordinate ruler of Città di Castello in Umbria, and in 1479 he campaigned against Florence after the Pope had tried and failed to assassinate Lorenzo de' Medici. Papal ambitions, however, soon became dangerous again when Sixtus began planning a conquest of Ferrara for yet another nephew. Federigo wrote to the Pope, urging him to turn against the Moslems who had just won a foothold in southern Italy; but the head of Christendom was more anxious to establish his family than to oppose the Turkish advance. As a result, war broke out over Ferrara, and Federigo aligned himself against papal aggression with Naples, Florence, Milan, Mantua, and Bologna, while his son-in-law, Roberto Malatesta, led the opposing papal forces. In the malarial swamps of Ferrara the rival commanders were stricken with the fever which was the greatest scourge of Renaissance Italy, and Federigo and Roberto died on the same day, 10 September 1482.

For a time Federigo's son and successor, Guidobaldo, was able to maintain the model state of Urbino, continuing his father's lavish patronage of the arts until his lack of success as a general lessened the profits of warfare upon which the economy depended. Then, in 1502, Pope Alexander VI persuaded Guidobaldo to loan the papal army his artillery, and at this crucial moment the Pope's son, Cesare Borgia, swept down on Urbino, forced its ruler to flee, and appropriated the priceless art collection, much of which he sold to pay his troops.

Perhaps Federigo himself would have fared no better. He had been the last of the great condottieri, and lived at a time when defence was much easier than attack. Shortly after his death that day had passed; heavy artillery became more common and more efficient, and when it did the fortified hill towns and castles were suddenly vulnerable. The superiority of new weapons spelled ruin for the small Renaissance princedoms. A decade after his death, the perennial conflicts between Italian cities and families led to an invasion of the peninsula by France and Spain, and it was these new, large nation-states which were to dominate the next period of European history. For three centuries

Italy was a convenient location where foreign armies could fight each other; and whereas Federigo had taken care to conduct his wars abroad, Urbino itself now became a battleground. By 1530 a series of invasions and counter-invasions had sacked Rome and Florence and desolated that world of small city-states which had engendered the Renaissance. Much of the surplus wealth which enlightened princes had once used for endowing culture and the arts was dissipated, and in this strange new world Urbino was too small and too awkwardly situated between rival empires to survive.

Federigo da Montefeltro is not remembered for his battles; he made no notable contribution to the art of war; his dynasty and dukedom disappeared. The one thing which survived intact was the memory of Federigo and his court of humanists and artists. In retrospect he and his son were spoken of alongside the magnificent Lorenzo. They were children of their time in a love of lavish display, in their burning drive for self-expression and a competitive urge for prestige. These instincts without doubt contributed in part to their devotion to art and learning, though both of them showed well enough that they also possessed a disinterested love of all things beautiful. Certainly they were far above all other contemporary rulers in character and intellectual refinement. Through them Urbino became a celebrated centre of culture which attracted men of talent and renown from all of Europe; it was the place to which the Doria, Orsini, and Farnese families, as well as wealthy parents in other countries, sent their children to be educated. Castiglione, nostalgically recollecting that Federigo, in his day, was 'the light of Italy', described life at Urbino in his delightful book *The Courtier*, in which he recorded a portrait of the model gentleman. As Vittoria Colonna wrote to him, 'I do not wonder that you have depicted the perfect courtier, for you had only to hold a mirror before you, and set down what you saw there.' The conversations recorded in *The Courtier* took place in the palace which Federigo had built at Urbino.

Books of all kinds were Federigo's greatest joy, and Vespasiano described his efforts to build the great library in Urbino:

We come now to consider in what high esteem the Duke held all Greek and Latin writers, sacred as well as secular. He alone had a mind to do what no one had done for a thousand years or more; that is, to create the finest library since ancient times. He spared neither cost nor labour, and when he knew of a fine book, whether in Italy or not, he would send for it. It is now fourteen or more years since he began the library, and he always employed, in Urbino, in Florence, and in other places, thirty or forty scribes in his service . . . There are numerous Greek books by various authors, which when he was not able to get them otherwise, he sent for them, desiring that nothing should be wanting in any tongue which it was possible to acquire. There were to be seen Hebrew books, all that could be found in that language, beginning with the Bible, and all those who have commented upon it, Rabbi Moses and other commentators. Not only are those Hebrew books the Holy Scriptures, but also on medicine, on philosophy, and in all branches, all that could be acquired in that tongue.

His lordship having completed this worthy task at the great expense of more than thirty thousand ducats, among the other excellent and praiseworthy arrangements which he made was this, that he undertook to give each writer a title, and this he desired should be covered with crimson embellished with silver. He began, as has been noted above, with the Bible, as the foremost of all, and had it covered, as was said, with gold brocade. Then beginning with all the Doctors of the Church, he had each one covered with crimson and embellished with silver; and so with the Greek Doctors as with the Latins. As well philosophy, history, and books on medicine, and all the modern Doctors; in such a manner that there are innumerable volumes of this kind, a thing gorgeous to behold.

In this library all the books are beautiful in the highest degree, all written with the pen, not one printed, that it might not be disgraced thereby; all elegantly illuminated, and there is not one that is not written on kidskin. There is a singular thing about this library, which is not true of any other; and this is, that of all the writers, sacred as well as profane, original works as well as translations, not a single page is wanting from their works in so far as they are in themselves complete; which cannot be said of any other library, all of which have portions of the works of a writer, but not all; and it is a great distinction to possess such perfection.

Vespasiano had helped to collect this library. He wrote:

Some time before, I went to Ferrara, being at Urbino at his lordship's court, and having catalogues of all the libraries of Italy, commencing with that of the Pope, of St Mark's at Florence, of Pavia – and I had even sent to England to obtain a catalogue of the library of the university of Oxford – I compared these with that of the Duke, and I saw that all were faulty in one particular; that they had numerous copies of the same work, but they had not all the works of one writer complete as this had; nor were there writers of every branch as in this.

Virtually the whole corpus of known classics was in the library, as well as Avicenna, Averroes, and medieval texts. Federigo was also a patron of contemporary literature. Ficino, Landino, Poggio, and Piero della Francesca dedicated writings to this man whom the humanist Piatti eulogized as *oraculum totius Italiae.*

The Duke was a competent Latinist in an age when close attention to the example of olden times was recommended for statesmen and generals. He was also an early enthusiast for Greek and hired instructors to teach it. He was able to discuss the Trojan war with Pius II and dared to contradict that learned scholar about the geography of Asia Minor. He liked to have Livy's histories read aloud at mealtimes, and was especially fond of Tacitus and the *Commentaries* of Caesar.

Vespasiano wrote:

To return to letters, the Duke of Urbino was well versed therein, not only in history and in the Holy Scriptures, but also in philosophy, which he studied many years under a distinguished teacher, Maestro Lazzaro, afterwards for his merits made Bishop of Urbino. He was instructed by Maestro Lazzaro in the Ethics of Aristotle, with and without comments, and he would also dispute over the difficult passages. He began to study logic with the keenest understanding, and he argued with the most nimble wit that was ever seen. After he had heard the Ethics many times, comprehending them so thoroughly that his teachers found him hard to cope with in disputation, he studied the Politics assiduously . . . Indeed, it may be said of him that he was the first of the Signori who took up philosophy and had knowledge of the same. He was ever careful to keep intellect and virtue to the front, and to learn some new thing every day.

With all this, the Duke was devoutly religious. He heard Mass daily, and delighted in discussing religion with the abbot or mother superior of the monastic houses which he had endowed. He not only knew the Scriptures well, but was familiar with the great Doctors of the early Church and possessed an extensive theological library. He developed 'a strong predilection' for the works of St Thomas Aquinas. He was no puritan, yet despite his four illegitimate children he was a moral man, and, as befitted a pupil of Vittorino, recognized no dichotomy between humanist and Christian ideals.

Federigo's taste and qualities of mind were embodied most obviously in his famous palace at Urbino, for to him architecture was not only queen of the arts but the very summit of intellectual as well as aesthetic activity. Beginning around 1450 and building slowly, Federigo gradually amplified his ideas, and in 1468, after searching and failing to find an architect in the Tuscany which he so admired, he chose Luciano Laurana as chief architect. After Laurana there arrived Francesco di Giorgio, the foremost engineer in Italy, who dedicated to the Duke a celebrated treatise on architecture and gratefully acknowledged an indebtedness to his employer for many technical hints about fortification. Five architects and engineers are mentioned in a surviving list of palace officers.

The same list reveals the royal scale of life in the great palace. There were five hundred people in the court: in addition to knights and men-at-arms, these included two hundred servants, four teachers, an astrologer, five 'readers aloud at meals', four men who transcribed manuscripts, two organists, the keeper of the bloodhounds, and a man who tended the camel-leopard.

But it was the buildings which struck people most. Lorenzo de' Medici admired them, and they were to astonish Montaigne and a long succession of travellers. Federigo had furnished his palace, Castiglione wrote, 'so well with every suitable thing that it seemed not a palace but a city in the form of a palace; and furnished it not only with what is customary such as silver vases, wall hangings of the richest cloth of gold, silk, and other like things, but for ornament he added countless ancient statues of marble and bronze, rare paintings, and musical instruments of every sort; nor did he wish to have anything there that was not most rare and excellent.' Vespasiano da Bisticci was even more enthusiastic. (As a Florentine, Vespasiano judged by the highest standards.)

As to architecture it may be said that no one of his age, high or low, knew it so thoroughly. We may see, in the buildings he constructed, the grand style and the due measurement and proportion, especially in his palace, which has no superior amongst the buildings of the time, none so well considered, or so full of fine things. Though he had his architects about him, he always first realized the design and then explained the proportions and all else; indeed, to hear him discourse thereanent, it would seem that his chief talent lay in this art; so well he knew how to expound and carry out its principles.

Vasari was another Florentine who commented admiringly on the commodious apartments of Urbino's palace, and its stairways which were 'more convenient and agreeable than any that had existed previously'. Windows and doorways in admirable proportion, a graceful court with slender columns, a hanging garden, the great library, and room after room with splendid decorations in stucco and marble relief – all testifying to the sensibility as well as the munificence of the Duke. Intarsia, marquetry, polychrome marble, and *trompe-l'œil* work on the walls represented what was best in current fashion all over Italy. Ambrogio da Milano and Domenico Rosselli of Pistoia were employed to design ornamental motifs on jambs, pediments, and chimney pieces, upon which the garter of England and the eagle of Montefeltro were frequently found. Typical of Federigo was that alongside his religious chapel, and with the same proportions, was another chapel dedicated to the Muses; and in his study were twenty-eight portraits of famous men in world history, among whom Homer was alongside Aquinas, Ptolemy with Saint Ambrose, and Seneca with Solomon. Typical also of this Renaissance prince was an inscription round the interior court which told how the great Federigo had raised this palace for his own glory and for his posterity.

In all respects Federigo had represented the best in his age, and his example endured long after he had passed away. Through his practice the teachings of Vittorino inspired a small but noble society which, even when conquered politically, made a conquest of all Europe. At Urbino could be found an intellectual élite which believed that an integrated and disciplined education would result in proper behaviour and a proper sense of duty towards God and man. Federigo's classical upbringing and intellectual curiosity in no way undermined, but rather reinforced, the teachings of orthodox religion. Nor did he tend to that all too common form of humanism which despised science; on the contrary, Vespasiano praised the Duke's skill in geometry and arithmetic. As for the arts, Federigo was enthusiastic about more than architecture. His musical tastes perhaps show the influence of contemporary Flanders, the same influence which brought Justus of Ghent and Flemish savants and textile artisans to his court. 'He delighted greatly in music,' Vespasiano noted, 'understanding vocal and instrumental alike, and maintained a fine choir with skilled musicians and many singing boys. He had every sort of instrument in his palace and delighted in their sound, also the most skilful players. He preferred delicate to loud instruments, caring little for trombones and the like.'

Anything loud and harsh was anathema at the court of Urbino. Dress had to be sober, demeanour quiet, conversation lively but gentle. Women were given an active and respected place in this world, setting new standards for polite society. Vittorino's educational goal had been to create the complete all-round person who was courteous, upright, sensitive, but at the same time active. Federigo himself was such a man. He possessed a robust physique which resisted wounds and great hardship, yet the rough practice of war left his finer feelings unimpaired. Everyone knew him to be a man of honour as well as courage. His official portraits show him not so much as a warrior but as an intellectual, either reading, contemplating, listening to a lecture, or at prayer. Unlike many Renaissance princes, he lived without excess, 'eating plain food and no sweetmeats', and the five hundred people who composed his court followed as orderly an existence as in a monastery: 'Here was no romping or wrangling, but everyone spoke with becoming modesty.'

What little we know about this court of Urbino gives us a precious insight into the civilization of the Renaissance in Italy at its most admirable. Piero della Francesca's work has partially perished, the superb ducal library was swallowed up by the Vatican, and Federigo's portraits were scattered to Florence, Milan, and Windsor. But time cannot easily erase his memory and example. Had he been more representative of his class, the course of the Renaissance might have followed a still more brilliant path.

THE SPREAD OF THE RENAISSANCE

I N the autumn of 1511 Erasmus, the most distinguished scholar of Northern Europe, took up his lodgings again in Queen's College, Cambridge – a cold, bleak room that overlooked the marshes of the fens. He was poor, he was frightened of the plague that raged about the University, he was very lonely. He had been swept to England by the tide of the Italian Renaissance, not for the first but for the third time. For five wearisome years Erasmus mouldered in Cambridge until he could stand the poverty and the ignorance no longer, and off he went on his journeys again, to the Netherlands, to Switzerland, to Germany, always carrying with him the memory of those years in Italy when he had discovered himself. The new learning had filled him with such hope that not even the sorrows and hardships of his personal life could eradicate it. In 1517 he could still write, 'Immortal God, what a world I see dawning! Why can I not grow young again?' Nor was Erasmus unique. In London one of the most gifted, yet wayward, of Florentine sculptors, Torrigiano, was modelling, under the soaring Gothic arches of Westminster Abbey, the first Renaissance tombs of Northern Europe, built to immortalize Henry VII and his wife, Elizabeth of York. For decades the currents created not only by cataclysmic events such as the invasion of Italy by the French kings, but also by the excitement of the new learning, had been drawing such men as Erasmus and Torrigiano into or out of Italy. And that sense of wonder, of a new world and a new dawn of the spirit, touched less sensitive men than Erasmus. Henry VII conferred the Garter, the highest order of English chivalry, on the Duke of Urbino, and the court of Windsor witnessed the embassy of Castiglione who came to receive it for his master. So profound was Henry VII's respect for the Italian scholarship that he asked Polydore Vergil to write what became the first serious and dispassionate study of England's history. Indeed, the presence of Erasmus in England was due entirely to a devoted band of humanists – Linacre, Grocyn, and Colet – who had studied in Padua, Florence, and Rome, seeking to acquire facility in Greek and a knowledge of the old as well as the new philosophies. Their attitude was deeply Christian, and their aim was to perfect their theology through a more exact knowledge of the early Fathers. The employment of Pietro Torrigiano was also due to the same band of humanists, which included Lord Mountjoy as its patron and John Fisher as its chaplain, both of whom were intimately connected with the English royal family. What was true of England was also true of the Netherlands, of Germany, and of Spain.

As the Renaissance spread beyond the Alps, it was checked in Italy. In 1495 Charles VIII invaded Naples and in so doing unleashed thirty years of carnage. In the Lombard plain battle followed battle, draining away wealth, disrupting trade, heaping up taxes, destroying conditions favourable to art and learning. Furthermore, the riches of the New World, so recently discovered, poured into Spain, the Netherlands, France, and England, but not into Italy; wealth went west, and with it art. And then came Luther, who in 1517 hammered his Protestant theses to the church door of Wittenberg. To hold off the Reformation, the Papacy needed a sterner spirit; the luxurious and wanton times of the Borgia and Medici were brought to an end, and a militant asceticism replaced the self-indulgence of Renaissance Rome. No wonder Vasari regarded the venerable Michelangelo as a relic of the age of heroes. This lonely, solitary artist had become the symbol of a time that had passed.

By 1500 Italy exerted a hypnotic influence, and just as the princes of the Western world wished to acquire the services of Italy's great painters and sculptors, so, too, did the artists of this outer world feel themselves drawn to Italy. The great Flemish school of painters might

296

be secure within its own great tradition and therefore possess little or no sense of inferiority when confronted with the brilliance of the Italian achievement; and in fact it contributed as much in technique and originality as it derived from Italy. The same was not true, however, of the French or the German artists. They had been ravished by the books of engravings of Italian pictures that had begun to circulate after 1470. Crude as these were, they sufficiently hinted the beauties of the masters they copied to excite an overwhelming curiosity. Albrecht Dürer, as a young apprentice at Nuremberg, somehow acquired engravings of Pollaiuolo and Mantegna. Already in a tentative, schoolboyish, and rather shocked manner he had begun to draw from the nude, but these engravings helped to release his spirit from the harsh, moral, and cruelly realistic treatment of naked women that had become traditional in Gothic Germany. Engravings were not enough, however, and try as he might, the secret of the Italian painters seemed to elude him. He believed that the formula for successful painting of the human figure, like some ancient mystery, was kept hidden by Italian artists. He sought the magic formula in Italy itself, deepened his imagination, improved his technique, but never found what he sought, and to his death the Gothic tradition into which he had been born held him in thrall. Yet without his Italian experiences and without his preoccupation with Italian art, his own achievement would have been less noble. As with Dürer, so with scores of artists great or small over the next four hundred years. They came to Italy as on a pilgrimage, for here was the source of their art. The painting of El Greco is as idiosyncratic as any artist's of Western Europe, yet his art is indelibly stamped with the years that he spent in Venice. The way he draws, the glittering light that runs along the edge of his figures, derives from Tintoretto, as his colour does from Titian. The two greatest French artists of the seventeenth century – Nicolas Poussin and Claude Lorraine – spent most of their working lives in Rome. Titian – his colour, his atmosphere, even his figures – entranced Poussin. Again and again, artists of the highest genius – Velázquez,

Rubens, Rembrandt, Goya, Renoir – paint the same themes, sometimes even copy the same pictures, that the artists of the Renaissance
had first conceived and executed. Giorgione's reclining Venus haunts
European painting like a dream. All who aspired to greatness in painting needed to make the long journey to Italy. Some, like Sir Joshua
Reynolds, went in great comfort under the patronage of the rich;
others, like Richard Wilson, went on foot and in poverty, painting
for their bread. Until the twentieth century, the traditions created by
the Italian Renaissance were those in which all Western European
artists worked.

The French kings and their courtiers during their invasions of Italy
were delighted by much that they saw in Milan and Venice: the Certosa of Pavia especially caught their imagination. On the other hand,
the austere and more truly classical buildings of Florence left them
unmoved. So at first Italian influences on the new luxurious hunting
lodges that the French nobility were building along the Loire combined, as at Chambord, the basic plan of a traditional medieval castle
with the sophisticated elevation and greater comfort of an Italian
palace. For a time this marriage of the old and the new satisfied Western Europe, but in the end, no matter how much inspiration might
twist and turn within its national traditions, or frolic in the riotous
decoration of the Baroque, it was drawn back, time and time again,
to the purity of classical achievement, to Brunelleschi, to Bramante,
to Palladio, and, finally – just before the Gothic revival destroyed
architectural taste throughout Western Europe – to the Greek. In the
visual arts, in its themes as well as its techniques, the achievements of
the Italian Renaissance permeated Europe like an indelible stain. They
expressed the world in which men wished to live – their dreams, their
aspirations, as well as their actualities.

The arts of the Renaissance were not the only achievements that
seeded themselves throughout the countries of the Western world.
Changes that had taken place in Italy generations earlier were happen-
ing in Western Europe in the sixteenth century, with the result that

Self-portrait, Dürer, 1484   299
Albertina, Vienna

a similar sort of society grew up with similar needs. Its basis, like Italy's, was mercantile and urban; and it was ambivalent towards the old feudal nobilities – longing for their grace, their courtliness, and their sense of privileged destiny, yet hating their special rights, their selfish and jealous independence that could cut so savagely across the needs of society as a whole, to the detriment of trade and profit. The

Sir Thomas More, by Holbein
Frick Collection, New York

new men longed for professional government, for a powerful person who could secure order and inculcate into a barbarous and anarchic society the *civilitas* of the ancients. For them the fountain of this political knowledge was Italy: there the wisdom of the classical world, of Plato, of Aristotle, of Cicero, had been sifted and refined and adjusted to modern necessities. Even more importantly, the University of Padua could teach them the secrets of Roman government through the study of its laws. Again, the Italians had made a profession of diplomacy in Europe of the fifteenth century which had come to be regarded as essential to good government as statistical analysis is in the twentieth. Men of affairs in London, in Paris, in Brussels, in Madrid, in the towns and states of Germany, thought that they could only manage their new and baffling societies if they or their subordinates had studied in Italy. Most of Henry VIII's ministers of state – Wolsey, More, and Thomas Cromwell – were fascinated by the new learning, and they encouraged scholarship whenever they could. Wolsey endowed Christ Church, Oxford, in order to establish the study of the new humanities in England. Thomas More became the life-long friend of Erasmus. Cromwell lent his rare and precious Italian books to his friends and encouraged young men such as Thomas Starkey, who had spent years studying civil law at Padua in the household of Reginald Pole. (Pole, who was a Plantagenet and a kinsman of Henry VIII, maintained a small court of English scholars at the University of Padua.) This interest in Italian learning certainly had its practical aspects, but it captivated them all – even Cromwell, that hammer of the monasteries – at a deeper level than practical usefulness.

This new learning seemed to hold the secrets of life itself for most of them and, for the more sensitive, some of the secrets of eternity. More and his friends – Colet, Linacre, Grocyn – were deeply religious men. So were Lefèvre d'Étaples and his colleagues in Paris; so were Ulrich von Hutten and Reuchlin in Germany. They reverenced Italian scholarship, for it took them, via a knowledge of Greek, to the purest texts of the New Testament. Here, they felt, they would find a faith cleansed from the impurities and evasions created by centuries of comment and explanation. By applying the new skills of philology and textual criticism which the Italian humanists had perfected, they would, they hoped, lay bare Christianity in its purest and most historical form and thereby strengthen the Church. This attitude towards religion fused with another, equally serious, but Flemish rather than Italian in origin. Before Renaissance influence had touched northwestern Europe there had been a strong revival of religious mysticism, led by the Brethren of the Common Life, which had been given literary and devotional form by Thomas à Kempis in his *Imitation of Christ*. This mysticism stressed the importance of the individual's direct relation with God, and, by implication, lessened the importance of the priesthood and the Church. The search for historical truth, through scholarship, became linked with this search for truth in the exercise of the individual's religious conscience; and both became the seeding ground of Protestantism.

No one is more typical of the linkage between Italian humanism and reformed Christianity than Erasmus, who prepared the ground for Luther. A bastard son of a priest, half-tricked into monastic life, sensitive, excluded both by his habit and temperament from an active life of the instincts, he concentrated his heart and mind on friendship with scholars of like tastes. A man of formidable intellectual ability and exquisite literary gifts, his vast reputation was built up not only by personal contact and familiar letters, but also by the new invention of the printing press. His sharp satire – *The Praise of Folly* – exploited the sensationalism which only the press can give, and his Latin translation of the Greek Testament established his reputation as a scholar with a rapidity that no one could have achieved in earlier centuries. For Erasmus, the institutions of the Church and its learning were encrusted with silliness, stupidity, and barbarity. Christian faith could never regain its pristine clarity until this dross of centuries was cleared away. Yet he was no Protestant, no revolutionary, and he retreated rapidly from the position towards which Luther with his furious denunciations and precipitate actions seemed to be dragging him. Naturally he refused to listen to Albrecht Dürer's ardent plea: 'O Erasmus of Rotterdam, where wilt thou tarry? . . . Hear, Christian knight, ride forth with the Lord Jesus . . . defend the right, obtain the martyr's crown!' He preferred to die in his bed: scared of the new age whose

Erasmus, by Holbein
Louvre

coming in 1517 he had welcomed with such joy. But for Dürer the reformation of religion was an inspiration greater and deeper than any experience of his life, greater even than his artistic experience in Italy.

Undoubtedly the scholars and critics had undermined, by their sharp attack on contemporary religious practices, the institutions of the Church; they mocked priests, bred resentment against papal taxation, and held the popes themselves up to the ridicule many deserved. Although some like Erasmus drew back, others such as Melanchthon and Peter Martyr, the Italian humanist, were prepared to go forward with Luther, feeling that he was leading them to the true dawn of a new age, to the rebirth of Christianity as Christ preached it. So the spirit of the Italian Renaissance, once it crossed the Alps, was diverted into new channels, plunging from the broad, sunlit meadows of secular delights into the dark ravines of religion.

Yet this political and religious twist to Italian influence was, for the early part of the sixteenth century, largely, if not entirely, confined to England, the Netherlands, and Germany. In France there were men like Erasmus, friends of his, deeply concerned with theology, deeply distrustful of scholasticism, as ardent as he was for pure religion. Yet they were not typical of French society as More and Colet or even Thomas Cromwell were typical of England. French society was more sophisticated, more secure, readier far to pursue that language of personal expression which lies at the heart of the Italian Renaissance. Much of Italian civilization – the gardens, the clothes, the furnishings and decoration of houses and palaces, the general civility of life, had entranced Philippe de Comines and many another noble Frenchman with the invading armies of Charles VIII and Louis XII. But it was Francis I who really fell in love with Italy and things Italian in spite of the fact that the greatest humiliation of his career – his defeat by the Emperor Charles V – took place at Pavia. He was the first prince outside Italy to begin a collection of paintings and sculpture by the great Italian masters. He persuaded Leonardo da Vinci to spend his last

Francis I, by Clouet
Louvre

years at Amboise, close to his great hunting lodges at Blois and Chambord. He did everything he could to entice Michelangelo to live in France and nearly succeeded. (He had to be content with a *Hercules* his agent bought.) With Benvenuto Cellini he was more successful. This fabulous rogue, a boastful, swashbuckling liar yet a craftsman of genius, entranced Francis, who tolerated his extravagance and forgave his bad temper for the sake of the embellishments (among them Cellini's superb gold salt cellar which is so justly famous) with which he was adorning his châteaux.

Francis I was not merely a collector; he wanted his court to outshine in literature and in manners, as well as in art, the most famous courts of Italy, and he flung his cloak of patronage on all who might bring distinction to his country. In this he was aided by his remarkable sister, Marguerite of Navarre, who can claim, perhaps, to be one of the most outstanding women of the Renaissance. She wrote the *Heptameron*, a bawdy collection of stories, after the style of Boccaccio; a mystical tract called *The Mirror of the Sinful Soul*, and a number of outstanding spiritual hymns. She corresponded with Erasmus, befriended Protestants, was accused herself as a heretic by the Sorbonne, and patronized Rabelais. Her court contained the whole world of letters, as complex and as strange as her own temperament. Indeed, many of the contradictions in her own self-expression reflected the contradictions of French artistic and intellectual society as it struggled to assimilate the achievements of Italy not only with its own Gothic traditions but also with those new horizons – intellectual as well as geographical – which the great discoveries had disclosed to the Western world. For Italian humanists, discovery lay in the past, in the art and history of their ancestors or their country's ancestors, the Greeks. With Frenchmen and with Englishmen, discovery also meant new worlds that knew neither Christianity nor Christian government nor Christian morality. To men such as Rabelais, Montaigne, Marlowe, Shakespeare, or Bacon, insecurity, anxiety, and elation mingled haphazardly and fused into art. Reverence for the past, a yearning for the safety of tradition, alternated with the intoxicating sense of the capacity of man, the uniqueness of his experience, and the splendour and freshness of the world about him.

In Rabelais, the greatest writer of the French Renaissance, this conflict was apparent both in his restless, troubled life and in his writings. Like Erasmus, he was a rebel monk who hated the ignorance and immorality of monastic life. He sought truth in the world. 'Abandon yourself,' he wrote, 'to Nature's truths, and let nothing in this world be unknown to you.' Rabelais followed his own dictum and it led him to strange places – to alchemy, to astrology, to the mysterious exoticism which seemed to offer new truth in the intellectual chaos of sixteenth-century Europe. And his great work *Gargantua and Pantagruel* is as odd and as moving as Rabelais' own quest for self-knowledge. Gargantua, Pantagruel, and Grangousier, the chief characters of this extraordinary fantasia, have the twisted extravagance of Gothic

Page from
La Navigation du compagnon
à la Bouteille
Lyons, 1532

gargoyles. They are gross representatives of the instinctive life, yet
full of satire and wisdom, capable of nobility and understanding.
Above all they are in search of life and truth. And in the midst of their
fantastic adventures comes the description of the Abbey of Thelema,
a Utopian world that might have been dreamed by Castiglione. The
turmoil and confusion of real life is stilled by the contemplation of
realized ideals; men and women achieve the noble life. The whole
book is written in a fabulous style, by a man utterly drunk with words.
It is almost as if Rabelais had himself discovered language. This mixture of barbarity and civility, of satire and sincerity, entranced the
French court. The Church might be scandalized, the Protestants outraged, but Pantagruelism became chic, the fashion of the aristocracy.
It was original, it was in tune with the medley and confusion of contemporary life, and above all, it was French.

Surrender of Breda, by Velázquez
Prado, Madrid

As soon as a literary renaissance began to flourish either in France or in England or in Spain, a strong nationalist sentiment rapidly infused it, and the delight that writers and artists took in the Italian achievement led not only to emulation but also to envy. In 1549 Joachim du Bellay published his pamphlet *La Défense et illustration de la langue française* (cribbed almost entirely from Speroni's defence of Italian) in which he exhorted Frenchmen to challenge in their own language the triumphs of antiquity. The same court circle that patronized Rabelais took du Bellay's exhortation as a battle cry. Fortunately, du Bellay could practise what he preached. He and his friend Ronsard and their group, *La Pléiade*, produced excellent lyrics. They, too, were preoccupied with the loneliness of men and their dependence on love and affection to save them from unbearable solitude. In Marguerite of Navarre, Ronsard, Rabelais, du Bellay, and the rest, the court of Francis I possessed a galaxy of talent that would have been a credit to any court of Italy. Owing vast debts to the Italian Renaissance, they nevertheless achieved a style, an idiom, and a theme that were distinctly French.

The same was to be true of the great efflorescence of literature that took place in England shortly afterwards. Plots, characters, in fact entire plays were lifted wholesale from Italian authors. The intentions of Edmund Spenser would have drawn from Castiglione nothing but his entire approval, and Spenser's debt to Ariosto's *Orlando Furioso* is as obvious as it is large. Yet there is no plagiarism: all is transmuted, Englished. Like Rabelais, the Elizabethans grew drunk on the discovery of their language. At the same time they were even less confined by tradition than the French, and their sense of achievement was far sharper, for the English were closer in time to barbarity and to anarchy. The great promise of the days of Chaucer, Langland, and Wycliffe had been checked by the maelstrom of the fifteenth century. The Wars of the Roses had ripped apart the fabric of English life. The violent class turmoil of the early Tudor period which followed, which had led men of affairs to seek guidance in politics and diplomacy in

Queen Elizabeth I and goddesses, by Hans Eworth
Hampton Court

Italy, had begun to settle by the reign of Elizabeth I into a new pattern
of society in which gentlemen – but not noblemen – predominated.
The break with the Church, combined with increasing knowledge of
the worlds beyond Europe, intensified this sense of a new age, of an
original time. Yet the very dissolution of the past created anxiety,
insecurity, a sense of isolation, and a longing to discover standards.
The dramatists held up a looking glass to this society in conflict. The
violence, the rapacity, the passion of their age was more acceptable
to the audience that thronged to see their plays if they were cast in
Italy, in ancient Rome, or more daringly in their own historic past.
For their crude audience, the crimes in the *Duchess of Malfi* or the
White Devil possessed a further dimension of evil and horror if set in
the criminal splendour of an Italian court where incest, riot, poison,
and murder were, everyone believed, commonplaces of life. As well
as stimulating the poetic imagination of a Webster or a Tourneur,

however, Italy and its Renaissance still possessed a serious purpose for Englishmen. Long after politicians had given up expecting to find the secrets of their craft there, and long after dramatists had exhausted the plots of its authors, Italy continued to exert the deepest influence.

Profoundly important as the influence of the Italian Renaissance might be on art and literature and learning, it was greater still in education, using that word in its widest possible sense. This possessed two aspects – one for the narrow circle of intellectually creative men, the other for the world at large. How far the intellectual scepticism of the Renaissance, with its search for truth in the evidence presented by men and events rather than in dogma and authority, stimulated the growth of a rational attitude to the world is difficult to know. Certainly without the greater stimuli of the discovery of the world beyond Europe and the revolutionary achievements of science in the seventeenth century it might easily have come to naught. However, to belittle the importance of those first broad cracks that were made in fifteenth-century Italy in the all-embracing dome of dogma is to falsify history. Ideologies were still to rage in the heart of man and haunt his destiny, but for Western man never again could there be two opposed worlds of Christians and heretics. Important though this impetus was to the habit of truth, to the growth of a scientific and sceptical spirit in the world of learning, it is of minor significance compared with the influence which the Italian Renaissance had on the social patterns which Western Europe adopted.

Italy, with Flanders, had been the first country in Europe to grow really rich on commerce, to throw up a middle class which could challenge the economic, political, and social power of the aristocracy. These merchants, bankers, craftsmen, found their first real security in economic life. This they knew; this they controlled. And so they organized their political and social life about their economic activity – in guilds – and ignored as far as they could the structure of the world about them. But the pressure of their wealth and the needs of their professions forced them from their exclusive habits, forced them into contact (and at time into conflict) with the aristocracy, whose sources of wealth, invigorated by the rise of commerce, remained large enough to maintain their privileged place in society. In the end a linkage was made between the aristocracy and the middle class: they remained distinct but joined by paths that men could traverse, and this mingling wrought a profound change in social customs, in manners, in education, in the images of man that seemed socially valuable. In its search for standards, Italy could look where the Flemish could not – into its highly sophisticated past, to the days of Rome and Greece when life had also been urban, rich, and aristocratic, yet commercially minded. Although antiquity could provide some ingredients, it could not provide all, and the merchants' hunger to belong drove them to accept readily many of the concepts of feudal aristocracy.

By 1530 or so, however, Italian society had brought into being an idea of a gentleman that was neither classical nor feudal, neither noble

Miniature portrait of a young man,
by Nicholas Hilliard
Victoria and Albert Museum, London

nor bourgeois, neither rural nor urban, but a fusion of all of these. The projection of this image acquired such intensity because western Europe had begun to undergo the same sort of violent social revolution that Italy had undergone between 1300 and 1450. In the sixteenth century commercial wealth poured into Cadiz, Lisbon, Bordeaux, Nantes, London, Antwerp, Hamburg. It raced through the veins of rural society, erupting, creating, destroying. The new men of this age – and there were thousands of them – felt great social insecurity. They had to learn to be gentlemen, to move at ease in the aristocratic world which they could not or would not eradicate. They adopted the pattern of compromise which the Italians had established. They wolfed down the courtesy books – della Casa as well as Castiglione. They adopted Italian clothes and Italian manners. They educated their children according to Italian precepts. A knowledge of a great deal of Latin and a little Greek became an absolute necessity for anyone who aspired to gentility, from the North Cape of Norway to the Strait of Gibraltar. And a gentleman was not only delineated by his education, he also required breeding – those aristocratic airs, that easy nonchalance, that assumption of privileged position lightly borne, which Castiglione had emphasized over and over again. A taste in the visual arts, or connoisseurship, was as essential a part of breeding as skill in sitting a horse. As Europe assimilated its vast wealth, and society became more ordered, so this image of a gentleman became more tenacious. It represented, as it did in Italy, the triumph of the aristocracy at the expense of the middle class, whose own merits – prudence, reticence, professional education – came to be regarded as either boorish or comic, from which the young not only wished to escape but were encouraged to do so. This is why the possession of land achieved such sanctity in western Europe – it was the way to salvation, the route by which a merchant's children might become gentlemen and gentlewomen. Excluded from true social power, hypnotized by the snobbery and sophistication of aristocratic life to which the Italian Renaissance had given such vivid definition, the merchant classes of Europe lost much of their dynamic and creative energy, and it took nearly two centuries of frustration before they challenged, in the age of Napoleon, the aristocratic foundations of European society.

During this period from the Reformation to the French Revolution the spirit of the Italian Renaissance pervaded Europe. It taught the rough and very raw provincial aristocracies of the West how to live, how to move at ease through a world of bourgeois delights, without being contaminated by it. Certainly it intensified snobbery, hardened the stratification of classes of men, and checked the scientific imagination by insisting on the education of character rather than of aptitudes. In return it gave much. It taught the new men of Europe that the purpose of art, the call of learning, were an essential part of the use of wealth. And it projected a theme – the uniqueness of personal experience, the idea of man caught in the jaws of Time – that has given rise to the world's greatest art and literature. The spirit of the Italian Renaissance broods over these centuries which link the age of feudalism to modern times, and makes them a part of itself.

INDEX

NOTE: Where page numbers appear in italics, it indicates that the subject is illustrated. Where the creator of a work of art is unknown, the work is listed by title.

Art and artists – *contd*
  In Florence, 77, 83–7, 89, 127, 134, 149–51
  In Milan, 77, 166
  New social position, 77
  In Rome, 77, 79
  In Venice, 77, 91–2, 239–43, 299
Astrology, 40, 95, 158–9, 167, 168, 217, 222
Augustine, Saint, *26*
Averroes, 290
Avicenna, 290
Avignon, 83, 189
  Art in, 79, 83
  Mentioned, 198
  Palace of the Popes, 189
  Papacy in, 36, 50, 189–90, 192

Bacon, Francis, 306
Baglioni, Simonetto, 50
Baglioni family, 50–2, 206
Bande Nere, Giovanni Delle, 269
Banking, 123, 129, 134, 137, 13., 141
Barbari Jacopo De'
  Plan of Venice, 226
Barbarigo family, 254
Baron, Hans, 57
Bartolommeo, Fra, 134
Basle, Council of, 211
Bastiani, Lazzaro,
  Francesco Foscari, 244
Belisarius, 18
Bellay, Joachim Du, 309
Bellini, Gentile
  Painting by follower of, *229*
  Miracle of the Cross, 242
Bellini, Giovanni, 24, 89, 240
  Feast of the Gods (with Titian), 96
  Paintings in Doge's Palace, Venice, 92
  Saint Francis in Ecstasy, 89
Bellini, Jacopo
  Design for a Venetian palace, *239*

Bellini family, 81
Bembo, Pietro, Cardinal, *241*
Benci, Donato, 151
Bentivoglio family, 31, 47
Berenson, Bernard,
  Quoted, 83
Bergamo, 236, 254, 259
Bernardino of Siena, Saint, *41*, 51, 79, 210
Bernini, Giovanni Lorenzo, 200
Berry, Duc De,
  Très Riches Heures of, 89
Bertoldo, 101
  Medal by, 149
Biadajolo, Il, 130
Bilheres, Jean, Cardinal of Saint Denis, 103
Blois, Château de, 306
Boccaccio, Giovanni, 46, 267, 306
Bologna, 31, 47, 56, 103, 109, 157, 160, 203, 213
  San Petronio, Church of, 109
Bonacolsi family, 43
Bonfigli, Benedetto, 52
Borgia, Alfonso. *See* Calixtus III, Pope
Borgia, Cesare, Duc De Valentinois, 60, 63–7, *65*, 201–3
  And Machiavelli, 60, 64–7, 71, 183, 201
  Mentioned, 43, 59, 192, 195
Borgia, Giovanni, Duke of Gandia, 63
Borgia, Lucrezia, 63, 203
Borgia, Rodrigo. *See* Alexander VI, Pope
Borgia family, 61, 195
Borgo San Sepolcro, 87
Botteghe (workshops), 81, 172, 240
Botticelli, Sandro, 103, 131
  Mentioned, 24, 81, 91, 129, 185
  Birth of Venus, 103
  La Primavera, 128

316

329